VOLTAIRE

EUROPEAN MASTERS

General Editor: John Lawlor
Professor of English in the
University of Keele

VOLTAIRE

HAYDN MASON

Professor of European Studies in the
University of East Anglia

HUTCHINSON
LONDON

Hutchinson & Co (Publishers) Ltd
3 Fitzroy Square London W1

London Melbourne Sydney Auckland
Wellington Johannesburg Cape Town
and agencies throughout the world

First published 1975
© Haydn Mason 1975

Set in Monotype Bembo
Printed in Great Britain by
R. & R. Clark Ltd, Edinburgh

ISBN 0 09 121490 4 (cased)
     0 09 121491 2 (paper)

To the memory of
my parents

Contents

Preface

Large and impressive volumes continue to pour forth on Voltaire, while the definitive edition of his collected works has begun to appear. Yet he remains for the undergraduate or the reading public at large an unknown writer, the author of *Candide* and perhaps one or two other short stories or the *Lettres philosophiques*, but little else. The intellectual and social historian will come across him hard at work in the cause of social reform during the last half-century of the *ancien régime*, but there too the battles which he fought seem long since won, at least in the circumstances in which he fought them. Enthusiasm tends to be tepid. Voltaire lacks the perverse originality of his contemporary Rousseau; he equally appears devoid of Diderot's unorthodoxy in speculation and literary form. So while Rousseau still seems vital to the present generation of philosophers and anthropologists in France, and Diderot has gained wide acclaim as the father of the *nouveau roman*, Voltaire seems outmoded and of interest only to a narrow band of disciples.

As ever, the accusations voiced from the very beginning are active. His thinking is second-rate, merely an elevated common-sense, and is purely negative to boot. He lacks unity. Everyone refutes Faguet's damning remark that his writings are 'un chaos d'idées claires', yet the comment has shown a remarkable capacity for survival. Quite simply, so the argument runs, Voltaire is flashy, like a paste diamond; and both are found wanting after a while. His attitude to life has a grubby mediocrity when set alongside those of the sublime Pascal and the brave Rousseau; for all his apparent rebelliousness, Voltaire is really conforming in all essentials to the pattern of a *grand bourgeois*. He lacks psychological insight in his narrative and dramatic works, his poetry is a stranger to lyricism, and all his literature lacks any sense of soul or elevation. In every direction he is without penetration and greatness. He has talent but no genius. It is a formidable indictment.

Books are not wanting to trace Voltaire's life chronologically, or to analyse the range and coherence of his ideas and actions; many of these are listed in the Selected bibliography. Within the space of this volume, a better means of considering the charges against Voltaire without simply repeating what others had said seemed to be to take a different approach. Instead of studying Voltaire period by period (England, or Cirey, or Berlin, or Ferney) as is usual, it seemed that some freshness might be possible if his work was examined in different lights: as that of a dramatist, historian, story-teller, poet, polemicist, philosopher and correspondent. The categories are not watertight, particularly those where he was not bound by formal conventions; nevertheless there is room for making useful discriminations. This approach, though, would merely degenerate into enumeration if we attempted to review the whole field; representative pieces have therefore been chosen in each case. We may in this way hope to convey something of the essence of Voltaire while also probing as much as space allows into particular works of importance, some of them unjustly neglected by most critics heretofore.

To Professor John Lawlor goes my appreciative recognition of his close reading and many constructive comments; to Miss Fiona Strange my warm thanks for typing the manuscript quickly and accurately under pressure of time; and to my wife my affectionate gratitude for being, as ever, patient, perceptive and forbearing.

I | Dramatic critic and dramatist

It might be well to preface Voltaire's drama by Voltaire's drama criticism. He had much to say on the theatre of other French dramatists, devoting a long and generally unflattering work to Corneille (*Commentaires sur Corneille*), pouring scorn on both Marivaux and the authors of the *drame bourgeois*, and according whole-hearted praise only to the eminence of Racine.[1] But the most illuminating confrontation is not with a fellow-countryman; it is with Shakespeare. The perspective is illuminating because it clarifies not only Voltaire but the literary climate of the age, caught between a dying classicism and a Romantic period waiting to be born.

Not that the picture Voltaire presents is wholly without merit. It is to him that the honour goes for making the first serious introduction of Shakespeare to French readers. During his years in England (1726-8), he saw, by his own avowal, several of the plays that were to come under his notice later on: *Othello, Hamlet, Macbeth, Henry V, Julius Caesar*;[2] and the *Lettres philosophiques* give generous attention to the Elizabethan dramatist. Shakespeare, he says, created the English theatre. Possessed of a genius both forceful and fecund, penetrated by the natural and the sublime, he none-theless 'had not so much as a single spark of good taste, or knew one rule of the drama'.[3] In that sentence is summed up the whole paradoxicality of Voltaire's position on Shakespeare, destined to remain with him throughout his life: how can a man of such grand imagination be so ignorant of the basic conventions? Furthermore, his influence has been disastrous; overshadowing the whole of sub-sequent English theatre, he has wrecked it. A man strangling his wife on stage, cobblers and shoemakers with their vulgar jokes, gravediggers drinking, singing and making abominable jests about

1. Superior figures indicate references listed under Notes and references (pp. 173-91).

the skulls they encounter—these episodes are lamentable. Yet when the English play the dramatic game according to sound classical rules, like Addison in his *Cato*, all the beauty of language and nobility of sentiment cannot rescue it from inflicting tedium. Perversely, the English race seems created only to produce irregular beauties. Like a 'tufted tree', growing strongly but fitfully, 'to lop and dress it' so as to suit a French garden is to kill it.[4]

The melancholy conclusion seems to be that Shakespeare is good only in purple patches, like the 'To be or not to be' soliloquy which Voltaire renders competently into French rhyming alexandrines, or the funeral speeches of Brutus and Antony over Caesar's body. The puzzle remains how an untutored man 'qui même ne savait pas le latin'[5] could rise to such sublime heights so often. In these earlier years Voltaire is still trying hard simply to understand; perhaps after all many of these conventions are merely the result of fashion.[6] One glimpses here, as in the metaphor of the tree, some stirrings of a relativist outlook. Even *Hamlet*, which reads like 'l'imagination d'un sauvage ivre', has 'des traits sublimes'.[7] Such as . . .? Such as the ghost—because the ghost is dramatically useful in making vital revelations, appears naturally (that is to say, is not forcibly contrived) and convinces us that there is an invisible power, the master of nature, which is concerned with avenging innocence and punishing crimes; finally, because he inspires terror. All these are the criteria of a good classicist: naturalness, utility, propriety, morality, catharsis. They do not extend to murder, drinking and low jokes.

Later on, Voltaire will put Shakespeare's defects down to the lack of taste in England. The popular curiosity in spectacles had triumphed over aristocratic manners. How then can one talk of universal rules when a whole nation manages without them and yet is delighted by its theatre?[8] Voltaire seems here to be adumbrating a primitive sociology of literature, as too when he argues that, like Lope de Vega in Spain, Shakespeare had genius in an age when taste was not yet formed. By contrast, French theatre is perhaps too refined; the ideal might be a combination of both styles:

J'ai toujours pensé qu'un heureux et adroit mélange de l'action qui règne sur le théâtre de Londres et de Madrid, avec la sagesse, l'élégance, la noblesse, la décence du nôtre, pourrait produire quelque chose de parfait.

(I have always thought that a happy, skilful blending of the action which dominates the London and Madrid theatre, with the wisdom, elegance, nobility, decency of ours, could produce something perfect.)[9]

These last, helpful comments date from 1764. Thereafter Voltaire draws back from new thoughts, and long-standing prejudices establish ascendancy over independent judgement, though it must also be remembered that his hostility had grown as the influence of Shakespeare (which he considered decadent) had become more widespread in France.[10] Unfortunately, Voltaire's lengthiest critical exercise on Shakespeare dates from this period. In a letter to the French Academy, intended for reading aloud at their main annual meeting in 1776, Voltaire sets out systematically to discredit his troublesome predecessor. Shakespeare is obscene; there are examples from *Othello*, *Macbeth*, *Lear* and *Henry V* to prove it. His language is vulgar. The charges are not surprising, but the evidence perhaps is: the sentry in *Hamlet* who when asked: 'Have you had quiet guard?' replies: 'Not a mouse stirring.' This little line draws down upon it the full weight of Voltairean wrath. It is true that a sentry might say that in real life; but he should never express such sentiments on stage before the leading people of the nation, who speak with nobility. The mouse is irrelevant to the tragedy. Compare the beauty of Racine's line from *Iphigénie*: 'Mais tout dort, et l'armée, et les vents, et Neptune' (But all is asleep, the army, the winds, Neptune), so evocative of the calm by which the Greek fleet is beset. It simply escapes Voltaire that the absent mice are just as evocative; mice, even non-existent ones, are not permitted in high tragedy.[11]

It is of course necessary to remember the context in which Voltaire wrote. Shakespeare was little known or liked in eighteenth-century France. Ducis's translation of *Hamlet* (1769) used the opportunity to refine the play for rational French taste. Gertrude is, at least technically, absolved of her crime; she had not meant to kill the King and simply went back too late to remove the poison. Nor has she married Claudius, and indeed she helps Hamlet in plotting against his uncle. In the end, full of remorse, she commits suicide, while Hamlet lives on. This was one effective way of scaling down what the French regarded as grotesque horrors, due as one critic said to the racial torpor of the English who needed sensationalism to shake them out of themselves. This travesty none-theless represents, argues F. C. Green, 'the closest approach to Shakespeare achieved by an eighteenth-century French dramatist'.[12] English critics were often scarcely more complimentary than the French. Thomas Rymer, Pope, even Dryden, saw Shakespeare as passing, in Dryden's words, 'beyond the bounds of judgement'.[13] Many felt, like Voltaire, that he was a freak of nature, whose excesses were integral to his genius.

Yet Voltaire strove all his life with Shakespeare, once he had encountered him in England; and though he became more hostile at the end his basic attitudes remained constant. He translated not only isolated passages, but also the first three acts of *Julius Caesar*. As early as 1726 he is using a line from *Hamlet* in a letter to express his grief at the death of his sister;[14] and the last observation is not till 1777, in another letter to the French Academy, which for all the unfavourable criticisms of these final years still concludes, as in the *Lettres philosophiques*, that Shakespeare is a savage with sparks of genius.[15] No Jacob wrestled longer with his angel.

Indeed, many of Voltaire's plays show signs of Shakespearean influence. *Zaïre* has similarities with *Othello*, *Ériphyle* and *Sémiramis* with *Hamlet*, the ghost included. But the closest analogy is between *Julius Caesar* and *La Mort de César* (written 1731), and a few comparative observations might be instructive.[16] Voltaire had been particularly impressed by *Julius Caesar*, and he wished to convey some of its wide sweep of political sentiments in a work of similar scope. But whereas Shakespeare's play has eighteen different settings, Voltaire's has only one; the former extends over two years, the latter over the mere length of the play itself. The English drama is almost entirely in blank verse, the French in rhyming alexandrines. There are forty-eight speaking parts in *Julius Caesar*, only ten in *La Mort de César*.

More significant still is the selection of plot. Voltaire ends with Caesar's death and the funeral orations, presumably taking to heart the commonplace criticism of *Julius Caesar* that, as one English critic put it, 'If it had properly been called *Julius Caesar*, it ought to have ended at his death, and then it had been much more regular, natural and beautiful.'[17] The crux of Voltaire's play is the drama resulting from Brutus' discovery that he is Caesar's son. Whereas Shakespeare takes in a large stretch of Roman history, his French imitator is essentially writing a psychological and even sentimental tragedy. The conflict here is not so much between a tyrant and a lover of freedom as within Caesar himself, between his paternal love and his political ambition, and particularly within Brutus, forced to choose between killing his father or betraying his principles. Voltaire felt that he was achieving greater depth than by simply concentrating on the political issues.[18] The most moving scene is in the mould of Corneille and Racine, where a human being is torn apart because he happens also to be in a public position of authority; Brutus does everything to save Caesar from himself, pleading with him to renounce power, betraying his fellow-conspirators by telling his father of the plot, and going down on his knees in a last vain effort (III. 4). But the other major characters lack density. Antony is a fanatic intent on power, Cassius a fanatic intent on revolution. There are no crowd scenes in the Shakespearean sense; when they speak, the bystanders do so in alexandrines like every-one else; and of course there is no blood shed on stage, nothing remotely like the barbaric magnificence of Shakespeare's Brutus and his fellow-plotters bathing their hands and swords in Caesar's bloody corpse. The worlds of *Caesar* and of *César* are completely unalike.

This play, like all others of Voltaire, seeks to eschew the irrational, the monstrous, the vulgar. One point should be made clear, lest those unfamiliar with his works commit the fatal error of thinking him a prude. The ribald jokes and the language in which he couches them in his correspondence, notebooks and humorous verse, should quickly dispel that impression. It is all a matter of time and place. The theatre set an example of noble behaviour, it mirrored back to the aristocratic audience its own conventions of elegance and *politesse*, confirming that the playhouse was a kind of sanctum where only high tone was acceptable. Although Voltaire goes so far as to suspect that the French might one day take to Shakespeare, as they were indeed to do in the following century, he can never overlook the fatal stumbling-block of bad taste. Taste was related to the capacity for critical discernment, which itself sprang from enlightenment and culture. It was based on an analytical, rational approach, not on sensibility, as so many of his contemporaries believed. True, he could on occasion make a frank appeal to sensibility, as in *L'Ingénu*; but his basic view is that ultimately all rational men can arrive at some general consensus of what is truly aesthetic and moral, because their minds have, through careful use of their intellect, been correctly formed.[19]

This approach should not, perhaps, wholly be decried simply because it failed to make due appreciation of Shakespeare or faltered in its more courageous insights into the English playwright. Admittedly, while Voltaire was retreating from his earlier more adventurous notions, it was left to critics like Herder to see the possibilities inherent in art forms such as folk poetry, precisely because they were the product of intense, even ecstatic, emotion rather than rational thought, and to try to approach Shakespeare on his own terms, reaching the conclusion that he was the supreme irrational creative genius of the Germanic race. The mote in Voltaire's eye is all too obvious, the great opportunity missed is saddening; he had an intuition of Shakespeare's genius long before almost all his continental contemporaries and he failed to make full use of it. Even so, the perception that taste might conceivably be an inhibiting barrier to every sort of wild subjectivist opinion can surely still commend itself to our age of artistic chaos; and Voltaire's own interpretations of it in his works should generally ensure our respectful attention, even if the example of Shakespeare proved its limitations. Furthermore, Voltaire's acquaintance with the English theatre helped him in his own attempt to renew French classical theatre in the direction of greater action and, to some limited extent, spectacle.

Œdipe (1718)

Voltaire was not quite twenty-four when his first play *Œdipe* was launched at the Comédie Française, and immediately it established him as a major figure in French classical tragedy. In three months it had thirty performances and attracted nearly 25 000 spectators, a record which few of his other tragedies surpassed.[20] It was hardly a case of the personage creating his own publicity, as might sometimes happen in later years; so far Voltaire was scarcely known to the public.[21] Yet with characteristic daring the young playwright[22] chose to begin his career by measuring himself on the same ground as Sophocles' *Oidipous Tyrannos* and Corneille's *Œdipe*. It was his triumph not merely to achieve competence in handling this great myth but actually to present an interpretation stamped with an original, clear-cut personality. The strong reactions evoked, the large number of brochures, for and against, which appeared in print, testified to the feeling that a new intellectual force had made itself felt in the theatre.

As he cannily made clear by his *Lettres sur Œdipe* (1719), Voltaire was fully aware of the technical problem inherent in the Oedipus story: according to strict logic, it should end in the first act, for it

runs contrary to nature that Oedipus should for so long be unaware
how Laïus had died. The dramatist's main response was to add a
new character, Philoctète, and to build a romantic sub-plot around
him and Jocaste. Philoctète returns to Thebes, still in love with the
Queen, only to find that he is accused of murdering Laïus. For the
first three acts, it seems as if the play will revolve around this
potential miscarriage of justice, especially since Œdipe cannot make
up his mind whether Philoctète is guilty, while the latter is too
noble to attempt a defence of his innocence. But when the
Grand-Prêtre reveals to Œdipe that he was the assassin, Philoctète
swiftly disappears from the play altogether, and the more traditional sequence of events in the Oedipus myth begins to
unroll. As Voltaire himself admitted, it made two tragedies out of
one.

This is a correct appreciation of a structural defect, one of
the main weaknesses in Œdipe. Alongside it must be placed a
flatness of characterization which will prove to be typical in
Voltaire's tragedies. But to judge Voltaire by the standards of
Racine or Corneille, or indeed by his own explicit criteria, is to
miss those qualities that stirred the audiences in 1718. For the theme
of the play is man's quest for self-liberation in the face of capricious
and vengeful gods. Œdipe's tragic weakness is laid bare long
before the revelations about his past unfold; he pleads a lack of
personal control over his actions. Trapped between the angry gods
and the fickle people, he can do nothing. He would have liked to
clear Philoctète of the accusation against him:

> Mais, seigneur, je n'ai point la liberté du choix.   (II. 4)

(But, my lord, I have not the freedom to choose.)

So he pleads a Sartrean *mauvaise foi*:

> Nécessité cruelle attachée à l'empire!
> Dans le cœur des humains les rois ne peuvent lire;
> Souvent sur l'innocence ils font tomber leurs coups,
> Et nous sommes, Araspe, injustes malgré nous.   (II. 5)

(Cruel necessity linked to empire! Kings cannot read in human hearts; they
often visit their blows upon the innocent, and we are, Araspe, unjust despite
ourselves.)

Araspe, his confidant, urges him in reply to have confidence in his own capacities:

> Ne nous fions qu'à nous; voyons tout par nos yeux:
> Ce sont là nos trépieds, nos oracles, nos dieux.

(Let us trust naught but ourselves, see all through our eyes: those are our oracles, our prophecies, our gods.)

But it is to no avail. Œdipe invokes the heavens' aid in determining his mind and, with suitable irony, it is the Grand-Prêtre who resolves it for him. For Oedipe, the revelation must be transcendental; it cannot come from within.

When the Grand-Prêtre utters his fearful news, Œdipe briefly rebels against him; but the priest is not disturbed. By merely hinting at the revelations still to come he frightens Œdipe into silence. Philoctète, now cleared of the crime, warns Œdipe about the dangers which priests represent for kings, stirring up discord and revolt among the people. He himself enjoys all the detachment of a free man, who had no ambition to reign[23] and is governed in all things by an inviolable sense of personal honour. This self-awareness finds an echo in Jocaste, who takes up the philosophic dialogue with Œdipe when Philoctète disappears from the scene, thereby providing a continuity of theme despite his absence. She too tries to persuade Œdipe that consultation of omens and entrails is no way to discover the truth; nor are priests infallible, as she points out in what is probably the most famous couplet in all Voltaire's drama:

> Nos prêtres ne sont pas ce qu'un vain peuple pense,
> Notre crédulité fait toute leur science.   (IV. 1)

(Our priests are not what a vain people think; our credulity is the basis of all their knowledge.)

To this Œdipe can only reply weakly:

> Ah dieux! s'il était vrai, quel serait mon bonheur!

(Oh gods! if it were true, how great would be my happiness!)

He goes to his doom like a man condemned long before, since he had already resigned all human initiatives to the gods and their priestly servants. He is 'vertueux', as he claims, but lacking lucidity, and his last long speech shows his explicit awareness of this defect:

> Et j'étais, malgré moi, dans mon aveuglement,
> D'un pouvoir inconnu l'esclave et l'instrument.   (V. 4)

(And I was, despite myself, in my blindness the slave and instrument of an unknown power.)

Jocaste's pleas have not been able to save him from the gods or from himself. When he dies, naught is left for her but despair and suicide. But unlike him she dies defying the odious gods who have imposed incest with her son upon her unknowing self. Her final commands to her Theban subjects are unambiguous on this point:

> Honorez mon bûcher, et songez à jamais
> Qu'au milieu des horreurs du destin qui m'opprime,
> J'ai fait rougir les dieux qui m'ont forcée au crime. (V. 6)

(Honour my pyre, and forever reflect that amidst the horrors of the fate that destroys me, I have made the gods blush as they forced me to crime.)

These are the curtain lines of the play, and by their tone of revolt they cast a light upon Œdipe's real tragedy, that he could not withstand his own guilt and self-horror even though called to it by a God of wrath.

Œdipe, then, makes a strong appeal to the audience to take its freedom seriously, to refuse the notion of fatality as being destructive of all human possibilities. Œdipe is a failed philosophic hero, who is virtuous but not courageous; Philoctète and Jocaste, by contrast, already announce something of the spirit of *Candide*. Voltaire is urging a radical approach to the supernatural; men are not meant for submission to inscrutable fate. It is little wonder that, beneath the classical façade, the play excited so much interest. Voltaire had already discovered his true bent in the theatre, and it lay, as elsewhere, in being a *philosophe*.

Zaïre (1732)

By the time he came to write *Zaïre*, the playwright had undergone the crucial experience of his stay in England. Many of the plays he had written since then show the influence of Shakespeare: *Brutus* (1730), *Eriphyle* (1732), *La Mort de César* (written in 1731 but not yet performed). Neither these nor the other Voltaire tragedies which had appeared since 1718 had however won the acclaim of *Œdipe*. The dramatist, ever attentive to the changing *Zeitgeist*, tried a new tack. Despite his conviction that tragedy was not the place for love, he bowed to the times and announced that since romantic heroes were fashionable 'il en ferait tout comme un autre' (he would create one just like anybody else).²⁴ He also switched to a new setting. Ancient Greece and Rome were replaced by the medieval Jerusalem of the Crusades, and French national history thus came into the canon of classical tragedy. Voltaire told his English friend Fawkener, to whom he dedicated the play, that it was the English theatre which gave him 'la hardiesse que j'ai eue de mettre sur la scène les noms de nos rois et des anciennes familles du royaume' (the audacity which I have had to put on the stage the names of our kings and of the ancient families in the realm).²⁵ Doubtless his knowledge of such plays as *Henry V* helped him to take this decision. Voltaire went on immediately to remark, with true prescience, that this could be 'la source d'un genre de tragédie qui nous est inconnu jusqu'ici, et dont nous avons besoin' (the source of a tragic genre which we have not so far known and of which we stand in need). National tragedy was perhaps not destined to reach the high peaks of literary achievement in eighteenth-century France, but it would prove increasingly popular as the country became ever more patriotic in the years leading up to and through the Revolution.²⁶

Zaïre moved into the realm not merely of love but of sentiment. At a time when Nivelle de La Chaussée was exploiting the new mood in the theatre with his mediocre but highly successful *comédies larmoyantes*, Voltaire, in the tragic mode, attained to something remarkably similar. Tears are shed on all sides (even the noble and courageous Orosmane weeps—for the first time in his life— as the crisis nears its climax),²⁷ the outpourings of virtuous and innocent hearts. The characters are driven by external institutions, which are the source of all their undoing and account for all their lapses from pure goodness. Like Othello (after whom he is in many respects fashioned), Orosmane kills out of jealousy; the fatal deed is however not bound up with his character as in Shakespeare's play but results from chance. If only Nérestan, writing to Zaïre the letter which Orosmane intercepts, had made clear that he was her brother and not her lover, all might have been well. Rousseau was surely echoing the feelings of many spectators:

Pour moi, je crois entendre chaque spectateur dire en son cœur à la fin de la tragédie: 'ah! qu'on me donne une Zaïre, je ferai bien en sorte de ne pas la tuer!'

(As for myself, I think I hear every spectator saying in his heart at the end of the tragedy: 'Ah! give me a Zaïre and I shall make sure not to kill her!')²⁸

But one might well experience also the same irritation as in Hardy's *Tess of the D'Urbervilles*, when the vital letter that might have resolved all is pushed under the carpet. These are avoidable disasters. A gratuitous element reigns. Lusignan is reunited with his children just before he died because Nérestan bears the appropriate scar and Zaïre her mother's cross on their respective breasts (II. 3); 'la croix de ma mère' has become a proverbial phrase in French for banal recognition scenes.[29] In this respect we seem to be nearer the picaresque novel than high tragedy; Joseph Andrews and his strawberry mark are just a decade away.

But once again the traditional criteria invoking Boileau and Racine will serve only to find out Voltaire's faults. The strengths are elsewhere, along the lines of the historical setting whose original possibilities he had glimpsed. There is some local colour, and the actors apparently tried to give verisimilitude to their costumes by spending thirty *livres* on turbans;[30] but the main value of the location lies in the scope it gives to a dramatic treatment of comparative cultures. Before his *Siècle de Louis XIV* and *Essai sur les mœurs*, Voltaire was already writing history as a *philosophe*. *Zaïre* presents a comparison of Christian and Moslem customs from which the Moslems emerge with credit. The Christians are brave and friendly—except about Christianity. No sooner has Lusignan been reunited with his daughter than he is urging her by emotional blackmail to resume the Christian faith and is stirring up the old hatreds:

> Tes frères, ces martyrs égorgés à mes yeux,
> T'ouvrent leurs bras sanglants, tendus du haut des cieux;
> Ton Dieu que tu trahis, ton Dieu que tu blasphèmes,
> Pour toi, pour l'univers, est mort en ces lieux mêmes;
> Et tu n'y peux rester, sans renier ton père,
> Ton honneur qui te parle, et ton Dieu qui t'éclaire. (II. 3)

(Your brothers, those martyrs massacred before my eyes, open to you their bleeding arms, stretched forth from the empyrean; your God whom you betray, your God whom you blaspheme, died for you, for the world, in this very place; and you cannot remain here without disowning your father, your honour that speaks to you, and your God who gives you light.)

This pressure will go on mounting, as Fatime and Nérestan add to it. When Zaïre asks the latter for advice on what the Christian law enjoins upon her, he explicitly tells her that it involves not only the love and service of God but also hating the Moslems:

> Détester l'empire de vos maîtres,
> Servir, aimer ce Dieu qu'ont aimé nos ancêtres   (III. 4)

(Hating your masters' rule, serving and loving that God beloved of our ancestors).

No contradiction between these two statements occurs to him; Moslems are demons, not men. His compatriot Châtillon, recounting the battle, reveals despite himself the horrors of war for both sides in a manner that anticipates *Candide* (II. 1). But he believes too easily that God is on their side; as for the Moslems, they are vile enough to seduce their captives into the religion of Islam while the latter are yet children.

No Christian escapes this vicious circle. On the Moslem side Orosmane, as generous and noble in nature as the Christian knights, outdoes them by liberating a hundred Christian captives instead of the agreed ten, then later releasing even Lusignan, despite the political dangers involved. When he is at last totally broken by the knowledge that he has killed Zaïre wrongly, his final act before killing himself is to order that all the prisoners be set free and escorted to the port of embarkation 'Comblés de mes bienfaits, chargés de mes richesses' (Showered with my benefits, laden with my wealth) (V. 10). It is the Moslem who achieves the great Christian act of redemption and forgiveness. As Zaïre puts it, 'S'il était né chrétien, que serait-il de plus?' (Had he been born a Christian what more might he be?) (IV. 1).

Yet Orosmane is not simply, as is sometimes claimed, a model Christian ruler in all but name; such a characterization would spoil the balance of the play. He is a primitive in temperament: transparent, spontaneous, proud, unsophisticated. When he suspects Nérestan of seducing Zaïre away, his fury at first knows no bounds. He will tear Nérestan apart before her eyes (III. 7). And though he recovers his senses enough to abandon this idea, he appeases his wrath by ordering the harem to be closed for ever to the outside world, with a consequent return to the ancient customs of oriental despotism and terror. A streak of cruelty strives with more lofty sentiments within his breast. The portrait, in fact, is of a European who has taken on Moslem customs, not of someone born and bred to despotism (III. 1). Voltaire sees dramatic advantages in presenting a man who enjoys the prerogatives of the harem and slavery, yet will readily sacrifice them all for Zaïre's sake. Although of rude Scythian stock, Orosmane is not sunk in the fatalist tyranny of Islam. Zaïre, herself a product of two cultures, would have made a fitting match for him.

In this international cockpit Zaïre is placed, the helpless victim whose love outweighs her religion, torn between the claims of her brother and dying father on the one hand and her passion for Orosmane on the other. She recognizes herself that her faith is not an absolute but the result of her upbringing (I. 1). By the end, she admits that she no longer knows what her desires or her obligations are (V. 3), and she is murdered before she has taken any decision. Her aim is somehow to combine loyalty to the Christian faith with telling Orosmane all, and one feels that, contrary to Fatime's forebodings (IV. 1), he would have pardoned the Christians if she had managed to do so. Zaïre is not a very interesting character in herself, but her situation is the crux of the drama. Here is another instance of human happiness destroyed by transcendental considerations. There is no good *philosophe* about, as there will be in the more relaxed world of *Le Taureau blanc*,[31] to turn the tables on behalf of mankind. The Christian God in practice encourages the basest instincts.

But the meaning of *Zaïre* is more indirectly conveyed than that of *Oedipe*. Voltaire tells us that it was called a *tragédie chrétienne*, and the portrayal of the Christians won applause from both Rousseau and Chateaubriand; so this can hardly be termed an anti-Christian play. Where the Moslems are not involved, the Christians' conduct is exemplary. Their defects arise not from being Christians as such but from the irrelevance of Frenchmen fighting in 'Des climats que pour eux le destin n'a point faits' (Climes that Fate did not create for them) (III. 1). Only in the closing lines when it is too late does Nérestan's fixed hatred of the infidels become affected by pity and admiration for Orosmane. Through evoking our tears for the pathos of Zaïre and the waste of her frustrated love, Voltaire is once more urging the claims of the natural over the supernatural.

Four years after *Zaïre*, Voltaire scored another great success with *Alzire*, where he experimented with one more unusual setting, this time the New World in the sixteenth century. As in *Zaïre*, he contrasts two cultures, though the Peruvians differ little in essentials from the 'civilized' Spaniards. Voltaire shows that Christianity is not in principle opposed to *philosophie*, since it is based on loving-kindness; but in practice the Christians from Europe are cruel and barbarous men who approve of torture and forced conversions. Once again it is the comparison of life-styles which carries more conviction than individual characterization, this contrast being enhanced by the exotic costumes of the Peruvians. *Alzire*, further-more, by suggesting that true religion lies in forgiveness and toler-ance, does not offend against Christian orthodoxy.

Voltaire's move toward more adventurous theatre was nonethe-less cautious, and the settings were less exotic than the places they represented. No attempt was made to show the reality of Jerusalem in *Zaïre* or of Lima in *Alzire*, and as late as 1748 the playwright experienced failure when trying to devise special *décor* for his *Sémiramis*.[32] Local colour came almost entirely from costume alone. We are still a very long way from Romantic drama; Voltaire's main concern with specificity of place is philosophic. He wants to convey the essentials in each society of what Montesquieu would later call 'l'esprit des lois'.

Mahomet (1741)

Thus it is that the next important tragedy, *Mahomet*, though set in Mecca, is even less preoccupied with exoticism than *Zaïre* and *Alzire*. The title, more precisely, is *Le Fanatisme, ou Mahomet le prophète*, and this gives a better idea of the play. Whereas *Zaïre* and *Alzire* radiate outward from the personal dilemma of the heroine, conveying a message whose precise significance it is often difficult to seize, this later tragedy announces its subject from the first as greater than its hero. And so it turns out. Mahomet is an arresting figure but lacking in subtlety. The true depth of the play lies not in him, nor in Séide, Palmire and Zopire, sympathetically drawn though they are, but in the awesome force that works through dedicated disciples and prostrates happiness beneath power.

Critics from Rousseau onwards have been given to pointing out that Mahomet is not a fanatic and that the play is about political rather than religious matters. This dichotomy is somewhat unreal. If Voltaire decided to *écraser l'infâme*,[33] it was because the evils of society and government stemmed from the fact that the Church dominated the State. Only by destroying the political power of the Church could society be properly reformed; it was, as Hugh

Trevor-Roper has pointed out, a revolutionary programme.[34]
Mahomet's precise religious beliefs are not clear, but evidently he
has faith in a God of some sort, as he indicates at the end of the play:

> Toi [Dieu] que j'ai blasphémé, mais que je crains encore. (V. 4)

(Thou [God] whom I have blasphemed, but whom still I fear.)

If therefore he is essentially interested in obtaining political authority
at the least one cannot call him a religious hypocrite. God seems to
be a conveniently easy assumption, of use essentially to the strong
who dare to frame a new society:

> Il faut un nouveau culte, il faut de nouveaux fers;
> Il faut un nouveau dieu pour l'aveugle univers. (II. 5)

(We need a new religion, we need new chains; we need a new god for the
blind world.)

But though lacking in blind religious enthusiasm, Mahomet is well-
endowed with that obsessive belief in himself and his right to
power which is no less characteristic of 'le fanatisme'. Objections
by his opponents and hesitations by his followers are to be broken
on the rock of this total will, expressing itself in single-minded
oppressiveness and intolerance. *Mahomet* is concerned with human
greed for power, it is true; but Voltaire is no less fascinated by the
use a man such as this makes of irrational elements, invoking the
divine to suit his ends.

This play is then an open attack upon the repressive forces operated
by superstition. Did Voltaire have Christianity in mind? Though
positive evidence for this is available in his correspondence,[35] we
hardly need it. The author had already made a tendentious analogy
between the birth of Quakerism and that of Christianity in the
Lettres philosophiques, even giving the founder of the Quaker group,
George Fox, precisely twelve disciples to drive home the point.[36]
Mahomet, like Christ, rose from a humble background—never a
matter for commendation to the aristocratic Voltaire, who feared
and despised the credulities of the masses—and his followers, like
Christ's, were outlaws

> errants de cités en déserts,
> Proscrits, persécutés, bannis, chargés de fers (I. 4)

(wandering from city to desert, proscribed, persecuted, banished, laden
with chains).

When Séide falters as Mahomet commands him to murder Zopire, the prophet flays him verbally; and one of the points he makes is to remind Séide of the exemplary obedience of Abraham when God ordered him to sacrifice Isaac. Long before Kierkegaard was to see Abraham's deed as the supreme act of a 'knight of faith', Voltaire was also invoking it, but for very different, more pragmatic purposes: to the one a sublime paradox, to the other simply a terrifying rejection of natural impulse and a submission to religious madness.

None of this explicitly equates Islam with Christianity; Voltaire would be unlikely to have done so in a public performance in 1741. Yet although the possible links apparently escaped the good people of Lille at its premiere there, Parisians were more vigilant (or fore-warned) when it reached the Comédie Française a year later, and it was withdrawn after three performances. The point was surely inescapable: religious fanaticism, even in one so essentially good as Séide, could be the motive for murder, it could overwhelm all natural impulses. There is no more subtle moment in the play than when Séide and Palmire try to reconcile their love for Zopire with Mahomet's order to kill him. Neither agrees that Séide should carry out the murder, yet both feel that Mahomet cannot be gainsaid. So when Palmire half-resigns herself to the deed, he seizes on her remarks as an order to go ahead. She for her part can neither confirm nor deny it; and so the pair find their excuse in each other, entering into a pact of bad faith so as to evade true responsibility. Mahomet carries all before him, because he is never irresolute; because he plays upon men's desire to commit philosophical suicide by rejecting free thought in the service of total authority; and, in the last resort, because luck favours him. He would probably have been destroyed by Séide at the end had not the poison intervened providentially to cast Séide down at his feet; but it is worth noting that Mahomet never wavers even at this worst moment. It is this total faith in himself which has enabled him to banish all thought of questioning or indeed discussing his commands.

The dramatic vitality of *Mahomet* rests, as in the earlier plays, not in the consciousness of individuals but in the play of forces. Mahomet himself is too overtly villainous to be convincing, Zopire is a touching old man but one who tiresomely prates, while Séide and Palmire, though moving when they are caught in the trap of choice, can hardly be said to reveal souls of great complexity. The strength lies in Voltaire's demonstration of charisma, conveyed, as usual, in lapidary phrases. It is not Mahomet the remorseful protagonist of the final lines who commands our attention so much as the colossus, free of all human flaws, who convinces the others that he is godlike and destined to rule without reservation.

In the final lines, nature may be said to gain a derisory triumph. Zopire, Séide and Palmire are all dead, but the manner of Palmire's dying has reminded Mahomet that he is a man after all. Henceforth he will reign, but in full knowledge that he has transgressed against humanity in a way for which atonement is impossible. He must hold command by fear, knowing that 'Mon empire est détruit si l'homme est reconnu' (My authority is destroyed if man's is recognized); this final line carries the same lesson as *Œdipe*. The circumstances are more pessimistic, since evil is left in the seat of power; Voltaire is more deeply aware of that negative spirit in human beings which is so readily available for exploitation by power-crazy tyrants. Yet the considerations are the same as before. This unnatural hold over others occurs because men lay claim to the transcendental, working beyond and therefore against the prerogatives of reason. Crush this infamous way of proceeding and the world can be a civilized place. Nor is *Mahomet* necessarily anti-Christian, though it has moved more closely to that position than its predecessors in Voltaire's theatre. Nothing in the play indicates that the Catholic Church must travel this road any longer. True charity and tolerance have nothing to do with Islam but they can find a place in Christendom. When Voltaire dedicated *Mahomet* to Pope Benedict XIV and the pope graciously accepted the dedication, it was clear that an enlightened religion was still possible.

Les Scythes (1766)

The best-known tragedies of Voltaire belong to the years before his *contes* began to appear. There may be a connection; if so, it was hardly intended by the author. Though from the late 1740s on he was acquiring fame as much for being the composer of *Zadig* and *Candide* as that of *Oedipe* and *Zaïre*, though the field of *philosophique* dramaturgy was far from an original one after 1760,[37] Voltaire never lost his dedication to tragedy, ten more examples appearing after this date. What is more, he could not rest on his laurels. The harsh statement that one is only as good as one's last production was

never more taken to heart by any artist; and no play caused him
more pain than *Les Scythes*.

At first Voltaire had apparently thought it would go down well;
he seemed delighted to discover that his inspiration had not withered
with age. Confident of its success, he extolled it to his friends the
d'Argentals: 'Des larmes! On en versera, ou on sera de pierre.'
(Tears! People will weep torrents, if they're not made of stone.)³⁸
But the tears did not flow when it was eventually put on by the
Comédie Française in March 1767 and it received only four performances. Voltaire had been warned of this possibility beforehand
when friends like the cardinal de Bernis had criticized it severely,
and for months he went on amending and correcting, hopeful that
he would be vindicated by the audiences over the critics. It was not
to be. Voltaire, despite his multifarious activities at this period, was
deeply wounded, as he dolefully confessed: 'Ils [*Les Scythes*] avancent
la fin de mes jours, ils me tuent . . . j'avais un besoin extrême du
succès de cet ouvrage.' (They [*Les Scythes*] are hastening the end of
my days, they are killing me . . . I utterly needed this work to
succeed.)³⁹ Although his characteristic resilience eventually came to
his aid and it did not take him ten years to recover, as he had
mournfully predicted, the love affair nonetheless lasted nine months.
Success in a myriad of polemical enterprises, fame as 'l'homme aux
Calas', these could not so easily erase the deep hurt that a beloved
tragedy should be spurned by his masters the Parisian audience.

Why this particularly deep commitment? The main immediate
reason, it would seem, lies in the wider social canvas presented.
Voltaire had undertaken, in his own words, 'une entreprise un peu
téméraire d'introduire des pasteurs, des laboureurs, avec des princes,
et de mêler les mœurs champêtres avec celles des cours' (a somewhat
rash venture by bringing in shepherds, farmers, alongside princes,
and mingling rustic manners with those of the courts).⁴⁰ He saw
this possibility of mixing widely different social classes on the stage
as 'un champ très fécond que de plus habiles que moi défricheront'
(a very productive field that men more skilled than I will bring into
cultivation).⁴¹ The opening scene, it is true, would have rudely
shaken a Racine. Four Scythians enter, 'couverts de peaux de tigres
ou de lions' (covered with tiger or lion skins), upon a *décor* repre-
senting a grassy bank, with huts set in the surrounding countryside.
But Voltaire's main concern, as in some of the earlier plays, is to
contrast two different life-styles. This time however religion is not

a factor but only political and social structures: on the one hand, the Scythians, republican, egalitarian, spontaneous and primitive (like the Swiss); on the other the Persians, proud, wealthy, hierarchical and sophisticated (like the French).

Unfortunately, the contrast is presented with some confusion, perhaps because Voltaire is involved not in one ambivalent relationship but two. The *conte L'Ingenu*, which he was to write shortly after *Les Scythes* and which contains certain analogies with it,[42] explores with some success its author's equivocal attitudes to French society. Voltaire saw that society as both cultured and heartless, and some of this feeling emerges here, especially in the first act where Voltaire is giving a barely disguised account of his own rejection by it; even Mme Denis is given a place in the tragedy, under the touching story of the heroine Obéide. The Persian hero Athamare, whom Voltaire likened elsewhere to a French marquis, has all the haughtiness of the Versailles Court. But the situation is more complex than this, for the play is full too of unresolved attitudes towards the Swiss. The Scythians are brave and public-spirited, and not unpredictably they defeat the less dedicated Persians in battle because they are defending

> La liberté, la paix, qui sont notre apanage,
> L'heureuse égalité, les biens du premier âge (IV. 2)

(Liberty, peace, which are our prerogative, happy equality, the possessions of the first ages).

But their sense of justice, though strong, is bereft of pity. Since Indatire has been killed, his wife Obéide must kill his murderer Athamare. This situation is complicated by the romantic plot: Obéide, Persian like Athamare but exiled to Scythia, has been obliged to marry Indatire even though she loves her compatriot. She is forced into an odious decision and avoids killing Athamare only at the cost of her own life. Her hatred and contempt for the Scythians, 'ces brutes humains pétris de barbarie' (these human beasts steeped in barbarism), iron-hearted souls of gloom and cruelty, are total (V. 4). Primitive man, she tells her confidante, is 'simple' and 'bon' provided he is not offended; then his vengeance is unchecked. Only in the last line of the play, when Obéide is dead, does the aged Scythian Hermodan remember that the basic precepts of morality include compassion quite as much as justice.

Voltaire wrote to the d'Argentals that in this scene he was

coining 'un petit portrait de Genève pour m'amuser' (a little picture
of Geneva to divert myself);[43] this is precisely what is wrong with
it. After a direct onslaught on Paris in the opening act, this further
riposte is excessive—in part because such personal statements,
though tolerable within the portmanteau form of the *conte*, do
harm to the aesthetic distance necessary for high tragedy; but even
more so because Voltaire, in calling down a plague on both houses,
muddies the structure. All that is left is a pathetic heroine, Obéide,
caught between two repressive societies; but that hardly bears out
the theme of the play. For a long while Scythia has been seen to be
a happy land, prey to the aggressions of a powerful neighbour; but
by the end it is Athamare who is endowed with humanity and his
enemies who are perverse. Obéide, lacking in depth, like most of
Voltaire's dramatis personae, fails to rescue the play from this basic
contradiction. *Les Scythes*, though not deficient in Voltaire's usual
effectiveness of linguistic statement, is thematically 'un fatras in-
compréhensible' (an incomprehensible hotch-potch).[44] Lacking a
controlling point of view, the play experiments with a broader set
of social conditions in a way that could hardly hope to succeed.

By now, in any event, such radicalism was being surpassed by the
drame bourgeois in the hands of those like Diderot and Sedaine. True,
they did not portray rude shepherds, but their middle-class characters were placed in context with a precision that Voltaire does not
seek. Hermodan may be wearing a tiger skin but he declaims
alexandrines with as much eloquence as his Persian counterparts.
The reform seems timid and incomplete. Likewise the staging is
limited in its adventurousness. Here however one feels a good deal
more sympathy for Voltaire's position, the more so as he appears
to have perceived it with a lucidity that did not inform his attempts
at social portrayal. In his Preface to the play, he gently takes issue
with Diderot: 'un plus grand appareil' and 'plus de pittoresque' are
certainly desirable on stage; nevertheless, one must not try to make
these elements perform the crucial task that only language can
undertake: 'quatre beaux vers de sentiment valent mieux que
quarante belles attitudes' (four fine lines of sentiment are better than
forty fine attitudes).[45] On this point, stage directors in the latter
half of the twentieth century would surely accord Voltaire the palm
over his fellow-*philosophe*.

The feeling is inescapable in a reading of Voltairean tragedy that
here was an important attempt at emancipation from the canons of

Corneille and even more so of Racine, but a limited and imperfect one. The dramatist judged correctly that the seventeenth-century giants had left untouched that area where classical tragedy could combine with reformist ideas, and he well knew the importance of theatre as a vehicle of social propaganda. His best plays, furthermore, are those which dwell more centrally on social patterns than individual predicaments. Voltaire's remarkable consistency in poetic statement of a cogent and luminous kind could only have furthered this development. But the latent possibilities were stifled, perhaps by the new-found energy available in the *conte* and its polemical counterparts. *Les Scythes* destroys the delicate balance, the more sadly because the basic theme was rich in possibilities, and Voltaire, sedulously avoiding vulgarity in language and characterization, achieves bathos by yielding to the temptation of mixing his picaresque life with his tragic work. Thereafter, the dramatic inspiration peters out, despite all his fervent wishes, and the *philosophie* becomes only more strident. It is a frustrating spectacle when one considers that the ingredients of a truly original contribution to classical tragedy were present in Voltaire's genius. Even so one must take account of the times. Diderot's dramatic prescriptions were more exciting but on the stage little of quality resulted from them. Even the great fervour of nineteenth-century French drama in its revolt against classicism has left a heterogeneous collection of curiosities rather than masterpieces. As late as 1944 Anouilh seems to feel himself greatly daring in mixing classical tragedy with comedy in *Antigone*; and one may argue that it was not until two foreigners, Beckett and Ionesco, presented plays on the Parisian stage that the inhibiting ghosts of the seventeenth century were at last exorcized from serious French drama. On this view, one should not lightly dismiss Voltaire's plays as failures. Quite the contrary; not once but several times he produced tragedies of absorbing interest and forcibly convincing expression. The real pity is that it has become almost impossible ever to witness any of them.

2 | Historian

The study of history preoccupied Voltaire the whole of his literary life; it is quite characteristic that his epic poem *La Henriade* (first published in 1723), should be based not on a classical or Biblical theme but upon the recent age of Henri IV. By 1727 he is producing his first historical work proper, the *Essay upon the Civil Wars of France*, which relates to the same period. Indeed, Voltaire's first interest was in modern history; the *Histoire de Charles XII* (1731), for instance, dealt with the life of its eponymous hero as king of Sweden in the early years of the eighteenth century. A year later, Voltaire had begun *Le Siècle de Louis XIV*, though its origins may date back even to 1729; this study was to occupy the next twenty years of his life, the full work not appearing till 1751 and undergoing important revisions in subsequent editions. Voltaire was also to write other historical works including an *Histoire de l'empire de Russie sous Pierre le Grand* (1759–63), a *Précis du Siècle de Louis XV* (1768), and an *Histoire de la guerre de 1741*; an authentic version of the last work (completed in 1752) has only recently been published in full for the first time.[1]

With the *Essai sur les mœurs*, however, Voltaire took a wider canvas, and extended his range backwards in time as well as in space. This historical enterprise appears to have begun as a sketch for his mistress and fellow-*philosophe* at Cirey, Mme Du Châtelet, and is first referred to by Voltaire in a letter to Frederick of Prussia of 1 June 1741. The work, like the *Siècle*, grows apace over the years. A pirated edition appeared in 1753, the first complete text officially authorized by the author was published in 1756, and he went on making substantial additions and changes until the very end of his life. In 1765 appeared *La Philosophie de l'histoire*, a work devoted wholly to ancient history which thereafter became attached as an introduction to the *Essai*.[2] The breadth of subject in the *Essai sur les mœurs* is even greater than for the *Siècle*, and it is not an exaggeration to claim, as does Theodore Besterman, that this is 'the work in which Voltaire concentrated the essence of his thought, on which he laboured the longest, and which he wrote with the highest seriousness'.[3]

THE PHILOSOPHY OF THE *Essai sur les mœurs*

To start with, this Essay is of colossal length, running to well over 1600 pages in the excellent modern edition established by René Pomeau: more than a half-million words. In the main body of the work (excluding *La Philosophie de l'histoire*) Voltaire undertakes what had scarcely ever before been attempted: a history of the world, such a project as no single writer would now attempt. Here we see the glory of the Enlightenment ideal of scholarship, handed on from the Renaissance but with more pragmatic intent: to encompass in encyclopedic fashion all that is proper for a gentleman of learning to know, so that reason and *philosophie*, developing their resources in the light of this new information, can increase the hopes of peace, prosperity and happiness, as old superstitions and prejudice are destroyed. As Voltaire put it in 1763, looking back on the *Essai*: 'C'est dans l'histoire de nos propres folies qu'on apprend à être sage, et non dans les discussions ténébreuses d'une vaine antiquité.' (It is in the history of our own follies that one learns wisdom, not in the obscure discussions of a futile antiquity.)[4]

But Voltaire was not the first to conceive of a universal history. The idea of a global 'histoire de l'esprit humain' with its consequences for 'les lois, et . . . les usages des nations' had been recommended by Pierre Bayle in his *Dictionnaire historique et critique* (1697).[5] A general world history had indeed been completed some years earlier by Bossuet in his *Discours sur l'histoire universelle* (1681), the author providing a broad survey of events from the beginning of the world to Charlemagne and the foundation of the French monarchy. Bossuet's vast study is however limited by its being a frank apologetic for Christian doctrine. The successive orders of history demonstrate, in Bossuet's view, God's for mankind working out His great scheme through the Judaic tradition, the Bible (His revealed word) and the establishment of the Christian Church. The nature of this aim dictates also the spatial limits of

Bossuet's work. Islam, India and China, regarded as peripheral to the essential meaning of human history, receive little or no mention.

This providentialist and parochial account could not appeal to Voltaire. He refers slightingly in *Le Pyrrhonisme de l'histoire* (1769) to Bossuet's

> prétendue *Histoire universelle*, qui n'est que celle de quatre à cinq peuples, et surtout de la petite nation juive, ou ignorée, ou justement méprisée du reste de la terre.

> (so-called *World history*, which deals with only four or five peoples, and especially the tiny Jewish nation, that is either unknown to the rest of the earth or rightly scorned by it.)[6]

In the *Essai* itself he will explicitly establish the different tenor of his work in dramatic fashion by beginning his narrative precisely where Bossuet left off, at Charlemagne's accession.[7] For Voltaire, there is no chosen race or creed. While he comes to regard European civilization as having unique qualities, he rebels against the Christian viewpoint that relegates all events outside Europe to manifestations of a secondary order. Human nature is the same the world over, so all history is basically alike: 'La terre est un vaste théâtre où la même tragédie se joue sous des noms différents.' (The earth is a vast theatre where the same tragedy is played under different names.)[8]

It is with this conviction that Voltaire sets out to write his great history. The title sufficiently indicates what he has in mind; he will expatiate primarily on 'les mœurs et l'esprit des nations'. This Essay is to give a strong emphasis to intellectual and social history. As in the *Lettres philosophiques*, the reader is wooed by flattery, being appealed to directly as an intelligent person weary of what passes for history and interested to know only 'ce qui mérite d'être connu de vous: l'esprit, les mœurs, les usages des nations principales, appuyés des faits qu'il n'est pas permis d'ignorer' (what deserves to be known by you: the spirit, manners, customs of the leading nations, supported by the facts of which one may not remain ignorant).[9] He will not want a mere chronology of all the dynasties,[10] or exclusive concentration on battles,[11] or a compilation of petty details like disputes over marriage contracts, genealogies and titles.[12] This is to be a history of peoples; kings will be of interest to the extent that they have improved the living conditions of their subjects. In short, Voltaire is writing a history of civilization.

But the term 'civilization' raises perplexing difficulties. What does Voltaire have in mind? Not the least problem is that he does not use the term itself; its first known appearance in French as a substantive dates from 1757, after the first editions of the *Essai*.[13] Voltaire tends to use 'police' in the modern sense of 'civilization', but even this word makes a relatively rare appearance. In general, he prefers to describe the salient characteristics of 'un peuple policé', often enough for us to distinguish them in the end with some measure of clarity. The essential elements appear to be humane government and tolerant religion, permitting the development of trade, affluence and consequently leisure, which give the necessary conditions for enlightened living in which the arts and sciences can flourish. From all this emerges a way of life that respects personal rights and individual freedom, accompanied by the equality of all before the law, such that every man's life and property are legally protected against arbitrary tyranny. The main theme of the *Essai* is that, amid a background of horrors and follies of every kind, mankind gradually makes progress. This is particularly true of Europe, which began late but has overtaken the civilizations of such as China and India. Starting in the twelfth century and spreading from Italy, culture makes an advance through all of western Europe. As true *philosophie* gains the ascendancy, belief in myth decays, and man's innate reason, encouraged to develop in the new climate, prefers to seek the truth instead of being seduced by the instinctive impulse to believe the extraordinary and marvellous.

This historical survey, then, ends on an optimistic note that may seem a little surprising after all the bloodshed that has gone before:

Quand une nation connaît les arts, quand elle n'est point subjugée et transportée par les étrangers, elle sort aisément de ses ruines, et se rétablit toujours.

(When a nation is acquainted with the arts, when it is not subjugated and bodily removed by foreigners, it emerges with ease from its ruins and is invariably restored.)[14]

But the correct balance has been struck a little earlier in this final chapter:

Il faut donc, encore une fois, avouer qu'en général toute cette histoire est un ramas de crimes, de folies, et de malheurs, parmi lesquels nous avons vu quelques vertus, quelques temps heureux, comme on découvre des habitations répandues, çà et là dans des déserts sauvages.

(We must therefore acknowledge once again that in general the whole of this history is a heap of crimes, follies and misfortunes, among which we have noticed a few virtues, a few happy times, just as one finds scattered dwellings here and there in wild deserts.)[15]

The implication seems to be that 'vertus', once thrown up, stand a good chance of attracting others, until they form a general climate much as the 'habitations répandues' may increase until they eventually form a town.

But how do such favourable circumstances come about in the first place? Here Voltaire's answer seems less clear. What he opposes is easier to discern than what he proposes. The hand of God which Bossuet had found to be ordering all things has no place in this resolutely secularist work. Civilization emerges fitfully, in response to certain needs and circumstances, without any finalist pattern becoming apparent. As for Christianity's contribution to civilization, the *Essai* is throughout at pains to show the baneful effect of the Church upon the whole of this period. Christian fanaticism has been more effective than wars in depopulating the earth.[16] In particular, the last five hundred years ever since the Albigensian massacres have been an uninterrupted history of bloodshed.[17] From time to time Voltaire may have words of commendation for certain Christian institutions: some of the monastic orders have an excellent record,[18] while the Church in Rome merits praise for the way it has based advancement on talent rather than on birth.[19] This does not prevent the *Essai* from being, as one critic puts it, 'un long réquisitoire contre le christianisme' (a lengthy indictment of Christianity).[20]

If then the history of the world reveals no external plan, how far do men make their own destiny? Voltaire seems to incline to the view that moral causes—human institutions and motives—are more powerful than physical. In the final summing-up, he discerns three constant influences on the human mind: climate, government and religion.[21] However, he is less keen elsewhere to give climate an important role in the development of European civilization. The *Avant-Propos*, indeed, makes a clear-cut distinction between East and West: 'Les climats orientaux, voisins du Midi, tiennent tout de la nature; et nous, dans notre Occident septentrional, nous devons tout au temps, au commerce, à une industrie tardive.' (Eastern climes, akin to southern Europe, derive everything from nature; and we, living in the northern part of the Western world, owe everything to time, trade, a late-developing industry.)[22] The accent is placed upon European freedom of action; and the impression one gains as the *Essai* advances is that certain great men can seize upon favourable circumstances and exploit them for the good of all.

To the 'great man' theory we shall return presently; for the moment let us consider what constitutes favourable circumstances. It rapidly becomes clear, as civilization begins to emerge in Europe, that it rests upon a bedrock of economic prosperity. It has survived in Constantinople because of that city's suitable geographical situation for commerce.[23] The only happy result of the Crusades is that certain towns achieve freedom and begin to build up trade and culture.[24] By contrast, medieval England was too poor to establish the middle class that will later on be seen as the backbone of English liberty; it is not so in the 'belles villes commerçantes' of Italy, where prosperity encourages freedom and culture.[25] The number of such examples could be multiplied indefinitely. Throughout the *Essai* Voltaire is attentive to the state of finances and commerce, delineating with care the particular amount of affluence in given countries at a particular time.[26] He does not, like his admired contemporary Turgot, try to establish a theory of economic progress; but the underlying assumptions are the same. Man's needs urge him on to make discoveries. Knowledge, once obtained, is a basis for further accretions. Trade, urbanization, a leisured class spring up, all of them increasing the place of culture.[27]

So it emerges that although the word 'esprit' appears with such prominence in the title and introductory chapter as to suggest an idealist view of history, in practice there is a strong material stress in the work. Voltaire's discussion of economic history lacks profundity, but at least he remembers to include it explicitly in his surveys of particular stages in a country's social development. Almost apologetically, he defends this emphasis: 'J'insiste souvent sur ce prix des monnaies; c'est, ce me semble, le pouls d'un Etat, et une manière assez sûre de reconnaître ses forces.' (I often insist on this matter of the currency's value; it is, I feel, the pulse of a State and a fairly reliable way of telling its strength.)[28]

But when it comes to determining who are the creators of civilization, then we find the tradesmen generally absent. Pride of place goes to those few great men who combine wisdom, enlightenment and strength of conviction. 'Il n'est point de véritablement grand homme qui n'ait un bon esprit.' (No truly great man is lacking a good mind.)[29] Military leaders like Genghis Khan are ineligible for this distinction, for they have left nothing constructive behind them that will improve society;[30] indeed, Voltaire throughout rejects any *mystique* based on military prowess, making it clear that courage is not a virtue but merely a fortunate quality to possess.[31] The outstanding heroes of the *Essai* are few: Alfred the Great, Pope Alexander III, perhaps Henry I of England, but above all Henri IV. For Henri IV was a giant among his contemporaries: not only a man of learning, as was the Emperor Rudolph, but a brave and bold warrior as well (unlike Philip II of Spain, who was merely a prudent tyrant); whereas Elizabeth of England had had fewer obstacles to overcome and had sullied her glory by the execution of Mary, Queen of Scots, while Pope Sixtus V, though a patron of the arts, was both treacherous and cruel.[32] In brief, Henri IV surpasses even Louis XIV in stature, though he had the disadvantage of living in a lesser age.[33]

It becomes clear from this summary that Voltaire is not merely awarding honours to those who promote the arts and sciences. The outstanding sovereigns are those with all-round ability, no less in the moral and political fields than in the cultural. Significantly, the first measure which Voltaire mentions as undertaken by Henri IV once war has been concluded is an economic one: he restores the financial situation. Thereafter, he undertakes judicial reforms and establishes religious toleration. 'Le commerce, les arts sont en honneur'; luxury objects reappear. A programme of public works develops Paris, making it more beautiful. Nor is this a matter of delegating authority to his minister Sully who, though capable and loyal, lacks the imagination of genius.[34]

This isolation of the great man exemplifies Voltaire's conviction about how progress is achieved: 'Il ne s'est presque jamais rien fait de grand dans le monde que par le génie et la fermeté d'un seul homme qui lutte contre les préjugés de la multitude . . .' (Almost nothing of greatness has ever been achieved in the world except through the genius and firmness of a single man at odds with the prejudices of the crowd . . .)[35] Strong government is the remedy to political disorders, as Elizabeth I demonstrated;[36] by this Voltaire means a certain firm integrity, not the ceaseless intriguing and steely vengeance such as kept Richelieu in power.[37] Given this strong affection for centralized power, it is not surprising to find the author antipathetic to feudal institutions, which in his view are both repressive and ineffective at the same time, permitting no room for free protest or trade or the arts, promoting lawless anarchy and consequent revolutions, in short destroying the conditions essential to the establishment of a civilized society.[38] By contrast, great men are treated by Voltaire with a respect which reminds one that he is also a classical tragedian; for they do not suffer as does the ordinary man with his 'petites prétentions' and 'vains plaisirs', but much more terribly.[39]

The enlightened king, as we saw above, 'lutte contre les préjugés de la multitude'. In the *Essai* the source of all the horrors is firmly identified as popular fanaticism; a king who sows the wind of superstition reaps the whirlwind of rebellion, as the populace, inflamed by blind prejudice, enslaves its masters.[40] Intellectual servitude gives not peace but war because it panders to man's blood-lust; therefore it is stupid as well as wicked to deny men the chance of enlightenment.

So we find a certain number of unresolved paradoxes in the *Essai*. Despite the repeated emphasis on economic aspects, Voltaire does not include them when he sums up the main motivating forces affecting mankind, and professes a more idealist line than he follows in practice. In the political realm, enlightened sovereigns are the saviours of mankind, firmly hauling their benighted subjects after them along the path of progress; yet one of the essential conditions of the civilized society is an insistence upon personal freedom and universal rights before the law. On the one side, Voltaire believes that men have a basic love of order[41] and can achieve progress, and he offers prescriptions for liberal rule which combine justice with enlightened self-interest; on the other, he has to admit that historical happenings are largely meaningless, that men have often plumbed the depths of savagery, that utter tyrants like Aurengzeb live to a peaceful old age,[42] that 'le maître le plus dur est le plus suivi' (the harshest master is the most popular).[43] It is the problem of the Enlightenment liberal, seeking to inaugurate a more civilized way of life but dealing with very imperfect institutions for accomplishing it, and wishing to believe that man's rationality is more truly human than his instincts. In fairness to Voltaire's 'great man' theory, he himself is the first to point out the dangers of such a simplistic view, which attributes all great things to a single man when he has performed only some of them; most of the time leaders merely profit from the conjuncture of events.[44] Few impose

a positive imprint upon history, and few emerge as heroes in the
Essai. Furthermore, as Peter Gay notes, in an age that antedated
universal literacy, universal suffrage and organized political parties,
dynastic politics counted for much more than now.[45] The nation
still appeared to be a political creation, infinitely malleable by a
strong leader, rather than a natural reality evolving organically, as
the nineteenth century would come to see it.[46] Meanwhile, despite
the discouraging world in which he lives, Voltaire sees his task as
to help improve the chances for civility, peace and happiness by
affecting public opinion. The *Essai*, in pleading for greater enlightenment, is itself an emblem of that enlightenment.

THE ART OF THE Essai sur les mœurs

For Voltaire history was quite as much a literary art as it was a
science, and his comments place it close to tragedy. As he said in a
famous letter to Shuvalov in 1758: 'J'ai toujours pensé que l'histoire
demande le même art que la tragédie, une exposition, un nœud, un
dénouement . . .' (I have always thought that history requires the
same artistic approach as tragedy, an exposition, a knot, a denouement . . .)[47] In the last months of his life he goes so far as to assert
that the only merit history can have is in the style.[48] Nor are these
isolated opinions.[49] As one might expect from someone who considered language an index of civilization,[50] formal presentation
would enter strongly into any writings by Voltaire.

Even so, the analogies with theatre are disconcerting. How far if
at all can a reliable historian treat personalities of the past as dramatis
personae and life itself as a vast stage *décor*? The most forceful statement of Voltaire's shortcomings in this respect has come in a
brilliant article by Lionel Gossman.[51] Professor Gossman bases his
case on the *philosophe*'s most 'theatrical' history, *Charles XII*, but
his argument is of general import since he asserts that Voltaire's
Charles XII 'is not . . . *fundamentally* different from his more mature
works of history'.[52] In this paper he argues that Voltaire reduces
history to a formal object, something that is only seen, never
penetrated intellectually, so that 'the inner substance . . . remains
enigmatic, like Watteau's *Gilles* . . .'[53]

It is certainly true that Voltaire very often uses the metaphor
of the world as a theatre; one such was quoted above.[54] Furthermore, the verb 'voir' or its equivalent plays a large part in the

narration.[55] But whether this reduces the *Essai* to a purely aesthetic display is not so simply resolved. For one thing, Voltaire's linking of history to tragedy does not imply an ironic distancing, as Gossman suggests. Quite the contrary, in fact; his plays suffer from the opposite defect of undue commitment to their subject. It is surely the same in the *Essai*. The ultimate weakness is not that it is too detached but that Voltaire can never forget he must write history 'en *philosophe*' (as he had put it long before in a letter to his friend Thieriot)[56] and cannot resist the urge to proselytize.

Considering first the ironic qualities, one would be surprised, with such a subject and such an author, not to find countless examples. Voltaire's skilful use of the antithetical paradox allows many a well-turned phrase. The complex quarrel over status and power between the medieval popes and emperors is well summed up when Frederick I goes to Rome in 1152:

Il fallut aller prendre à Rome cette couronne impériale, que les papes donnaient à la fois avec fierté et avec regret, voulant couronner un vassal, et affligés d'avoir un maître.

(It proved necessary to go to Rome in order to take this imperial crown, which the popes bestowed with mingled pride and regret, since they wanted to crown a vassal but were distressed at having a master.)[57]

The death of Charles VII of France is tragic bathos:

Le malheureux Charles VII mourut, comme on sait, par la crainte que son fils ne le fît mourir; il choisit la faim pour éviter le poison qu'il redoutait.

(The unfortunate Charles VII died, as we know, from the fear that his son might kill him; he chose hunger to avoid the poison that he dreaded.)[58]

Voltaire is master of the ridiculous detail that deflates all human dignity. One such is the papal ceremony at which the new emperor is to kiss the pope's feet, then hold his stirrup and lead his palfrey by the bridle for nine Roman paces. The nonsense is increased when the emperor agrees to the kissing of feet but not to the other more dignified obligations—the first was acceptable because customary, the second was revolting because new.[59] Voltaire rings a further change on this later when Durazzo, king of Naples, takes the pope's bridle, but only to lead him into prison.[60] On occasion Voltaire strings together a concatenation of senseless horrors, entirely devoid of causal conjunctions, in a way that is reminiscent of *Candide*. One of the best such examples is an enumeration a page long of murders and mutilations in eighth-century Constantinople. The details are horrifying—eyes put out, tongue and nose cut off, a murdered man's skull used as a cup by his killer—but the senseless succession, heightened by the meaningless list of names, downgrades the protagonists to absurd puppets in a grotesque Punch and Judy show.[61]

If this were all, then Voltaire would merely be writing an historical *Candide*. But the atmosphere is not the same. Mordant irony is the exception, not the norm; the more constant tone is one of sadness tinged with horror at such madnesses. Typically, the enumeration of horrors in Constantinople mentioned above does not end with some devastating pirouette of black humour but in a direct appeal to the reader's judgement: 'Quelle histoire de brigands obscurs, punis en place publique pour leurs crimes, est plus horrible et plus dégoûtante?' (What story of obscure brigands, punished in the public square for their crimes, is more horrible and more disgusting?)[62] Flaubert commented on one eloquent passage that here 'éclate d'une façon presque lyrique la tristesse de Voltaire en songeant à la barbarie des siècles qui suivirent la splendeur de l'empire romain' (bursts forth in almost lyrical fashion Voltaire's sadness when he thinks about the barbarism of the centuries which followed the splendour of the Roman Empire).[63]

This statement could be widened to take in the whole work. Sometimes the author explicitly avoids facile wit, as when talking about the Catholic accusation that Luther was in the Devil's employ:

Il ne faut point plaisanter sur les sujets tristes. C'était une matière très sérieuse, rendue funeste par le malheur de tant de familles et le supplice de tant d'infortunés . . .

(One must not jest about sad subjects. This was a very serious matter, turned into catastrophe through the unhappiness of so many families and the torment of so many unfortunates . . .)[64]

History is not futile nor to be mocked at, though many of its participants and happenings are foolish to a degree. The picture should rather evoke our compassion and sense of justice which, says Voltaire, are the two feelings on which society is founded;[65] for this dual attitude will save us from useless scorn and urge us instead to work for a better society.

Comparison of the way the same material is treated here and in the *contes* helps to show that the style of the *Essai sur les mœurs* is not basically caustic. The most suitable for our purposes is the *Histoire des voyages de Scarmentado* (written probably 1753–4), partly because some of the episodes are also found in the *Essai*, partly because this *conte* is one of Voltaire's most brilliant demonstrations of irony and the only one to rival *Candide* in this respect. In *Scarmentado*, the Mogul Emperor Aurengzeb makes an appearance as a pious figure who receives a present of the broom which had swept out the temple: 'Ce balai est le symbole qui balaye toutes les ordures de l'âme.' (This broom is the symbol which sweeps away all the filth of the soul.) Being such a devout man, Aurengzeb did not seem to be in need of such a gift. But Voltaire adds, almost as though it were an afterthought:

Il est vrai qu'il avait égorgé un de ses frères et empoisonné son père. Vingt rayas et autant d'omras étaient morts dans les supplices; mais cela n'était rien, et on ne parlait que de sa dévotion.

(It is true that he had slit a brother's throat and poisoned his father. Twenty rayas [non-Moslem subjects] and as many omras [Mohammedan lords] were executed; but that was nothing, and people spoke only of his devoutness.)[66]

The treatment of Aurengzeb in the *Essai* displays none of this ferocious humour:

Aurengzeb, dans le Mogol, se révoltait contre son père; il le fit languir en prison, et jouit paisiblement du fruit de ses crimes.

(Aurengzeb, during the Mogul period, rebelled against his father; he let him languish in prison and peacefully enjoyed the fruits of his crimes.)[67]

The other comments on this figure are similar. Once again, it is a matter for melancholy wonder that such a villain should enjoy success: 'Nul homme n'a mieux montré que le bonheur n'est pas le prix de la vertu.' (No man has demonstrated better that happiness is not the reward of virtue.)[68]

It would therefore seem unfair to apply to the *Essai* Gossman's conclusion about *Charles XII*: 'The princes and potentates of the world are revealed in the last analysis as the playthings of destiny and the victims of their own roles. The true heroes and conquerors are the intellectuals, the spectators of the great comedy.'[69] Few though they are, the true heroes of the *Essai sur les mœurs* are kings like Henri IV who embrace the intellectual world as but one of their many domains of action; and they move in a tragic, not a comic, universe.

The defects of the history as an art form are therefore similar to those of Voltaire's tragedies. In a work where the writer pays so much attention to individual leaders, the psychological analysis is too flat for the reader to gain any clear insight into their make-up. While the few heroes are idealized beyond belief, the villainous majority are equally unbelievable, being stupid or malicious or both. If these characters have any vitality, it is not so much in isolation as in the dramatic oppositions which Voltaire contrives between some of them: Pope Gregory VII and the Emperor Henry IV; François I and Henry VIII; Elizabeth I and Mary, Queen of Scots. To some extent the faults stem from Voltaire's persuasion that all men are alike under the skin; but there is an aesthetic weakness too. As one critic has put it, he lacked the historical imagination to enter into the feelings or cares of a medieval cathedral builder.

Fortunately this is not the whole story. Voltaire has strengths well suited to a historian of civilization. The structure of the *Essai* is not built upon pure narration, for every so often Voltaire interrupts the chronological account to give us a panoramic view, comprising tableaux of the different countries at a particular point in time. After the meaningless succession of wars and disputes, these portraits come as a welcome relief; and they fit in well with Voltaire's tendency, evident in so many of his works, to break down a continuous flow into sharply-defined episodes. Furthermore, they allow Voltaire to bring into play his extraordinary ability to sum up a complex situation in a brief space, as when he unravels the complexities of the Crusades or the Reformation. Here his lucid mind removes all ambiguity and paints the picture plain (albeit with the danger of superficiality). As we shall see with *Candide*, there is a price to be paid for such clarity; but the virtues should not be minimized. Voltaire is masterly at picking the representative detail which sums up a whole situation or period in striking fashion: details about affluence, as we noted earlier; the primitive climate of fifteenth-century Paris captured in the religious tableau played at Charles VII's entry into the city in 1437;[70] the crudity of morals in Sweden a hundred years later, seen in the way King John gets rid of his brother in prison by publicly sending him poison.[71] The *Essai*, like many of Voltaire's other writings, is a remarkable piece of popularization.

THE SCIENTIFIC QUALITY OF THE *Essai sur les mœurs*

Capitalizing upon the growth of historical scholarship in the seventeenth century,[72] Enlightenment historiography displayed as strong a scepticism in this field as Descartes had shown for metaphysics when he wrote his seminal *Discours de la méthode* (1637); indeed, the emphasis upon 'methodical doubt' as a means for constructing new avenues of approach to knowledge may be placed squarely in the Cartesian tradition. But Descartes's edifice of doubt had removed history from the field of knowledge and it was left to others to make this particular link. Inheriting the legacy of erudite sceptics like Pierre Bayle,[73] Voltaire applies Cartesian principles to the historical domain. As he had put it in his 1748 Preface to *Charles XII*, 'L'incrédulité . . . est le fondement de toute sagesse . . .' (Incredulity . . . is the basis of all wisdom . . .)[74] Scepticism will help one to seek out falsity, to separate the dross of myth and fable from the gold ore of true fact. The historian must avoid partisan views; in particular, Voltaire objects in the *Essai* to sycophantic professional writers who praise leaders like Charlemagne[75] or Alfonso III of Spain,[76] or spread false stories such as the ridiculous rumour that Henry V of England died of haemorrhoids as divine punishment for sitting on the French throne.[77] The weaknesses of Voltaire's position are all too clear to modern scholars, who will take his scepticism one stage further in asking what he means by a true historical fact. At the same time, in his laudable desire to avoid repeating the unverified details of sectarian historians, Voltaire does not fall into the opposite error of those nineteenth-century writers who believed that a godlike perspective on the past was possible, all prejudice removed. By deciding that one must take a *philosophe*'s point of view, he commits himself to a consistent historical perspective that does not pretend to the aspirations of pure positivism.

For Voltaire it is above all written sources that count. He explicitly rejects the faked speeches and harangues of oral traditions[78] and only rarely falls into the trap of supplying a patently contrived anecdote.[79] Extra-literary sources are scarcely considered;[80] and scepticism is shown towards such evidence as contemporary medals.[81] In consequence of such views, the farther back one goes into the past the more difficult it becomes for Voltaire to discover truth. Nonetheless, although so much of his research must be based on second-hand compilation (much of it faulty, as for instance on ancient Indian history),[82] Voltaire reads widely, though in haste. Brumfitt shows that he is thoroughly documented on the history of religion as background to *La Philosophie de l'histoire*.[83] Furthermore, his standard of accuracy in using sources is high, as Pomeau has shown in an illuminating check on various sections of the *Essai*.[84] (A similar conclusion had emerged from a careful study by Lanson of certain chapters in *Le Siècle de Louis XIV*.)[85] And as Lanson points out elsewhere, Voltaire had the rare merit for his time of appreciating that no history can be written without a critical examination of evidence and documents.[86]

The criteria for this examination, however, are unreliable, since they are based on a rationalist view of what is likely to have happened. The dangers are manifest; Voltaire can so easily conclude that what is accurate is what supports his own outlook. He rejects the idea that temple prostitution could have existed in Babylon and elsewhere, on the *a priori* grounds that no man would do such a thing in the presence of those he respected.[87] For similar reasons Voltaire denies that any religion has ever been set up which encourages men to vice;[88] he would doubtless have found voodoo and black magic difficult to fit in with this optimistic outlook. Even the rule, inherited from Bayle and others, that when a historian admits a fact contrary to his interests it must be right[89] does not take account of the possibility that unknown to him it could still turn out later to be false.

Nor does this approach protect the writer from sharing the fashionable view of his time. The Enlightenment's scant regard for the Middle Ages is notorious and it constitutes one of the greatest weaknesses of Voltaire's *Essai*. The price to be paid for his admirably secularist approach is a refusal to see any cultural hopes in the medieval Church, with the rare exceptions of isolated monasteries or a quite exceptional pope like Alexander III. It is this tendentiousness which most deforms the work as history; examples are the disturbingly ferocious onslaught on Jewish civilization because above all 'ce sont nos pères!',[90] the reduction of the Reformation to simplistic causes and the exaltation of non-Christian civilizations above their merits. In respects like these Voltaire is most the prisoner of his age.

But let us conclude on a more positive note. The *Essai*'s claim to count among Voltaire's most important writings rests on firmer foundations than these. What most distinguishes this history is the ability to see how a civilization can become an object of study. Escaping from servitude to a plethora of inconsequential details, Voltaire demonstrates that here is a topic rich for future exploration as the most complex and sophisticated of human enterprises, to the charting of whose fragile and gradual beginnings he has devoted such formidable energy.

3 | Conteur

Voltaire came late to the *conte*, for his first published essay in the genre, *Zadig*, did not appear till 1747, by which time he was well over fifty. It is one of the paradoxes of Voltaire's career that he took so long to establish himself in the form for which he is now best remembered. With very little exaggeration, one can say that his *contes* are an old man's genre.

Two considerations, however, affect this view. Voltaire's whole writing career is unbalanced. It took him nearly sixty years to develop his bent as polemical author. The *Lettres philosophiques* (1734), for all their *succès de scandale*, had no immediate successors. Forced to leave Paris by the subsequent storm, their author went underground at Cirey, and the next decade was essentially one of maturation as a *philosophe*.[1] So when the *contes* begin to appear, they form part of Voltaire's output at the height of his intellectual and literary development. The other point is a corollary. Voltaire had, under other forms, been practising the techniques of the *conte* for some time. In his light verse, his correspondence, his *Lettres philosophiques*, his historical writing, sharpness of observation, quickness of wit, ability to sum up a situation or character in a few words, are already present.[2] At least one *conte*, *Micromégas*, had been drafted earlier, by 1739. The Voltairean *conte* might then be better described as a mature genre. There are no prentice pieces; Voltaire's style was already fully fashioned.

Micromégas (1752)

Although *Micromégas* was not published until 1752, the evidence for believing that the tale as we have it was in large part written by 1739 is strong. In that year Voltaire sent Frederick of Prussia a

48

story entitled the 'Voyage du baron de Gangan'. Frederick's reply
on 7 July indicates that the basic framework of *Micromégas* is already
present:

il m'a beaucoup amusé, ce voyageur céleste; et j'ai remarqué en lui quelque
satire et quelque malice qui lui donne beaucoup de ressemblance avec les
habitants de notre globe, mais qu'il ménage si bien qu'on voit en lui un
jugement plus mûr et une imagination plus vive qu'en tout autre être
pensant . . . un ouvrage où vous rabaissez la vanité ridicule des mortels. . . .

this celestial traveller has much amused me; and I have noticed in him some
satirical malice which makes him seem like the inhabitants of our globe in
many ways, but which he handles so tactfully that one finds in him a more
mature judgement and livelier imagination than in any other thinking
being . . . a work in which you belittle the ridiculous vanity of mortals. . . .)[3]

Furthermore, *Micromégas* arises out of Voltaire's main preoccupations in the 1730s (science, philosophy, metaphysics) and bears
affinities with other works of that period. Pretty certainly, it is with
Micromégas that Voltaire's ventures into the *conte philosophique*
began.[4]

    Voltaire uses the tradition of the philosophic voyage, later to
serve him in such good stead; but here the hero wanders the cosmos
rather than the earth. Disgraced at the Court of Sirius, Micromégas
takes off on what might now be called his trans-stellar journey. So
far the element of personal suffering is muted. In *Zadig* such an
upset will be distressing; not here. Micromégas merely accepts the
incident as a good reason for undertaking on his Grand Tour of the
heavens. Unlike some of the later heroes, he is no simpleton. Travel
will teach him some surprising lessons, notably about the folly of
men on our planet, but his original philosophy, based on sound
principles of empirical reasoning and an absence of intellectual
arrogance, is well equipped to stand the test. This is not so for his
fellow-traveller from Saturn; the latter is much too impetuous in
jumping to conclusions, keeps reasoning deductively from unverified principles, and so naturally falls victim to his prejudiced
assumptions.

    Micromégas is sub-titled *Histoire philosophique*. It takes place in an
essentially intellectual world, one of logic and scientific method.
The basic problem is how to distinguish between good and bad
reasoning. Little is known about the hero, simply that he is a giant
(which is necessary for the theme of the *conte*) and intelligent. What

he does is to travel, observe, think. Existentially he is never involved. His role is always that of a spectator; at most he is moved to anger by the stupidity of others. But all is centred on him, and he is never absent for a moment from the stage. This is a world of simple structure. The scene is acted out before Micromégas, who, sometimes with the dubious aid of the Saturnian, acts as a philosophic chorus interpreting correctly for the reader. All the significant happenings are reducible to intellectual discussion (and the metaphysical domain is rejected precisely because the human mind can make nothing useful out of it). There is dialogue, but it is cerebral. The vocabulary itself denotes mental actions rather than physical movement.[5] This is the *conte philosophique* in its purest, most abstract form.

As one might expect, then, no time is spent on romanesque adventures in space. The universe through which Micromégas and his friend travel is homogeneous, friendly, understandable by human intelligence: created by God, interpreted by Newton. No sense of an alien void here; it is more like the countryside (to which Voltaire, as befitted his classicist's background, paid little attention) whose dullness one must endure as one goes from town to town:

ils côtoyèrent la planète de Mars . . . nos gens trouvèrent cela si petit qu'ils craignirent de n'y pas trouver de quoi coucher, et ils passèrent leur chemin comme deux voyageurs qui dédaignent un mauvais cabaret de village et poussent jusqu'à la ville voisine.

(they skirted the planet Mars . . . our heroes found it so small that they feared they would not find a place to sleep, and they went on their way like two travellers who scorn a bad village inn and push on to the neighbouring town.)[6]

Despite his occasional ironies at the expense of Fontenelle, there can be little doubt that Voltaire shared the older philosopher's belief in the probable existence of other inhabited worlds like our own. Wherever they travel, Micromégas and the Saturnian will meet people with whom they can, if not reason, at least converse. Both possess 'le don des langues'; there are no problems on that score. The two giants, for all their size, are just earthmen writ large.

The story is built upon a dual operation. Man is first deprived of his self-centred conceit, then built up to his true role. Earth does not appear till nearly halfway through, and its entrance on stage is pathetic: 'Enfin ils aperçurent une petite lueur: c'était la terre: cela

fit pitié à des gens qui venaient de Jupiter.' (At last they perceived a
small gleam: it was Earth: it looked pitiful to men coming from
Jupiter.)[7] Yet this humble planet turns out to hold men capable of
noble work, not, as they generally prefer to believe, in metaphysics
but in the more modest world of science. Here is a place for agreement on incontrovertible evidence, unlike discussions on the nature
of the soul that lead only to discord. Like Locke, one must dare to
doubt; like Newton, one may rejoice in the powers God has given
man to reduce his environment to rational order. The delight in
scientific discovery that belongs to the Cirey years comes through
here: 'Quel plaisir sentit Micromégas en voyant remuer ces petites
machines . . .! comme il s'écria! comme il mit avec joie un de ses
microscopes dans les mains de son compagnon de voyage!' (What
pleasure Micromégas felt at seeing these little machines move . . .!
how he cried out! how joyfully he put one of his microscopes into
the hands of his travelling companion!)[8] Similarly, the puny dwarfs
of Earth exalt themselves when they show that they can measure
their giant visitors. Newton is not only sublime but useful too.

The mood of the tale reflects this calm optimism; even so, the
darker side is already present, if muted. 'Sur notre petit tas de
boue' (on our little heap of mud), to cite a phrase that repeatedly
comes to Voltaire's pen, humankind are indeed wretched. Men
ignore their best possibilities and prefer quarrels, war, massacre;
they destroy themselves through hunger, fatigue, intemperance. It
is some little comfort to know that on Saturn, too, even on Sirius,
'the acme of magnitude among the planets' in Voltaire's eyes,[9]
death comes at last; and when it comes, 'avoir vécu une éternité, ou
avoir vécu un jour, c'est précisément la même chose' (to have lived
an eternity or a single day comes to precisely the same thing).[10]
One *never* has world enough, and time; Time's winged chariot is
always hurrying near. For all his intellectual delights, the much-
travelled Micromégas has to confess: 'Je n'ai vu nulle part le vrai
bonheur.' (Nowhere have I seen true happiness.)[11] The seeds of
Candide are already present.

Yet the tale ends in laughter and irony. Homeric ridicule is
reserved for the idiotic little theologian from the Sorbonne who
claims that the whole universe is made uniquely for man. The
ultimate truths are not for us; 'le bout des choses' turns out to be a
'livre tout blanc'. Locke's disciple speaks the last sensible words: 'Je
révère la puissance éternelle; il ne m'appartient pas de la borner:

je n'affirme rien; je me contente de croire qu'il y a plus de choses possibles qu'on ne pense.' (I revere the eternal power; it is not for me to limit him: I assert nothing; I am content to believe that more things are possible than one thinks.)[12] In that statement, with its reminiscence of *Hamlet*, lies the recipe for a sane and worthwhile existence.

Zadig (1747)

Zadig, probably written about 1746, is a more extended attempt at the *conte*, and the *philosophique* aspect is now revealed somewhat less directly. The eponymous hero here is much more than a mind at work; his personality is more precisely indicated, while keeping within the restrictive limits on individualization common to the contemporary novel. He is, like Micromégas, an ideal figure, but the accent falls more heavily on his moral than on his intellectual prowess. Furthermore, he is less worldly. Time and time again he has to learn that virtue does not necessarily win happiness. Nonetheless Zadig acts, he does not merely look on, and with the exception of the most famous chapter, 'L'Ermite' (to which we shall come presently), it is through his actions that Voltaire's ideas are revealed. The perspective opens out more widely in this story. The stage is set with a multiplicity of figures, most of whom are not mere foils to Zadig but offer resistance to him, dramatically speaking, from within their own nascent individuality. Zadig does not have to be omnipresent like Micromégas. He can be subordinated briefly to the delightful Almona outwitting the lascivious old priests, or the cheerful brigand who delights in interpreting moral fables to his immoral profit.

What is *Zadig* about? The subtitle, *La Destinée*, is not very precise; the work really centres on the question of Providence, as Voltaire made clear when he wrote that he would have preferred this subtitle if he had dared to 'se servir de ce mot respectable de providence dans un ouvrage de pur amusement' (to use that respectable word Providence in a work of pure entertainment).[13] Providence, in fact, is closely linked from the start with the personal matter of happiness:

Zadig, avec de grandes richesses, et par conséquent avec des amis, ayant de la santé, une figure aimable, un esprit juste et modéré, un cœur sincère et noble, crut qu'il pouvait être heureux.

(Zadig, with great wealth, and consequently with friends, possessing health, a nice face, a just and moderate mind, a sincere and noble heart, believed he could be happy.)[14]

It is 'la destinée' of Zadig to be disabused on this point, at least until the very last chapter. He painfully acquires the knowledge which Micromégas already possesses, that evil resides in human nature; but the theme is more explicitly and more pessimistically stated here: 'L'occasion de faire du mal se trouve cent fois par jour, et celle de faire du bien, une fois dans l'année'. (The opportunity to do evil occurs a hundred times a day, the chance to do good, once a year.)[15] Sixty-three out of sixty-four applicants for the royal treasurership prove themselves dishonest, ninety-nine out of a hundred women. On his way through the tale Zadig meets judicial abuse and venality, sectarian dogmatism, Arimaze's envy, Moabdar's jealousy, Itobad's crowning deceit. Women are if anything worse than men. By 1748 Voltaire, his idyll with Mme Du Châtelet over and engaged in a turbulent love affair with his niece Mme Denis, is at his most misogynist; *Zadig* displays a veritable rogue's gallery of women. Sémire is unfaithful and so too the fisherman's wife, Azora intolerant, Missouf capricious. Life at Court is equally productive of malice; *Zadig* seems to represent a literary revenge for the many humiliations Voltaire had suffered at Versailles.[16]

So when Zadig is forced to flee the Babylonian Court, he perceives that all his well-meaning gestures have led only to trouble; and it is at this moment that a true intuition of the world appears to him:

Il se figurait alors les hommes *tels qu'ils sont en effet*, des insectes se dévorant les uns les autres sur un petit atome de boue. *Cette image vraie* semblait anéantir ses malheurs, en lui retraçant le néant de son être et celui de Babylone.

(He pictured to himself men *as they really are*, insects devouring each other on a little atom of mud. *This true likeness* seemed to wipe out his misfortunes, as it reminded him that he was nothing and so was Babylon.)[17]

As usual, the author helpfully tells the reader what to think; and the 'petit tas de boue' returns with added emphasis. But in the moment of 'néant' hope arises from the ashes. For one thing remains constant, the cosmic order, as the stars shine forth before his eyes, and Zadig passes from despair to a brief sense of the sublime: 'Son âme s'élançait jusque dans l'infini, et contemplait, détachée de ses sens, l'ordre immuable de l'univers.' (His spirit soared into the infinite, and, detached from his senses, contemplated the unchanging order of the universe.)[18] True, his own miseries soon return and wipe out the vision splendid, but the revelation is of significance for later developments. There is some consolation too if one can share one's misfortune with another. Zadig is able to comfort the fisherman, who greets him as an 'ange sauveur'; but he himself wonders what angel God will send to help him. The scene is set for the appearance a brief while later of the Leibnizian angel Jesrad, in a moment even darker than this.

The chapter devoted to 'l'ermite' Jesrad (based largely, though not wholly, on Parnell's poem of 1721, *The Hermit*) has caused more controversy than the rest of the book put together, not surprisingly since its interpretation crucially affects the reading of the whole story, and also because it must be allowed that ultimately a certain irreducible ambiguity remains at the heart of this episode. But some strong presumptions may be made. Although Voltaire criticizes Leibniz on various points before 1748, he never (with but one exception that has been perhaps over-stressed) attacks Leibnizian Optimism, the reconciliation of personal liberty with cosmic necessity that is at the basis of Leibniz's *Theodicy*.[19] It is difficult to see the *Zadig* chapter as an all-out attack on Jesrad. Zadig from the first respects and admires him, an essential point in a story where the hero's philosophical reactions are a faithful guide to the reader. The trouble begins, of course, when Jesrad moves to action. His first two deeds, eccentric though they are, can be fairly easily accepted as moral lessons on vanity and avarice. The third, where he burns down the good philosopher's house only to reveal the treasure lying beneath, is merely a case of *reculer pour mieux sauter* of which no worldly man would entirely disapprove; one might however have some reservations about Jesrad's downright effrontery! But the final act where he kills an innocent boy is bewilderingly enigmatic. According to Jesrad, there was no other way out. The cosmic plan, while it seems to leave room for alternatives, had determined that in any event the boy was doomed.

Perhaps in all the attempts to interpret Voltaire's attitude not enough attention has been paid to the fact that he does not so much answer the question of evil as dare to pose it in its most acute form. In this incident he anticipates Camus, for whom the supreme scandal of our world was the death of innocent children. Zadig puts to Fate the most difficult of questions; it is not surprising that he receives no clear-cut answer. It must be noted that Zadig is not satisfied with Jesrad's replies, for when Jesrad calls upon him to cease arguing, he interjects a bewildered 'Mais . . .' At the same time, one should not overlook that the angel has placed this terrible dilemma in a wider context which somewhat mitigates the murder while not explaining or justifying it. Human life may appear tragic; nonetheless the universe is majestic, awesomely beautiful, immensely rich in its diversity.[20] It is as well, too, to note who gets the last word, another significant indication in Voltaire. Zadig may not immediately give up the dispute at Jesrad's behest, but when Jesrad departs for his heavenly domain, he accepts: 'Zadig, à genoux, adora la Providence, et se soumit.' (Zadig, kneeling, worshipped Providence and submitted.)[21] On his side, Jesrad utters words of unambiguous helpfulness: 'Prends ton chemin vers Babylone.' Zadig takes the road to Babylon, with the happiest of consequences.

Voltaire has gone to the brink of the precipice and looked over, but no more. Any temptation to believe in the absurd is always counteracted by the unchanging prop of Voltaire's deism, the argument from cosmic design. Zadig's earlier vision is now confirmed. Man is miserable, but God is great: small consolation in the darkest hours, as Zadig himself had discovered, but one that preserves a value for human action. The ambiguity in the chapter 'L'Ermite' is that of any man who, like Voltaire, apprehends with equal force the existence of God and the existence of evil.

Zadig is saved from futility and goes on to a happy, useful life in the true domain of human activity, the non-metaphysical. He submits to Providence, as we have seen, but his resignation is not fatalistic. At the end of the *conte* he is governing Babylon 'par la justice et par l'amour'. This bears out the whole lesson of the tale. In good and bad times alike Zadig has practised generosity, peacemaking, tolerance. 'Son principal talent était de démêler la vérité, que tous les hommes cherchent à obscurcir.' (His chief talent was to distinguish the truth, which all men seek to obscure.)[22] Well-endowed with intellectual and moral qualities, informed by reason and *bienfaisance*, he observes nature carefully and learns that it teaches wisdom. Just as he alone, with a sagacity presaging Sherlock Holmes, knows by examining the ground whither went the queen's dog and the king's horse, so too he alone can show, when he meets the Babel of conflicting creeds at the international fair, what their holders have in common. One critic cogently sums up Zadig by saying that 'il résout le merveilleux en termes de clarté' (he resolves the marvellous in terms of clarity).[23]

It is along these lines that one may discern a true optimism in the *conte*. The ironic insistence upon the world's vices gradually dies down as Zadig's exemplary character holds ever greater sway. At first he is unsophisticated, particularly where feminine wiles are concerned, but he quickly learns. Against the fickle women one must set the virtuous Almona and Astarté; even the rascally courtiers seem subdued by Zadig's rationally benevolent rule at the end. Besides, Voltaire chooses not to dwell upon some of the more bitter aspects of life. War, for instance, which always aroused his horror, plays a very muted role here, while reference to natural catastrophes over which man has no control is virtually non-existent. It is noteworthy that when Zadig finds Astarté again she is untouched by her tribulations, both physically and morally; not so will be Cunégonde, all her loveliness horribly aged and her purity defiled many times over when Candide eventually redis-covers her. In spite of the malicious characters in *Zadig*, the world in which they are set is much more full of hope than *Candide*'s.

The structure of the *conte* is loose and there is some negligence in detail and continuity, but a unifying element is provided by Zadig's quest for happiness, and there is a progressive movement towards a climax as his problems grow in scale and demand answers in wider terms. The chapter 'L'Ermite', indeed, provides a sort of philo-sophical denouement, as the detached insights into evil-doing are grouped into a systematic perspective. Once these questions have been aired, the *conte* can proceed to its conventional romantic ending. For the first time Voltaire has chosen the oriental tale as vehicle; so all is refracted through Babylon, Zoroaster and the setting of *A Thousand and One Nights*, which Voltaire knew and drew upon. By removing his hero to a never-never land of mystery and magic, the author acquires greater detachment for him. Such swift changes of fortune are acceptable in a world where the marvel-lous intervenes at every moment. Against this fantasy Zadig is set, nominally a Zoroastrian but in fact a civilized man such as one could hope to meet anywhere; Babylon is essentially Paris. Given this core of lucidity, a hero who has 'le style de la raison',[24] Voltaire surrounds him with a fantastic narration where the storyteller can indulge his surprised mirth at human folly. He combines the virtues of the Arabian tales, 'des contes qui sont sans raison, et qui ne signifient rien' (tales which lack reason, and are meaningless),[25] with the qualities of the philosophic story. In the words of the mock-official 'Approbation' with which Voltaire prefaces the *conte*, *Zadig* is (and the order of the words is doubtless not haphazard) 'curieux, amusant, moral, philosophique'.

Even so, the philosophical element looms disconcertingly large. The lessons are too straightforwardly didactic; either Zadig is imparting lessons or receiving them. At times one feels that the case is being overdone. In one of his most desperate moments, Zadig meets the fisherman, who has lost wife, house, business, and has now nothing but his fishing to maintain him; he is not exaggerating greatly when he describes himself as the most unfortunate of men. But Zadig, whose losses are objectively by no means as great, tells the fisherman that he himself is 'plus malheureux que toi cent fois';[26] and there is no suggestion that Voltaire has his tongue in his cheek here. In the last resort, only Zadig counts, and the backcloth, though richer than in *Micromégas*, is still pale in comparison.[27] We are yet some way from the density of *Candide*, even further from the emotionality of *L'Ingénu*. Such irony as exists tends to be directed only at the patently absurd devices of the oriental tale. Chapter viii 'La Jalousie', for instance, which describes Zadig's growing love for Queen Astarté and her husband's jealous revenge, parodies the traditional romance in its conventional language, hyperbolic sentiment and outlandish stratagems, but not to the point of alienating our sympathy for Zadig.

Candide (1759)

A dozen years pass between *Zadig* and *Candide*, years in which Voltaire's experiences and reading had not conduced to a brighter view of existence. Climactically, the Lisbon earthquake (1755) and the onset of the Seven Years War in 1756 confirmed this growing disenchantment. Voltaire had already given a foretaste of the astringent tone which was to come in *Candide* when he had written the *Histoire des voyages de Scarmentado*, probably in 1753–4. But *Scarmentado* is only an abbreviated blueprint, lacking the authorial control of *Candide*. As all the world knows, *Candide ou l'Optimisme* (to give the *conte* its full title) is a satire on Optimism, in which the philosophy of Pope's *Essay on Man* and Leibniz's *Theodicy* received their quietus at last.[28] The complex details of this philosophic filiation need not be examined in order to understand why Optimism was so hateful to Voltaire.[29] Its basic defect is summed up by Candide at a moment when he can no longer overlook the horrors of this world. Optimism, he explains in answer to Cacambo's question, is 'la rage de soutenir que tout est bien quand on est mal' (the mania for asserting that all is well when one is not).[30] In its unrealistic cheerfulness, it is not merely an absurd philosophic view-point but a cruel one to boot, as Voltaire had made clear in a letter some years before.[31] It is awful because it invites man to acquiesce in the existing situation, to say Yes to the universe (as Camus would put it), to give up hope and practical effort. The point is demonstrated by Pangloss, preventing Candide from any attempt to rescue Jacques with his thesis that 'la rade de Lisbonne avait été formée exprès pour que cet anabaptiste s'y noyât' (Lisbon harbour had been formed expressly for this Anabaptist to drown in it).[32] Pangloss, in his useless passivity, waits for events to happen in order to prove them right. In the best of all possible worlds, there would be no point to a *Candide*, nor indeed to any literary work except perhaps hymns of pure praise and exultation.

The *conte* is in the first place a protest against any such nonsense. Its world is full of abominations, in which man's misfortunes are exceeded only by the absurd figure he cuts; dignity is as rare as happiness in *Candide*. One critic speaks of Voltaire's satanism, of his delighting in the horrible when at work on this canvas.[33] Of this there can be little doubt. But to see the tale as purely a savage attack would be to limit its resonance most seriously. J. G. Weightman has seized upon the special tone of *Candide* precisely when he writes:

> In this one book, the horror of evil and an instinctive zest for life are almost equally matched and it is the contrast between them . . . which produces the unique tragi-comic vibration. . . . an unappeasable sense of the mystery and horror of life is accompanied, at every step, by an instinctive animal resilience. . . . *Candide* throbs from end to end with a paradoxical quality which might be described as a despairing hope or a relentless charity.[34]

This quality is explicitly stated by La Vieille, when she has concluded her personal recital of atrocities suffered. From this tale of horror, perfidy and humiliation one gains a vivid impression of nonsensicality. The Moors break off their hideous massacres only to observe the five times of prayer ordained by Moslem ritual each day. The janissaries swear never to surrender to the besieging enemy and in order to keep their pledge begin to dine off their captive women when stocks run low. La Vieille, like the others, has lost one buttock when the attackers carry the fort and kill all the male defenders. This nightmarish ridiculousness is in keeping with the basic perception which La Vieille has made of human existence: however many miseries and humiliations we incur, we never give up clinging to life:

je voulus cent fois me tuer, mais j'aimais encore la vie. Cette faiblesse ridicule est peut-être un de nos penchants les plus funestes: car y a-t-il rien de plus sot que de vouloir porter continuellement un fardeau qu'on veut toujours jeter par terre? d'avoir son être en horreur, et de tenir à son être? Enfin de caresser le serpent qui nous dévore, jusqu'à ce qu'il nous ait mangé le cœur?

(I wanted a hundred times to kill myself, but I still loved life. This ridiculous weakness is perhaps one of our most lamentable inclinations: for is there anything more foolish than to want to carry around continually a burden that one is forever wanting to cast down? To hate one's being, and to cling to one's being? In brief, to caress the serpent that devours us, until he has eaten our heart?)[35]

It is by rational standards a folly indeed, though whether it renders the human condition more tragic or more comic is hard to tell. Perhaps *Candide* is best of all described as a *sotie*.

The tone is consistent with these remarks. It has often been pointed out that *Candide* is a story where the characters do not die, or if they do are resurrected.[36] Though generally true, this statement must be treated with caution. Apart from the death of Jacques (the exception which proves the rule), a few minor characters do disappear for good: the first one referred to in the *conte*, the Baron of Thunder-ten-tronckh, and his wife, who both perish horribly, as too does La Vieille's mother; the wicked Vanderdendur is drowned at sea, and all the major characters witness scenes of carnage and destruction. In brief, the people on the forefront of the stage all have ample experience of death; but death is, as Sartre once put it, something that happens to others. At times the leading characters come perilously close, and Candide even requests at the very beginning of his career that he be put out of his misery when

he can run the gauntlet of the regiment no more; but once we have
seen the improbable way he is saved from this fate we can guess
what will be his destiny and the destiny of his friends: to survive.

Cunégonde impresses this point upon him when they meet in
Lisbon. She has indeed been raped, her stomach ripped open,
'mais on ne meurt pas toujours de ces deux accidents' (but one does
not always die from these two accidents).[37] Suicide is so eccentric a
practice as to be of little relevance to mankind as a whole; in all her
odyssey of tribulations La Vieille has known only a dozen people
who took that way out. Hope springs eternal; although Candide
comes to realize, especially after seeing Eldorado, that Pangloss
cannot possibly be right, he still has Cunégonde to seek for, and that
is enough to sustain life. His *naïveté* is fatuous too: 'quand il songeait
à ce qui lui restait dans ses poches, et quand il parlait de Cunégonde,
surtout à la fin du repas, il penchait alors pour le système de Pangloss.'
(When he thought of what remained in his pockets, and when he
spoke of Cunégonde, *especially at the end of the meal*, he inclined
towards Pangloss' system.)[38] On such a fragile material basis as a
good dinner theories like Optimism are constructed and upheld.
But Candide is not merely a figure of fun. He is in his foolish hopes
Everyman. By contrast 'Martin n'avait rien à espérer';[39] and Martin
turns out to be a cardboard figure, a walking version of philosophical
pessimism, much more devoid of human sensibilities than Pangloss.
Martin never acts save to opine, and his opinions, though often right
because there is so much misery and malice in the world, are also on
occasion wrong; for Martin is as morally blinkered as Pangloss:
'Il y a pourtant du bon, répliquait Candide. —Cela peut être, disait
Martin; mais je ne le connais pas.' ('However, some good does
exist,' replied Candide. 'That is possible,' said Martin; 'but I am
not aware of it.')[40]

This unawareness of good is as disabling as unawareness of evil.
Martin is cynical about friendship and loyalty, wrong in thinking
that Cacambo, once possessed of riches, would never return to his
master Candide. He fails to perceive that, however miserable, one
human being can find consolation in the company of another;
indeed, he does not seem to notice that this sense of consolation
comes over him too ('ils se consolaient')[41] on the journey across the
Atlantic with Candide. Martin is an excellent person for pointing
out how little there is of virtue and happiness in the world, but he
overlooks the fact that there is some. He serves a useful function as

Candide's philosophical mentor in the second half of the story, Voltaire endowing him with a vivid gift for summing up a situation. When the rascally Vanderdendur, who has stolen most of Candide's wealth, is drowned at sea with all his crew, Martin makes a precise distinction: 'Dieu a puni ce fripon, le diable a noyé les autres.' (God has punished this rascal, the Devil has drowned the others.)[42] But Candide is not persuaded of such a Manichean arrangement, any more than he shares Martin's belief that the world has been formed 'pour nous faire enrager.'[43]

A much more likely hypothesis, and one which appears to carry more weight with the hero, is that of divine indifference to the human lot, as outlined by the

derviche très fameux qui passait pour le meilleur philosophe de la Turquie: Quand Sa Hautesse envoie un vaisseau en Egypte, s'embarrasse-t-elle si les souris qui sont dans le vaisseau sont à leur aise ou non?

(very famous dervish who was reputed to be the best philosopher in Turkey: 'When His Highness sends a ship to Egypt, is he concerned if the mice in the ship are comfortable or not?')

The best solution in the dervish's view is not to go on philosophizing as do Pangloss and Martin, but in reply to Pangloss' question to 'te taire'.[44] Martin is wrong too about the basis of human character in equating men's rapacity with the predatory nature of sparrow-hawks, and even though Candide's objection is feeble—'Oh! dit Candide, il y a bien de la différence, car le libre arbitre . . .' ('Oh!' said Candide, 'there is a great deal of difference, for freewill . . .')[45]—he is right. There is a difference, as the saintly Jacques, or Cacambo's loyalty, or the old Turk in the final chapter, demonstrates. The world contains a stupendous amount of evil but some good; the only satisfactory picture is one which does justice to this blend. By the end Candide has gone beyond his second philosophical tutor Martin just as much as he has rejected Pangloss. Despite his ingenuousness he has always been practical-minded, wanting to rescue Jacques, turning to help cure Pangloss of his syphilis instead of uselessly arguing with him over the philosophical reasons for such a disease. By nature he is equipped to 'se taire', once he is convinced that metaphysical discussion is forever useless. At the close of *Candide* he has become an agnostic, totally emancipated from the teachings of his dogmatist friends.

The final resolution of the *conte*, in the garden near Constantinople, should be seen along these lines. It is not a wholly satisfactory solution, but in the nature of things it could hardly be, since the world of *Candide* is one of intractable problems. At any time thieves could break in to murder and destroy, or an earthquake could wreak the same havoc as at Lisbon, even without human intervention. But it is as suitable a spot as any, not at all a mythic place but one where a viable community could be realistically envisaged in the mid-eighteenth century.[46] A fugitive from the Old World whose hopes are as quickly dashed in the New, Candide returns a wealthy man to try the European experience afresh; but he is to discover that life for the rich and powerful is as miserable as for the poor.[47] The final stay is to be made in a place where a limited form of civilization can exist in a small community, as the old Turk has shown; as for Parisian theatre or Venetian society, these possible delights fade into insubstantiality. If *Zadig* is anti-Versailles, equally *Candide* is anti-Europe.

The aim of the characters in this book has been to survive; such will still be the situation at the end, though now they face a further problem arising from their new-found calm and prosperity, the problem of boredom. It is a skilful stroke of Voltaire's imagination to show this little community as thoroughly discontented in the garden at first. They seem to have learnt nothing. Cacambo is overworked and curses his fate; the three 'philosophers' seem by contrast to have endless time on their hands for disputations over metaphysics and morality; while Cunégonde and the old woman are thoroughly out of sorts. Only their discussions, useless though they are, punctuate the ennui, which is so great that the old woman wonders whether after all the atrocities of the past were not preferable. Martin draws the appropriate conclusion from their mode of existence: 'l'homme était né pour vivre dans les convulsions de l'inquiétude, ou dans la léthargie de l'ennui' (man had been born to live in the convulsions of anxiety or the lethargy of boredom). The only mistake he makes is his usual one: he generalizes too readily. Candide alone of the group has some doubts about this viewpoint ('n'en convenait pas'), but he too has no positive ideas about how to alter the situation ('il n'assurait rien').[48] They have come to the best place in the accessible world and they do not recognize its qualities; they have not heeded the king of Eldorado's advice that 'quand on est passablement quelque part, il faut y rester' (when a man is tolerably well off somewhere, he should stay there.[49]

Everything depends in the last resort on the right attitude. It will require the brusque philosophic advice of the dervish, followed by the practical demonstration given by the old Turk as to what work can achieve, to open their eyes. Candide, Pangloss, Martin all recognize at last the benefits of work, even if Martin's reasons are cloaked in habitual gloom and Pangloss characteristically thinks he has found a new final cause of man's existence. The important change is that 'chacun se mit à exercer ses talents'. Cunégonde will still be ugly, Pangloss loquacious, Martin presumably unchanging in his views: but there is room for good harvests and even (more significantly) for moral improvement: 'frère Giroflée . . . fut un très bon menuisier, et même devint honnête homme' (Brother Giroflée . . . was a very good carpenter, and even became a gentleman).[50] Martin's total fatalism has been disproved, while Pangloss' teleological explanations of their better state are self-evidently as false as all his earlier opinions. Only Candide has achieved the difficult task of renouncing metaphysics and absolutes and settling for relative values. There is no transcendental goal whatsoever at which to aim. It is sufficient if they have created a little light for themselves in a brutish world.

Flaubert, who admired *Candide*, regarded this conclusion as a work of genius, because, he felt, Voltaire had captured the sense of platitudinous existence: 'cette conclusion tranquille, *bête comme la vie*' (this quiet conclusion, *stupid as life is*).[51] People who have run before the storm for so long can hardly hope for more. The ethic of work is proposed as the only adequate response, but that does not turn Voltaire into a banal exponent of European capitalism as such. If the garden helps by providing food for the world, well and good, but the main aim is still to find a *modus vivendi*. The European social order, as we have seen, is rejected. Here Voltaire puts together a few fragments from the wreck as a kind of raft against total despair. It is this dark vision, this awareness of the absurd, which gives *Candide* a special place amongst Voltaire's works. With a recovery of more positive goals in his own life after 1758, *écrasez l'infâme* becomes the keynote. It is a stirring call and it set the seal upon Voltaire's position in his own century; but it is not the note of *Candide*.

Voltaire has a heightened sense of man's absurdity; he is not for that an exponent of *l'absurde*. Candide is often an absurd but never an absurdist hero. We find ourselves here in difficulties of nomen-clature, since the word 'absurd' has been expropriated by the existentialists. Candide's world is full of ridiculous and meaningless elements, it is one where history appears to be devoid of sense, yet it is not the world of Sartre or even of Camus. For, despite all appearances to the contrary, there is the possibility of cosmic harmony, limited though it may be. God appears to be indifferent to individuals but makes general provisions for an overall stability. Eldorado has shown what can be done, and even if much in Eldo-rado, the place itself included, is unattainable, not everything there is beyond man's reach. The development of science, the construction of beautiful and splendid buildings, the courtesy of manners, are all within the capacity of those who are not completely benighted. Above all, Eldorado has an inner sense because it has a God, the God of deism whom all adore and never cease thanking for His many blessings. True, Eldorado seems curiously free of the natural disasters which plague the rest of the world, but that does not nullify the lessons to be drawn. Human life must, after all, proceed on the assumption that natural disasters will not occur, even though they threaten constantly. In the rarefied atmosphere of Eldorado Voltaire can demonstrate a lesson capable of application in an inevitably more unsatisfactory way within our less well-arranged world.

So, even if this world seems utterly mad, no suggestion exists that it lacks a final arbiter of order and sanity. Even the most pes-simistic figure, Martin, never denies God, espousing rather a philo-sophy according to which the Devil seems on level terms with Him. Candide's worst moment of despair after being cheated by Vander-dendur revolves around human wickedness alone; the possible dangers for a deist belief are not considered. As we have seen, the dervish's chilling view of man's situation conjures up a hidden, aloof God, but a God all the same. Voltaire's pessimism will go no further. Men may be at odds with the world, but they are not, in Sartrean terms, entirely *de trop*. By work and civilized human intercourse they can discover for themselves that the world is not wholly out of joint. To see *Candide* as a prefiguration of *l'absurde* adds no illumination and indeed distorts the specificity of its mean-ing. Its value lies in its special reaction to an eighteenth-century context rather than in being the precursor of a world-view which Voltaire would have disowned. The *conte* advocates purely human values in a world from which God seems to have withdrawn; but the final sanction of those values lies, incomprehensibly, in that unknown and enigmatic deity.

The socio-political attitude that emerges from *Candide* is similarly moderate. History, as we have seen, has no meaning, and the final garden does not claim to confer any; it is merely a better solution than the various gardens in the work (Westphalia, Jesuit Paraguay, Pococurante's) which enjoyed a favourable situation yet, for one reason or another, went wrong.[52] Roland Barthes cogently sums it up as exemplifying the morality of the small individualist landowner, hostile to history and its rationalizations.[53] Voltaire, as we noted, is not proposing a system of capitalist productivity for its own sake; but neither does he ever threaten to revolt against the existing capitalist society in favour of some other order. Eldorado has a hierarchical system where, quite simply, masters and servants alike are happy. Perhaps the most persuasive critic of the *status quo* is Jacques, who by his actions proclaims an ethical Christianity which none of the Christians in the *conte* achieves. But Jacques is part of his society, a factory-owner whose charitable actions include giving Candide a job in his 'manufactures' and making Pangloss his book-keeper. The journey to Lisbon is not for purposes of vague philanthropy but 'pour les affaires de son commerce'.[54] His exemplary conduct stems not from any kind of socialism but from an individualist outlook that refuses to see men as inherently evil. On the moral plane, Martin equates men with sparrow-hawks and regards their nature as unchanging; by contrast, Jacques feels that men have degenerated from their original state:

Il faut bien, disait-il, que les hommes aient un peu corrompu la nature, car ils ne sont point nés loups, et ils sont devenus loups. Dieu ne leur a donné ni canons de vingt-quatre, ni baïonnettes; et ils se sont fait des baïonnettes et des canons pour se détruire.

('Men,' he said, 'must really have corrupted nature a little, for they were not born wolves, and they have become wolves. God did not give them 24-pounder guns or bayonets; and they have made themselves bayonets and guns to destroy one another.')[55]

The theory sounds Rousseauist, but the remedy is not Rousseau's. Instead of seeking a new social contract on radically different lines, Jacques works within the existing system, demonstrating that man's primeval qualities have not been wholly corrupted and awakening a similar sense in those like Candide who are not beyond redemption. Candide's actions at the end of the book are in line with the lessons he has absorbed from Jacques. As has been recently pointed out, with two exceptions 'all the members of the little society set upon the shores of the Bosphorus are in the most literal way purchased, not only Cunégonde and *la vieille*, but Cacambo and the baron as well'.[56] In similarly modest terms, Candide works to improve those few he can reach; like Jacques, he may yet fail.

In this regard, one of the cruxes of *Candide* lies in the hero's encounter with the negro slave in Surinam. The slave, miserably clad, has lost a hand because it was caught in the millstone and a leg because he tried to escape. He utters one of the most memorable lines in the tale: 'C'est à ce prix que vous mangez du sucre en Europe.' (It is at this price that you eat sugar in Europe.)[57] Nowhere else in *Candide* is the reader's complicity in suffering brought home so clearly. The experience makes a deep impression on Candide, and for the first time he openly denounces Optimism.

But what, in practical terms, does Candide do for the slave, having finished his brief tirade? 'Et il versait des larmes en regardant son nègre, et en pleurant, il entra dans Surinam.' (And he shed tears as he looked at his negro and, weeping, entered Surinam.)[58] Why does he make no attempt to free him? Why, even at the end, does he not employ at least one symbolic slave in his garden? The little group is, significantly, made up of people who have been enslaved, but all in an exceptional, unsystematic way, and all Europeans. The author seems to regard the problem as so large and horrifying that a practicable course of action cannot affect it; as with the death of someone beloved, one can only weep and go on one's way, or presumably, continue to eat sugar with a guilty conscience. This conclusion is not wholly fair to the writer if one looks outside *Candide*, for Voltaire had already attacked slavery in other works. One should note too that the only suicides ever encountered by La Vieille who were not slightly ridiculous are the three negroes. But curiously enough, in a work that catalogues so comprehensively man's inhumanity to man, the episode of the negro slave comes into the story at a very late date, since it does not appear in the manuscript which Voltaire despatched to the duchesse de La Vallière and represents one of the very few important revisions which Voltaire made to that text.[59] The lateness of the addition (probably in November–December 1758) seems to reinforce the impression left by Candide's reaction to the slave; Voltaire appears uncertain how to integrate this scene into the work. As we have seen, Candide is, most unusually, indignant; yet the effects of the indignation wear off. Jacques's passage through his life teaches him an abiding lesson; the slave's does not.

We should not fall foul here of a modish tendency in criticism to impale eighteenth-century writers upon the ambiguities which they reveal in discussing problems like slavery and colonialism, whose complexity they were just beginning to understand. Voltaire was to denounce slavery as vigorously as other abuses, and he like other contemporary *philosophes* prepared the way for the *Société des Amis des Noirs*, formed on the eve of the Revolution, and the emancipation of slaves in the following years. But Voltaire was not prepared to tear down the social fabric for any reason however good, believing that revolution was necessarily worse than what it replaced. In this view he never wavered, and *Candide* offers no reason for concluding, as some critics have suggested, that this *conte* is unique in its social outlook among Voltaire's works.

There still remains an element of hesitation. Candide, however compassionately, leaves the slave to lie there. The same uncertainty may be detected in the final garden on the Bosphorus. A way of life is adumbrated but only in general terms: 'Toute la petite société entra dans ce louable dessein [i.e., de travailler sans raisonner]; chacun se mit à exercer ses talents. La petite terre rapporta beau-coup.' (The whole of the little community joined in this laudable scheme [i.e., to work without reasoning]; each member began to exercise his talents. The little property yielded a very fruitful harvest.) We can speculate upon the extent of social commitment implied in those few lines, but we shall always end up against a blank wall, for we simply do not know. The vagueness seems to relate to Voltaire's own state of mind at the time of writing *Candide*. He is beginning to emerge from a period largely composed of doubts into the final phase of his life, the glorious Ferney epoch filled with enough activity in social protest and reform, by word and deed, to satisfy even so restless a figure as Voltaire. In this regard, both the nature of the negro slave episode and its late in-clusion are of significance. Voltaire is just beginning to involve himself actively in such matters; it is interesting to find that in November 1758 he writes a letter describing the poverty of Ferney's inhabitants, a letter which Besterman notes as the first example of 'a trumpet-call of social protest'.[60] The Bosphorus community is a provisional solution which can be retrospectively infused with the Ferney programme; but that is an extra-literary gloss, irrelevant to the value of the work. The uncertainties of *Candide* are those of a thinker who sees the problems of the human condition but has yet to evolve his own answer to them.

To this extent *Candide* is not a 'réussite parfaite',[61] and we do it little good by pretending that it is; indeed, much present-day criticism of this work begins with the assumption that it is the acme of the Enlightenment, either going on to confirm the view (which is misleading) or to dismiss it and mark Voltaire down heavily for having been so marked up in the first place (which is unfair). Suffice it to say that *Candide* is one of the greatest works of an age rich in philosophic literature; that said, let us, like Voltaire, refrain from dealing in absolutes. Nor is it essential to make one's total view of the work rest upon the final statement by Candide that 'il faut cultiver notre jardin'. Though important it is not crucial. What is crucial is the panorama we have previously been watching. Voltaire's technique in *Candide* has been analysed so often that it would be otiose to reproduce those observations at length. From beginning to end illusions are systematically deflated. Candide first learns, like Zadig (though much more bitterly), that goodness of intention is useless against the world's evils. Hounded across Europe, he takes ship for the New World where, characteristically, he expects at last to find Paradise. But the New World is no better than the Old, as he quickly discovers.

Voltaire appears to have seen the advantage for his purposes of copying the denouement in Prévost's *Manon Lescaut*, where the young lovers also hope for a new life in America and quickly discover that the corrupting effect of power is as fundamental as back in France.[62] Just as des Grieux is threatened with the loss of his Manon because he is not married to her, so too Candide with Cunégonde; but whereas *Manon* ends in poignant tragedy, Candide is allowed little time for elegiac regrets, and his few romantic sighs are quickly ridiculed by the businesslike Cacambo. The only difference between the New World and the Old is that the former contains Eldorado. The difference is however largely academic, seeing that Candide and Cacambo reach it only by a marvellous stroke of luck, and having reached it cannot restrain the urge to re-enter the 'real' world with their new-found riches. Eldorado thereafter affects all subsequent events. It shows that not all is illusion and that a civilized life may be possible. It also permits Candide another kind of exploration, this time with greater detachment since, although often cheated, he always has money to cushion him against the more basic brutalities. But Europe with money is as disenchanting as without, and the only dignified existence lies in a humble and remote garden.

This betrayal of illusions finds its parallel in the form used to narrate it. Like Swift, though for the most part less savagely, Voltaire undercuts the reader's expectations, generally in the final phrase of the sentence or final sentence of the paragraph. The technique begins early. Already in the first paragraph, even if unprepared, one may begin to suspect that the reason for Candide's name is not quite consonant with what one might find in a conventional romance. The opening sentence of the second paragraph leaves little room for doubt: 'Monsieur le baron était un des plus puissants seigneurs de la Vestphalie, car son château avait une porte et des fenêtres.' (The Baron was one of the most powerful lords in Westphalia, for his castle had a door and windows.) Assuredly, the irony is gentle, no more than traditional mockery of aristocratic pretensions in Germany; but the manner of it is fresh and promising. Later, it will be used with more resounding effect. An impressive paragraph describes the *auto-da-fé* in Lisbon where Candide and Pangloss are punished (Candide beaten, Pangloss hanged) as a propitiatory rite to prevent another earthquake. The fluent rhythms of the passage are impressive, albeit horrible. The sting is in the tail: 'Le même jour, la terre trembla de nouveau avec un fracas épouvantable.' (The same day, the earth trembled anew with a frightful thunder.)[63]

The same method is used freely in assaults on our orthodox thinking at every turn. La Vieille, almost the only survivor of a terrible massacre, encounters a fellow-Italian who has had the misfortune to be castrated as a choirboy and who is mournfully crying: 'O che sciagura d'essere senza c . . .!'[64] The nature of the encounter may arouse our suspicions, for she awakens from unconsciousness to find him uttering this sad phrase as he 's'agitait sur mon corps'— and her body is at this stage still fresh and appetizing. Even so, it is no more than a hint, and the eloquent lament is memorable (Beckett has thought fit to resurrect it on several occasions);[65] and most readers (certainly male ones) will find their hearts going out to him.

He offers to take La Vieille back to Italy, and reiterates his despairing cry. Her reaction is dangerously predictable:

Je le remerciai avec des larmes d'attendrissement; et au lieu de me mener en Italie, il me conduisit à Alger, et me vendit au dey de cette province.

(I wept tender tears as I thanked him; and instead of taking me to Italy he bore me to Algiers and sold me to the chief of that province.)[66]

Almost always (but it is the 'almost' which makes the world so complicated) people are not a whit better than they are obliged to be. So romantic sighing is a foolish luxury. Zadig had departed from Astarté in a sombre mood, which is described with sensibility;[67] not so Candide, whose dilemma is most prosaically recorded: 'Il n'y avait pas un moment à perdre; mais comment se séparer de Cunégonde, et où se réfugier?' (There was not a moment to lose; but how to part company with Cunégonde, and where to take refuge?)[68] He thinks he has killed Cunégonde's brother and is forced once again to flee. Past the frontiers of the Jesuit community, when they can at last pause, Cacambo urges his master to eat. Candide rounds on him indignantly: 'Comment veux-tu . . . que je mange du jambon, quand j'ai tué le fils de monsieur le baron, et que je me vois condamné à ne revoir la belle Cunégonde de ma vie?' (How do you expect me . . . to eat ham, when I have killed the Baron's son and see myself doomed never again to look upon the fair Cunégonde while I live?) And so on, to a typical anticlimactic end: 'Et que dira le Journal de Trévoux?' (And what will the Journal of Trévoux say?) But this oft-quoted gibe at the Jesuit review is less cunning than the following remark which opens the next paragraph: 'En parlant ainsi, il ne laissa pas de manger.' (While speaking thus, he did not neglect to eat.)[69] Life must and will go on. To this end, the past definite tense is, as here, used in a distorted way, creating what one critic has called an 'aspectual parody' of the conventional narrative form, so as to reduce the sequential and logical tone.[70]

Irony, then, at expense of character and situation is ubiquitous. In *Zadig*, as we saw, Voltaire used a parodic device, but it was still somewhat facile and consorted uneasily with the more serious tone. Here the mock-romance effect suggests by its very tone the folly of expecting knights to be noble or even damsels to be distressed. As every commentator on *Candide* must point out, Voltaire carefully distances us from the characters, so that every time there is any danger of arousing our sympathy they are reduced to proper proportions again. Both Cunégonde and her brother lose none of their snobbishness because of their sufferings, La Vieille tells her awful tale as if it had happened to someone else, Pangloss is unteachable, Candide, though more attractive a personality than anyone save Jacques, is slapped down repeatedly once his assumptions begin to rise above the reality of his surroundings. Voltaire has realized that the most effective way to evoke a sense of the world's injustices is to display them before our gaze with lucid irony. *Candide* perfectly exemplifies Camus's view of the narrative art: 'Le roman . . . est d'abord un exercice de l'intelligence au service d'une sensibilité nostalgique ou révoltée.' (The novel . . . is primarily an exercise of the mind in the service of a sensibility pervaded by nostalgia or revolt.)[71]

Hence Auerbach somewhat misses the point when he argues that Voltaire over-simplifies, that there is no relationship between character and destiny and that the 'sole standard of judgment is assigned to sound, practical common sense'.[72] True, we cannot walk round Voltaire's characters, know their thoughts except by the resulting actions (there is a moment of interior monologue as Candide kills one of his rivals for Cunégonde in Lisbon, but it is handled in such an objective manner that Voltaire clearly sets no store by the technique), or watch them existentially making choices. Nor do they suffer *Angst* or make stoical preparations for death. But then Voltaire is no Richardson (to name one contemporary who seeks to convey some awareness of an inner spirit), still less a precursor of the nineteenth-century novel. He is writing a *conte philosophique*, and what matters is the mental reaction to events. It is a classic example of what R. S. Crane called a 'plot of thought', where the change in the protagonist's thought conditions all else.[73] Another useful distinction, by Ramon Fernandez between *roman* and *récit*, is of value here. The novel, he argues, is the representation of events taking place in time, a representation subjected to the development of these events. The *récit*, by contrast, is 'the presentation of events which have taken place, and of which the reproduction is regulated by the narrator in conformity with the laws of exposition and persuasion'; it tends to substitute a conceptual order for the order of living production, and the idea rather than the concrete representation of reality determines the narrative.[74] So it is in most of Voltaire's *contes* and pre-eminently in *Candide*. The authorial presence is supreme, though in *Candide* it is related to a more perceptive view of reality than elsewhere. Time is of no consequence, is even reversible in the sense that characters are resurrected; when the plot imposes the need for Cunégonde to age horribly at the end, she makes the transition with suitable swiftness. To calculate the dating of events in *Candide* would be a singularly futile enterprise.

So then aesthetic distance is paramount. It operates at several levels. As we saw, only one important major character dies. In addition, Candide is more sheltered from atrocities than most, Voltaire appreciating that if we were too near to a protagonist who cannot be allowed to become antipathetic we would become too sensitive to his sufferings. He feels the rough edge of life, of course; but the full dimensions of misery in the world are left to others to relate: mainly, La Vieille, Cunégonde, Martin, Paquette and Giroflée. Voltaire's attitudes to his characters are not wholly unambiguous. There are autobiographical elements in the Pangloss who believes, like Voltaire, in final causes (albeit not the ridiculous examples Pangloss cites), in the pessimistic Martin with whom Voltaire concurs in letters at this period,[75] in the disillusioned Pococurante who has lost the taste for life and who bears some resemblances in thought, age and life-style to Voltaire in Geneva. But these represent no more than temptations of his personality; the future lies with Candide, vague though it may be.

This relative lack of ambiguity is one of the most striking aspects of *Candide*. Some uncertainties we may have uncovered but they are few. For the most part, the tale is handled with a mastery that all too automatically brings the word 'brilliant' to the critic's pen. Auerbach appropriately calls Voltaire's technique 'the searchlight device',[76] though he then goes on unfairly to deduce that it falsifies. Voltaire's great capacity for seizing on the essentials of a problem and exposing them so that the meanest intelligence cannot fail to understand was never better demonstrated. But a price is to be paid for such strong light: chiaroscuro effects are wanting. That *Candide* is not the greatest work of the French Enlightenment has become an almost heretical opinion, but justified: its logical dissection of illogicality is too cut and dried, its clarity, while admirably free of sloppy thought, is lacking in that sense of the unknowability of life which makes Diderot's work so alive for us today and his *Rêve de d'Alembert*, for instance, a masterpiece. After *Candide*, one might put Q.E.D., a dangerously abstract annotation to award any work of art. Diderot's sense of the confusion of life is more evocative to the contemporary reader, and I suspect from my own students' reactions that *Candide* is an object to gaze on more with awe than affection, like the great Château at Versailles; both are imperishable monuments to French classicism, in a world to which the classical precepts do not speak with such immediate force. The excellence of the achievement, in both cases, nonetheless remains, and surely no civilized man could imagine our culture as complete without *Candide*.

L'Ingénu (1767)

Did Voltaire himself sense some of these limitations? Whatever the case, *L'Ingénu* eight years later was constructed on a different formula.[77] Voltaire is now fully the man of Ferney, 'l'homme Calas', famed crusader for justice throughout the European world; he has totally realized how to cultivate his own garden. *L'Ingénu* becomes a work of propaganda within that cause, an eloquent cry against a system in which innocent people can be imprisoned or abused without justifiable cause by overweening power. The Huron who is *l'ingénu*, his beloved St Yves and his friend Gordon are all victims of authority; and that authority is no longer general-ized to take account of the whole world's wickedness, it is precisely the ruling government of Church and State in France, though set in 1689 to give at least the semblance of indirectness to the attack. The theme of *L'Ingénu* is essentially persecution, whether the target be Protestants or Jansenists or *parlementaires*, and it evolves out of the author's growing horror at all the scandals of the 1760s, notably the Calas and Sirven cases and most strikingly of all the La Barre affair. The way in which, for all the growth of *philosophie*, the nineteen-year-old chevalier de La Barre was condemned to burning because of a few acts of sacrilege that could charitably have been ascribed to the follies of adolescence made an indelible impression on Voltaire's mind. At the time of writing *L'Ingénu*, memories of La Barre's execution were particularly fresh, and many of the details of the case are integrated into this *conte*.[78] Calas and Sirven were Protestants, La Barre was, at least nominally, a Catholic. It made little difference, for in the end they were all 'persécutés', as Voltaire indicated in a letter to the duc de Richelieu at the time.[79] He was composing various polemical works to expose these and similar scandals: the *Commentaire sur le livre des délits et des peines*, the *Avis au public sur les Calas et les Sirven* and the treatise *Des conspirations contre les peuples*, all concerned with abuse of judicial authority, date from this same year.

L'Ingénu was to achieve, by different means, the same end. Instead of appeal to rationality (albeit couched often in emotive form), Voltaire decides this time that the *conte* can persuade more directly by the actual portrayal of suffering. Voltaire seems to have conceived the notion of *L'Ingénu* in a letter of late 1766:

Ne pourrait-on point faire quelque livre qui pût se faire lire avec quelque plaisir, par les gens mêmes qui n'aiment point à lire, et qui *portât les cœurs à la compassion*?

(Could a book not be composed to be read with some pleasure by the very people who do not like reading, and to *move hearts to pity*?)[80]

The basic motif is set down in the *Avis sur les Calas et les Sirven* where, discussing the 'Causes étranges de l'intolérance', he begins: 'Je suppose qu'on raconte toutes ces choses à un Chinois, à un Indien de bon sens' (I shall imagine that one is telling all these things to a Chinese or an Indian of common sense);[81] the Huron merely has different origins.

So Voltaire in this *conte* follows the same path as in the *Avis*, showing how the absurdities of dogma and religious practice can become lethal by unloosing hatred and aggression. Nothing could be more ridiculous, to Voltaire's pragmatic point of view, than the prohibition upon the Huron to marry St Yves because at his conversion to Christianity she acted as his godmother; yet from this farcical state of affairs the whole tragedy ensues.

But this time Voltaire has no room for detachment. This time pity must be evoked for the characters as positively as it was withheld from those in *Candide*. When *L'Ingénu* was completed, the author claimed that it was superior to *Candide* because 'infiniment plus vraisemblable'.[82] Sub-titles, as we have seen before, are worthy of attention in Voltaire's *contes* and we should not overlook the significant fact that *L'Ingénu* was also titled *Histoire véritable*. *Vraisemblance* (verisimilitude) is a central feature of Voltaire's aesthetics; indeed, the term is for him essentially bound up with the conventions of classical tragedy. Significantly, *L'Ingénu* bears the marks of a careful attempt to achieve a tragic tone. Nowhere is this clearer than in Voltaire's recourse to a patent device of noble drama, by aiming at a cathartic effect through the evocation of pity and terror. St Yves' dying words are 'tendres et terribles', the crisis arouses 'l'effroi et l'attendrissement', 'douleur et . . . pitié', while the Ingénu's state likewise provokes 'compassion et . . . effroi'. The effect of fear and pity upon our soul was, he had claimed in his *Commentaires sur Corneille*, to produce 'un plaisir très noble et très délicat, qui n'est bien senti que par les esprits cultivés' (a very noble and delicate pleasure, which is really felt only by cultivated minds). In such a manner 'on . . . remue . . . l'âme'.[83]

There is some evidence for believing that Voltaire's employment of tragic effects in *L'Ingénu* is in part a reaction to the disappointment he suffered when his play *Les Scythes* proved a failure; in many details *L'Ingénu* looks like a compensatory attempt to succeed where *Les Scythes* had gone wrong.[84] But clearly this cannot of itself account for the great difference in tone from that of *Candide*. the ways in which the *drame bourgeois* could be socially didactic on the ways in which the *drame bourgeois* could be socially didactic and Sedaine had shown by *Le Philosophe sans le savoir* (1765) what could be achieved by a success in this field, Voltaire appears to have seen the possibilities to be exploited, in a more strictly classical mode, by a *conte sensible*.

Not that the story begins with tears. At first it reads like a typical Voltairean sally against Catholic superstition, and some critics profess dissatisfaction at a work whose beginning is so different from its end. But even the early chapters do not at all read like *Candide*. The introduction is keyed more to pure narration, the philosophical element is more subdued. The cruel sharpness, especially at the characters' expense, has gone; at most we may be permitted an indulgent smile. Apart from the very minor figures of the *bailli* and his son, there are no puppet-like caricatures such as we had become used to in the earlier work. Mademoiselle de Kerkabon is a 'dévote' and one can imagine where that quality would have placed her in *Candide*; but here her character is 'bon et sensible'.[85] Almost everyone, even the villain of the piece, can be touched by compassion. After all, 'St Pouange n'était point né méchant'; and when he learns of the tragedy he has caused by his abuse of St Yves, 'il connut le repentir'.[86] The abbé de St Yves, who has also, but to a lesser extent, aided in the catastrophe, likewise sees the error of his ways.

These last details, out of context, sound like the direst stuff of melodrama and recall to mind all too uneasily the worst excesses of the *drame bourgeois*. But, weak devices though they are, they must be seen in relation to the more important characters and the general philosophical attitude of the story. For *L'Ingénu* is an exercise in metamorphosis, as *Candide* is not. The Huron's evolution is the most obvious; as he says of the experience which he has undergone in prison, thanks to reading and the company of Gordon, 'Je serais tenté . . . de croire aux métamorphoses, car j'ai été changé de brute en homme.' (I might be tempted . . . to believe in metamorphoses, for I have been turned from a beast into a man.)[87] But this evolution is an ongoing process, not to be completed so quickly. Intellectual growth does not of itself bring social sophistication. Although when he leaves prison, 'l'Ingénu . . . n'était plus l'*Ingénu*',[88] he is still ingenuous enough not to guess at the reason for St Yves's grief and to believe that virtue is enough to bring happiness. Only her death forces him to change his opinion, and then the wild impulsiveness that characterized him at the outset of the *conte* reasserts itself, so that but for the surveillance of others he might well have killed St Pouange and himself. At the end of the story we take leave of a man who has passed the great crisis of his life and will henceforth live as 'un guerrier et un philosophe intrépide'.[89] The situation is, in human terms, more complex than Candide's; the latter has discovered, it would seem, the one tolerable place on earth and the one way of making it tolerable. By contrast, we leave the Huron, the crisis over, *disponible* for a more open-ended existence. As in other respects, *L'Ingénu* is here approximating more to a novelistic depiction of reality than to a philosophic construct.

Similar changes occur in St Yves, educated, like l'Ingénu, by 'l'amour et le malheur'.[90] A perfectly normal young girl, 'tendre, vive et sage',[91] with a healthy admixture of passion and modesty, she is thrust into a tragic situation all the more pathetic because her youthful life-force rebels so completely against the death which the destruction of her moral principles imposes upon her. The Jansenist Gordon too has evolved, the harshness of his earlier opinions modified by his knowledge of the unhappy lovers: 'il était changé en homme, ainsi que le Huron' (he was transformed into a man, like the Huron).[92] Here the contrast with *Candide* is particularly clear. Like Pangloss, Gordon holds to a providentialist view of life and maintains it to the end, since in the final lines he is still maintaining that 'malheur est bon à quelque chose' (misfortune is good for something).[93] Gordon, however, is no cardboard philosopher, but a character who becomes increasingly humanized when acquainted with the sad complexity of life. It is characteristic of *L'Ingénu* that he should turn out to be better than his philosophy.

These ambivalences of life come under repeated scrutiny. In *Candide*, Voltaire had concentrated upon the supreme absurdity that men cling to a life they should rationally despise. Such is not the picture left by *L'Ingénu*; indeed, when the hero is tempted to suicide but saved from it because he loves St Yves (Chapter vii) the contradiction is registered with sympathy. There is, it is true, only one death in the tale, but that death is central, and besides it is not caused by some accidental shrug of the universe but intimately relates to what the human spirit can tolerate without being broken. The appetite for survival revealed in *Candide* was, as we saw, hard to classify in literary terms, but it could scarcely be called the stuff of high tragedy. In *L'Ingénu*, however, the important paradoxes of existence are all tragic. One discovers, for instance, the educative function of pain, in particular for the three main characters and in general for the world in which they move. The knowledge of suffering leads to wisdom, understanding and tolerance; it leaves people better than it finds them. The *conte* evolves from satiric flippancy (though muted here) to the nobility of high drama. Perhaps Voltaire himself felt that his own art had progressed; as has been noted, he expressed a preference for the *vraisemblance* of *L'Ingénu*.

Be that as it may, posterity has not ratified the author's judgement of his work. It is difficult to read *L'Ingénu* without feeling that the sensibility becomes excessive by the end. Voltaire's feminine psychology, never one of his strongest points, is not subtle enough to gain our sympathy for a heroine who, rather improbably, falls into a fatal decline because she has been seduced, even though she knows that the seduction has secured the Huron's release from prison and that he would be the first to condone the act. Voltaire's characterization of women was always better when somewhat detached, whether it be Cunégonde in *Candide* or Mme Du Deffand in real life; in seeking to be serious, he falls back upon a hackneyed trope like the loss of virginity and cannot elevate it to the stature of tragic seriousness.

Jacques in *Candide* had glimpsed the possibility that men were not inherently evil. In *L'Ingénu* Voltaire builds his plot upon the thesis that man is good, corrupted only by institutions, and the world he creates is not wholly convincing, because essentially, it would seem, such pure Rousseauism runs counter to his real views. The device to win pity fails to come off because it is at odds with his more complex view of human beings. Besides, St Yves is not La Barre. The eloquent indignation he felt for this unhappy victim cannot be transmuted into the portrait of a girl who has done nothing to get herself into trouble except to be beautiful and dependent upon authority. It is in the last resort the total innocence of St Yves which makes her so uninteresting.

Even so, *L'Ingénu* has much to recommend it. The main character, after all, is the eponymous hero, and here Voltaire is much more effective. The Huron is yet one more of Voltaire's 'natural men', devoid of experience but possessed of a judicious mind. With his straightforward common sense, he deflates the mysteries of confession and baptism; but he is a wild man who believes that marriage is fornication and that burning down the convent where St Yves is interned is the best way to release her. Such is the portrait, full of interestingly selected detail, which Voltaire gives us of this character before real misfortune refines him and elevates him to a higher but still believable plane. Unlike Candide, who starts in European society and is driven out of it, l'Ingénu comes from the wilds of Canada but is destined, as a true Frenchman, to settle down in France. It is through the acquaintance of books and of civilized people like Gordon that he himself grows in knowledge and morality. His early life had been of value in saving him from a prejudicial upbringing: 'Car, n'ayant rien appris dans son enfance, il n'avait point appris de préjugés.' (For, having learnt nothing in his childhood, he had learnt no prejudices.)[94] The *tabula rasa*, having survived the vulnerable years of childhood, can now admit of true perceptions; like St Yves in her Breton home he has not been contaminated by the worst effects of society.

Voltaire is making no primitivist claims, nor applying the same reductionist principles to European culture as in *Candide*. Books pre-eminently have value, as we have seen, and there is a useful existence for the Huron to lead henceforth as an army officer. If men's hearts are visited by pity and justice, then one's garden can be within the confines of France. The Huron's struggle with and triumph over adversity, described in sympathetic terms, provides a firm central structure. It is rather unfortunate that the novelistic attempt to widen the canvas by giving St Yves an autonomy denied to earlier heroines is not crowned with greater success. Nonetheless, the didactic aim of *L'Ingénu* (to provide a fable for the times about persecution in France) has largely been achieved through the figure of this romantic, exotic hero who receives, as one critic put it, an 'éducation sentimentale', and to more positive effect than Flaubert's hero.

Le Taureau blanc (1774)

L'Ingénu remains unique, however, amongst Voltaire's *contes*, an isolated venture, with mixed success, into the more realistic field of what one might call the *roman philosophique*. But it must be borne in mind that the author never ceased experimenting with the formal possibilities of the *conte*. *L'Homme aux quarante écus* (1768) is more a *philosophe* discussion than a story; the *Histoire de Jenni* (1775) begins with recounted events and turns into dialogue. The permutations are many and varied, the author mixing narrative and reflection experimentally without concern for purity of genre. *La Princesse de Babylone* (1768) is a more conventional tale, but here Voltaire appears to be copying too mechanically the devices of earlier stories: the world voyage as in *Candide*, the fantasy romance as in *Zadig*; only the section on England rises above the level of mere competence. But with *Le Taureau blanc* the author showed once again that he had not lost the narrative gift.

This tale may not be quite the swan-song which the date of its appearance, less than four years before Voltaire's death, seems to indicate; internal evidence suggests that the genesis of the story dates from as early as 1766, with additions made over subsequent years before the final revision in 1772–3.[95] The author has gone back to a mode of stylized fantasy, but the setting is new. For the first time (surprisingly, in view of his tireless interest in Biblical criticism), he uses the world of the Old Testament. To heighten the absurdity of these surroundings, Voltaire settles upon what he regards as one of its more improbable episodes. When Nebuchadnezzar had recounted a troubling dream to Daniel, the latter had seen it as a prediction that 'they shall drive thee from man, and thy dwelling shall be with the beasts of the field, and they shall make thee to eat grass as oxen' (Daniel 4:24–5). And so it came to pass; the king underwent this fate, 'till his hairs were grown like eagles' feathers, and his nails like birds' claws' (Daniel 4:33). The passage had long proved an embarrassment to Biblical exegetes.[96] Voltaire, adept at fishing in troubled waters of this sort, simply assumes that Nebuchadnezzar literally turned into a white bull and thereupon builds up his fantasy.

The result is a magical world, a stylized version of Voltaire's views about the way of life described in the Old Testament. Supernatural happenings are everywhere; the unlikely dramatis personae include the Witch of Endor, the 'gros poisson' that swallowed Jonah, and a snake and ass both of whom can speak fluently. The author enjoys himself mixing incongruities in the most arbitrary way. Whereas the charming Princess Amaside is just twenty-four years old, her counsellor 'le mage Mambrès' is around 1300; the snake and ass can talk but not the noble bull; the snake has a 'physionomie . . . noble et intéressante';[97] Mambrès turns the bull into a god; God himself alters the three filthy, ragged and loquacious prophets Daniel, Ezekiel and Jeremiah into magpies. As in *L'Ingénu*, this is a world of metamorphosis, but the changes are all based on irrational accidents. Mambrès reminds Amaside that in his youth he accomplished even finer transformations: 'On ne marchait dans mon jeune temps que sur des métamorphoses.' (In my young days one trod only upon metamorphoses.)[98] No oriental fairy tale could be more fanciful; but such fairy tales made no pretence at being reality. The pre-Christian Biblical world, on the other hand, is Anti-Reason made manifest in its ridiculous claims to truth.

It would be bad enough if this chronicle of the Israelites, a race supposedly chosen of God but unknown to the rest of the world, merely contained absurdities. Unfortunately, as usual in Voltaire, irrationality cannot be harmless, since it always appeals to the human capacity for intolerance and persecution. One character bears the odium: King Amasis, one of the *conteur*'s most lively representations. This king sees himself as possessing the God-given right to kill his daughter in righteous wrath, even though he claims to love her: 'Il est juste que je vous coupe le cou.' (It is right that I cut off your head.)[99] But he too is not entirely free to choose; once he has sworn to kill her he must go through with it, otherwise he is condemned to Hell for breaking his oath—'et je ne veux pas me damner pour l'amour de vous' (and I do not want to damn myself for love of you).[100] The full horror of Old Testament religion emerges nowhere more clearly than here. In this awful world human beings must destroy one another to avoid the divine wrath that is worked out in eternal Hell. If the reason for such a punishment is no more than that she involuntarily uttered the taboo name of her beloved Nebuchadnezzar, that merely heightens the cruel nonsense. It is illuminating to compare the Biblical source of this episode with Voltaire's reconstruction. He clearly has in mind the poignant tale of Jephthah's daughter, whom her father had unwittingly pledged to God if he should defeat the Ammonites (Judges 11). There could be no greater contrast than that between Jephthah's anguish and Amasis' conduct; but then Voltaire would surely have rejoined that the Israelite leader should never have made such an inhuman vow in the first place, and that the victory over the Ammonites was itself a typical Old Testament blood-bath.[101] The one direct allusion to Jephthah is not complimentary; Voltaire speaks of the 'puissant bâtard Jephté, qui coupa le cou à sa fille parce qu'il avait gagné une bataille' (the powerful bastard Jephthah, who cut off his daughter's head because he had won a battle).[102] For this *philosophe* the justice of the Old Testament is based on retribution, not love. Amasis himself is a surrogate figure for the hateful Jehovah.

Even so, the tale is invested with a calm urbanity; these nightmares have been conjured. At the worst moment, when Amasis is ready to cut off his daughter's head, she blithely replies: 'Mon cher père, allez couper le cou à qui vous voudrez; mais ce ne sera pas à moi.' (My dear father, go and behead anyone you like; but it will not be me.)[103] Sanity has prevailed, thanks to Mambrès; the bull is restored to human form and all ends happily. The pursuit of human wisdom and happiness has been confirmed in opposition to the grandiose falsity of Amasis and the priests. This resolution of the tale is matched by the tone; instead of the devastating wit of *Candide* or the satiric pathos of *L'Ingénu* one finds an attenuated irony, the quiet deflation of a world so ridiculous that it destroys itself by the merest exposure to ridicule. Such antiquated absurdities have not the power to evoke indignation as does the contemporary world. After a lifetime of Biblical commentary, Voltaire is crowning his efforts with a tale that conveys the essentials of his criticism in imaginative form.

Through this crazy society moves one wise man, Mambrès: like his author a 'vieux solitaire' better than his environment, helpful, prudent, discreet, persuaded like Voltaire that 'ce monde-ci subsiste de contradictions'.[104] But Mambrès, like Candide and the

Huron, is not wholly a mouthpiece. Since he was born into a totally un-Voltairean time, his attributes are often to be mocked. As a 'divin mage, divin eunuque',[105] he acts like an Old Testament prophet—except that he cannot prophesy! The mixture of 'sage' and 'mage' in Mambrès would be bewildering if Voltaire were aiming at psychological consistency; but after the single venture into the psychological novel represented by *L'Ingénu* the author has returned to the terrain he knows best, where the improbable plot rules, the overriding presence is the author's, the final goal a polemical victory.

Nowhere is this clearer than in the role of the snake, a humanized character worthy of La Fontaine. Here is a gallant gentleman with the ladies but doomed to get them into trouble through no fault of his own. So it had been with Eve in the Garden of Eden. How could he have guessed that God would actually disapprove of her wanting to gain more knowledge by tasting the fatal apple? But the snake serves other purposes as well. For he is also the Devil who charmed Eve, and as such he can say ominously: 'J'oserais presque dire que toute la terre m'appartient.' (I would almost dare to say that the whole earth belongs to me.)[106] Thus Voltaire gets full value out of a Protean character, demonstrating the same genial scorn for the Garden of Eden hypothesis of evil as for the rest of the Old Testament, yet allowing, like Mambrès himself, that the riddle of the power of evil in the world is beyond him.

Whichever character is speaking, Voltaire controls the utterance and reminds us all the while that he does so. Amaside has read Locke, the snake knows about *Paradise Lost*, Mambrès anticipates the 'Venite adoremus' of Christ's Nativity. *Le Taureau blanc* lacks that sense of philosophical urgency which gives force to the best of Voltaire's earlier *contes*, and to that extent it is slighter. But it is one of his most polished products in the genre, radiating an uncommon charm and freshness and possessing perhaps the most imaginative setting of any *conte*. If the reach is not as ambitious, the grasp is more consistent; the tale is devoid of those *longueurs* which disfigure even *Candide*. Voltaire has created a myth of the Old Testament more persuasive by its stylization than all else he has to say on the subject.

Le Taureau blanc contains what is possibly Voltaire's most important pronouncement on the aesthetic of the *conte philosophique*. The serpent has been telling Amaside stories to distract her from her distress at the thought of Nebuchadnezzar's impending death.

These tales are all about horrors or absurd miracles out of the Old Testament, Voltaire exploiting the opportunity to show some of the more notorious examples. As a young lady who has read Locke, the princess is understandably bored by this recital. She seeks another sort of story:

Je veux qu'un conte soit fondé sur la vraisemblance, et qu'il ne ressemble pas toujours à un rêve. Je désire qu'il n'ait rien de trivial ni d'extravagant. Je voudrais surtout que, sous le voile de la fable, il laissât entrevoir aux yeux exercés quelque vérité fine qui échappe au vulgaire.

(I want a tale to be based on verisimilitude and not always resembling a dream. I wish it would contain nothing vulgar or extravagant. I should like above all that, under the disguise of fable, it might allow practised eyes to glimpse some subtle truth that escapes the common people.)[107]

Once again we encounter the principle of *vraisemblance*, which Voltaire apparently considers to be as relevant here as in *L'Ingénu*. Clearly it is not intended to refer merely to characterization. While *L'Ingénu* approaches the realist novel and *Le Taureau blanc* is a fantasy, the differences are ultimately secondary. The fabulous or dreamlike element in so many *contes* is only a façade, encouraging the truly enlightened reader to look deeper and discover the 'vérité fine' beneath; one does not need to stress the aristocratic notion implicit here. Whatever the extravagances of a story like *Candide*, it is not 'extravagant', for it always adheres to the classical notion of imitating nature. Voltaire had no patience with the conventional plots of romance and exploits them for parody; as he had written in his *Notebooks* early in his career, probably while still in England: 'All that is old topik. No more digging in these exhausted mines.' He added, however: 'But let us stik to nature.'[108]

VOLTAIRE'S TREATMENT OF THE *conte*

In these respects, then, Voltaire remains a classicist. The *contes* intrigue and amuse in order to lead the reader to the moral and philosophical purpose. Furthermore, they diffuse general truths relating to Man, not men. Zadig in Babylon or Micromégas on Sirius act according to the same principles as Voltaire in Paris or Geneva. Reason is dominant. Disorder and folly are always observed with lucidity, which itself constitutes, even at the most desperate hours, an assurance that life has a unique value and man a unique role in the universe. As we have seen so often, catastrophe and malice arise from poor thinking; the philosophic hero, though aware that virtue does not lead to happiness, discovers a mode of conduct that will make for a civilized and tolerable existence. With the exception of *L'Ingénu*, this is scarcely ever a tragic world; the final attitude of *Le Monde comme il va* (1748) holds true for all of them: 'si tout n'est pas bien, tout est passable' (if all is not well, all is tolerable). Voltairean style mirrors this view. It is all balance, harmony, elegance, the triumph of mind over formless matter.

In all this Voltaire is the perfect classicist. And yet. . . . Consider the brilliant mixture of registers ranging from the sublime to the farcical, so contrary to classical precept. Consider the picaresque development of plot, the loosely organized accumulation of episodes. For those who know of Voltaire's devoted reworking of his tragedies in order to find the right turn of phrase, his casual attitude to the *contes* comes as a surprise. Chapter xxii of *Candide* contains an interpolation, added two years after the first edition, where the author lapses into a critique of tragedies being performed in Paris. Critics generally find this section inferior to the rest of the tale; besides, Voltaire indulges here in personal polemics in a way generally avoided elsewhere in *Candide*. Why this insertion? For no better reason, it would appear, than that the author's play *Tancrède* had met with harsh criticism when put on in 1760. All for this Voltaire, unhappy about one of his tragedies in which he generally made such a deep psychological investment, tampered with his masterpiece! The structure of these stories is always very informal, as if at any late moment another episode could be added without noticeable strain. Compared with such models of classical organization as *Manon Lescaut* or *Les Liaisons dangereuses*, one may say that Voltaire's *contes* lack any careful framework.

We are confronted, then, with a paradox. Starting with classical concepts, Voltaire moves a good distance away from orthodox interpretation of them in his narratives. But the history of the eighteenth-century French novel is one of literary experiment, and Voltaire is no exception. He tries numerous variations of the form, always, it seems, looking for a new way of conveying the philosophic narrative. Nonetheless, it always comes back to a lesson in *philosophie*, generally imparted through wit and laughter rather than tears. The Voltairean *conte* is an essay on the human condition, elucidated with the author's surpassing gift for clarity. Dialogue reinforces description as pointing the moral; this is quintessential conversation, going succinctly to the heart of the matter. Just as the Huron's stay in prison revolves around an extended philosophical dialogue with Gordon, so do Candide's questions in Eldorado elicit a discourse on the ideal state. There are picturesque details, it is true, but the author is always tending toward the expression of ideas, of which the recounted actions are merely the instrument. Voltaire's *vraisemblance* here is essentially philosophical, based on true ideas; by contrast, the perception of the individual human temperament matters little.

Since there is a lesson to be learned, there is a master to teach it, Voltaire himself. As one critic puts it, 'Voltaire was never willing to trust to the story alone; the lesson had always to be made explicit.'[109] His presence is constantly felt, as we have discovered, and his attitudes are generally not hard to define. Indeed, it is this very element of clarity which may limit even a *Candide*. But Voltaire's virtues, in the major *contes* at least, prevent that spotlight from becoming merely crude. His capacity for seeing through the banal and exposing with deadly precision the folly that makes it so dangerous was eminently suited to this genre. Drawing upon the traditional *conte* with its far-fetched plot, flat characters and remote setting, and the imaginary voyage with its philosophic potential, he fashioned a form new and unique to himself. Perhaps the reading of *Gulliver's Travels* was seminal, though he went on to create a style more concise, more direct and more exclusively philosophical than in Swift's work. The form, wide-ranging and flexible, allowed him all the freedom he needed. Perhaps the only wonder is that he took so long to discover and elaborate it.[110]

4 | Poet

The grudging attention which posterity grants to his poetry would have caused Voltaire particular displeasure. For most of his life, and especially up to 1750, this was his essential claim to renown with the French public.[1] In particular, his epic poem *La Henriade* was the source of prolonged praise throughout the century: 'l'auteur de *La Henriade*' was one of the most banal periphrases employed in referring to Voltaire. But from about 1830, as O. R. Taylor reminds us in his superb edition of the epic, '*La Henriade* cessa d'intéresser les Français';[2] nor does Professor Taylor wish to argue that the decision of posterity is unjust: he finds the poem, for all its qualities, lacking the inventiveness and sensibility of true heroic verse.[3]

However, as Lanson points out, the more one descends the scale of formality in poetic styles, the freer Voltaire grows and the more individual.[4] Even more frigid in his odes than in his epic, Voltaire appears however to become less inhibited as he moves away from the domain of *genres nobles*. His philosophical poems, if lacking the rhetorical trenchancy of Pope's *Essay on Man* (which Voltaire admired and helped to have translated into French), achieve a consistently high standard of clarity, precision and vigour, three qualities that their author prized highly in prose as much as in verse.[5] In particular, the *Poème sur le désastre de Lisbonne*, written as an immediate reaction to the earthquake at Lisbon on 1 November 1755 that had taken about thirty thousand lives, not only discusses with lucidity the meaning of evil but contains passages of lyrical sensitivity rare in Voltaire's work:

> Quel crime, quelle faute ont commis ces enfants
> Sur le sein maternel écrasés et sanglants?
> Lisbonne, qui n'est plus, eut-elle plus de vices
> Que Londres, que Paris, plongés dans les délices?
> Lisbonne est abîmée, et l'on danse à Paris.

(What crime, what fault have these children committed, crushed and
strangled on their mothers' breast? Did Lisbon, now vanished, have more
vices than London or Paris, steeped in revelling? Lisbon is destroyed, and
people dance in Paris.)[6]

But here too the language is formal and unsurprising; the heightened
tone comes above all from the phrasing, the flowing movement
which comes itself as a climax to the opening section and its brief
survey of the horridly devastated scene.

By contrast, Voltaire's light poetry is among the very best
examples of such verse in the whole century. Here the man-about-
town and society wit comes into his own. Frivolity and gracefulness, playful eroticism tastefully portrayed, such are the hallmarks
of this minor art. One such instance, apparently written in 1716
when he was just over twenty, is *Le Cadenas*, addressed to Madame
de B.[7] The lady is married to an old man who jealously watches
over her; and it is this odious figure who has equipped her with
the padlock of the title, which is none other than a chastity belt.
The theme, potentially unsavoury and vulgar, is handled with
perfect discretion. Once the nature of the 'cadenas' has been made
clear by tactful periphrases, Voltaire devises a conceit of classical
lineage, in which he narrates how the invention came from Hell
when the abominable Pluto sought to monopolize the attentions of
the charming young wife Proserpine whom he had abducted. From
Hell knowledge of the device spread to Venice, Rome and now
Paris. But all is not lost; love will find a way, as the final lines make
clear:

> Car vous m'aimez: et quand on a le cœur
> De femme honnête, on a bientôt le reste.

(For you love me: and when one has the heart of a worthy woman, one
soon has the rest.)

This charming piece, with its light suggestion of the scandalous, is
ideally suited to the elegance of Voltaire's pen. The whole poem,
eighty-two lines long, flows smoothly, with a transparent art that
conceals art. Quoting brief excerpts gives little idea of the poet's
skilfulness, for the chief qualities are not specific highlights so much
as the balance and benevolent irony of the complete work, conveyed
with an apparent ease of expression and phrasing. A detached
humorousness plays over the surface, leaving no room whatever
for sentiment; here is no cause for tears or brooding.

Clearly, Voltaire's genius lay with the more worldly sorts of poetic invention, an invention which took delight in amusing the reader as it mocked at repressive authority. But his propagandist side was never to be obscured for long; the best of his verse is that which combines the light touch with the serious thought. Many of his Epistles, for instance, belong here, ranging from the early *Epître à Uranie* (1722) with its eminently quotable affirmations of deism ('Je ne suis pas chrétien; mais c'est pour t'aimer mieux' (I am not a Christian; but so that I can love Thee more) sums up his religious position)[8] to the *Epître à Horace* fifty years later, which allies to Horace's Epicurean detachment a satisfaction at having brought some good into the world. More ambitious is *Le Mondain* (1736), where Voltaire delivers a brilliant apology for a life of civilized ease. In the brief space of 128 lines a complex movement in economic and intellectual history is encapsulated. Adam and Eve appear as wretched inhabitants of a poverty-stricken wilderness, ugly and unkempt, eking out a miserable existence;[9] the force of the paradoxes was to guarantee them long notoriety and some personal trouble to their author.[10] Voltaire returns to the attack a few months later with his *Défense du Mondain*, of identical length and even more comprehensive in its argument than its predecessor. Here the poet sets the stage by introducing a dinner-table companion who attacks his views on luxury, pausing awhile during this discourse on austerity to moisten his parched throat with a wine of the finest quality![11] Having arrested the reader's attention by this vivid cameo, Voltaire goes on to develop his paradoxical theme that vanity and idleness can be the source of industrious prosperity:

> Ainsi l'on voit en Angleterre, en France,
> Par cent Canaux circuler l'abondance.
> Le goût du Luxe entre dans tous les rangs;
> Le Pauvre y vit des Vanités des Grands;
> Et le travail, gagé par la Mollesse,
> S'ouvre à pas lents la route à la richesse.

(Thus you see in England or France wealth flowing through a hundred channels. The taste for affluence pervades all classes; the poor man lives off the vanities of the great; and hard work, in the service of soft living, slowly opens the road that leads to wealth.)

La Pucelle d'Orléans

These two poems on luxury are perhaps the most effective instances of Voltaire's poetic talents operating on a broad front. But in his mock-epic poem *La Pucelle d'Orléans* he achieves distinction of a different order. The *mondain* poems are brilliant but brief. By contrast, *La Pucelle* is vast in scope and length, over 8500 lines long and spanning more than thirty years of Voltaire's life, equalled by few other works in the amount of commitment which he brought to it. By its epic dimensions it fulfils, if indirectly, that liking for the large canvas which *La Henriade* had already demonstrated in more sterile vein. By its comic tone covering an intention of moral seriousness it joins together those two strands of the author's temperament which we have seen to give the most fruitful results in his verse. Yet the work has been consistently neglected until recently and has only rarely received the critical appraisal which is its due.

One of the reasons for this harsh treatment is quite straightforward. The textual history of *La Pucelle* is of a complexity unequalled even by the impressive standards in that respect of other Voltaire works. The long period of creation (from 1730 to 1761), the various manuscripts which Voltaire circulated among friends, the pirated editions in 1755 and 1756 which eventually induced him to publish an official version in 1762 that was subsequently modified in later editions—all these factors have turned the bibliographical problems attending *La Pucelle* into a nightmare. Thirty-one extant manuscripts and a hundred editions (many of them pirated) merit attention; the variants fall into seven broad categories, ranging from fourteen to twenty-four cantos. A rough working version has however been available ever since the Kehl edition of 1785, but widespread doubts about exactly what constituted Voltaire's contribution and what came from other hands have made scrupulous critics hesitate to offer detailed comment. *La Pucelle*, one might say, like its eponymous heroine Joan of Arc, was a vague vision rather than a clearly defined individual.

The recent critical edition by Jeroom Vercruysse[12] has fundamentally changed all this. With rare skill and energy M. Vercruysse has brought order out of chaos, unravelled the tangled web of the poem's genesis and subsequent history, and given us at last a reliable version to make informed criticism possible. Some of the problems of attribution are presumably for ever beyond our reach, and even this masterly edition cannot decide whether certain passages are or are not by Voltaire; but the area of irreducible doubt is now relatively small. Above all, M. Vercruysse has performed the signal service of removing from Voltaire's responsibility many of the grosser sections which, appearing in the pirated editions, continued Voltaire's iconoclasm along paths that the *philosophe* regarded as vulgarly distasteful. By segregating these as being not the author's work he has rescued *La Pucelle* from the disrepute it has suffered when critics, otherwise favourably inclined, have been embarrassed by what they considered a disastrous breach of taste on the poet's part.

The other reason for the sad neglect of *La Pucelle* is however more complex. With his unerring aptitude for seizing on the most effective symbol for developing his views, Voltaire chose that most sacred of characters for every loyal Christian Frenchman of his own day and for very many thereafter.[13] M. Vercruysse enumerates a list of melancholy length, extending down to this century, of those who excoriate the writer for betraying morality, religion and country all in the same work. These critics, in varying degrees of indignation, wax eloquent about the mud of obscenity and sacrilege which Voltaire has cast upon that emblem of purity. Indeed there can be little doubt that, if one were disposed to see the hand of God in French history, one could look to no better instance than Joan of Arc. The twentieth-century dramatist Paul Claudel, convinced of such a view, evokes the sense of miracle admirably in *L'Annonce faite à Marie*. One moment France is hopelessly divided, reeling under the English and Burgundian assaults; yet out of imminent destruction come a new sense of purpose and the creation of a united France, thanks to the intervention of one simple country girl. What could be more improbable or mysterious?

Furthermore, the essential purity of this girl became an integral part of the legend. General de Gaulle, himself a confirmed believer in France's noble destiny, summed it up pithily during the Liberation of France in September 1944. Ever mindful of the need to give France an unbesmirched ideal to revere, he was thinking of resigning before the name de Gaulle had become hopelessly compromised by party politics; and, characteristically, it was to Joan of Arc that his mind turned: 'La France peut avoir encore besoin un jour d'une image pure. Cette image, il faut la lui laisser. Jeanne d'Arc, si elle était mariée, ce ne serait plus Jeanne d'Arc.' (France may still one day stand in need of an image of purity. This image one must bequeath to her. Joan of Arc married would no longer be Joan of Arc.)[14] It is precisely this cult of unspotted virginity which Voltaire chooses for attack when he comes to write his long poem.

The Joan whom Voltaire conjures up is not the martyr who burned at Rouen. For that historical figure the author showed a proper sense of admiration and pity in the *Essai sur les mœurs* and elsewhere. In his view, she became a political tool in the hands of the French military leader Dunois. A simple, good-hearted provincial maid, she was brought to the Court of Charles VII and thereupon presented to the world as sent by God in order to restore the morale of the French. Voltaire speaks eloquently of her extraordinary courage and resolution. About her death, his comments are more perfunctory, apparently because this is of less interest historically than her triumphs; even so, he makes clear that her fate was undeserved. There is no doubt in his mind, however, that the supernatural thesis does not hold water.[15]

But the protagonist Jeanne of *La Pucelle* is a deliberately fictitious invention. The author gives clear warning the moment she is introduced, by announcing that she was the bastard daughter of a 'certain curé du lieu';[16] but an accompanying footnote by Voltaire himself gives the lie to this, stating flatly that her father was not a priest and that this is a 'fiction poétique'. Surely here is a clear indication to the reader not to refer all subsequent observations on Jeanne for comparison with historical fact. The Jeanne we see at the outset is still in her native Lorraine. A servant-girl in the local inn, she is fresh, gay, spontaneous and attractive, fending off audacious overtures as all traditional barmaids are supposed to do. She is a happy child of nature, earthy and direct in a Rabelaisian setting, strong as a man in riding horses bare-backed. It is this healthy animal who will go on, when she is summoned by Saint Denis, to save France. Though transformed by divine grace with the most improbable speed, so that from a simple chambermaid she becomes 'un héros . . . une âme guerrière',[17] she remains in all essential respects the character we have seen at the outset. Indeed, the change itself is made to appear entirely understandable; a girl so strong and resolute might very naturally have become a military heroine under the right influences. In short, the paraphernalia of saintly intervention explains nothing; but we shall return to Voltaire's views on metamorphosis later.

The animal-like quality of Jeanne is explicitly stressed more than once. When listening to Saint Denis's stirring call to arms

> Jeanne étonnée ouvrant un large bec,
> Crut quelque temps que l'on lui parlait grec.

(Joan, opening her large beak in astonishment, thought for some time that he was talking Greek.)[18]

All contemporary readers of Voltaire would have recognized the obvious reference to La Fontaine's *Le Corbeau et le renard*, where in that well-known fable the crow, listening to the fox's seductive speech, 'ouvre un large bec, laisse tomber sa proie' (opens his large beak, lets fall his prey).[19] When later Jeanne wards off one of many assaults on her virginity, the poet in an extended simile compares her action to that of a mare refusing to mate.[20] So it is not out of keeping with the tone of the poem when we arrive at its most notorious episode to discover Jeanne beset by the supplications of her muleteer who has been transformed into an ass. If she nearly succumbs,[21] it is partly because her strong animality is awakened by this creature, ludicrous though his appearance is, as we shall later see. In the end Saint Denis, who has temporarily deserted her, returns to rescue her from temptation, and she gently puts the ass aside in words that link the tones of Corneille to a situation far removed from classical tragedy:

> bel âne,
> Vous concevez un chimérique espoir,
> Respectez plus ma gloire et mon devoir,
> Trop de distance est entre nos espèces

(handsome ass, you are forming fanciful hopes; pay more respect to my fame and duty; there is too great a distance between our species).[22]

In brief, as this passage indicates, Jeanne cuts a ridiculous figure at times in *La Pucelle*. But she is the victim of circumstances, in ways that rob her of any real autonomy. First of all, she is a woman, and a woman in an army of men is a constant prey to licentiousness; even when she is at her most inspiring as a leader, she is arousing lust along with admiration.[23] It is part of a basically absurd situation, as Voltaire is keen to impress upon us. The other, and even more ridiculous, side to this affair is that she is constantly under Saint Denis's tutelage and protection; without him, we are led to believe, she would long since have satisfied her natural instincts and ceased to be 'la pucelle'.

Jeanne, then, is essentially a puppet, serving the wider interests of the author. The reader is not permitted to sympathize with her—indeed, she is in the strictest sense of the word not a sympathetic character. To start with, she is seen to be quite capable of looking after her own affairs with hard-headed common sense. She understands that her maidenhead has as it were been placed out of bounds for the duration of the war, and with straightforward candour she points this out to her lover Dunois, asks him to be patient, and promises herself to him once the English are defeated;[24] as soon as the victory is won, she straightforwardly fulfils her pledge.[25] The same lack of subtlety applies to her military exploits. Her natural sanity makes her reject even Saint Denis when he urges her to kill sleeping soldiers;[26] but in battle she has no compunction about putting the enemy to the sword:

> Jeanne en volant inonde la campagne
> De flots de sang, de membres dispersés,
> Coupe cent cous l'un sur l'autre entassés.
> . . .
> Jeanne d'en haut étend son bras vengeur,
> Poursuit, pourfend, perce, coupe, déchire.

(Joan in flight drenches the land with torrents of blood, with scattered limbs, severs a hundred necks heaped one on another . . . Joan on high stretches forth her vengeful arm, pursues, cleaves, pierces, severs, rends.)[27]

The narrator's tone is not one of admiration; rather, the details chosen evoke a general distaste. Jeanne tends to live for war, quixotically mistaking, for instance, a bunch of rascals for a band of knights waiting to be freed.[28] Significantly, on an earlier occasion we find Jeanne slaughtering the enemy while herself stark naked. The absurd and erotic overtones need no stressing; but the picture is also well chosen to conjure up a certain untamed quality in this girl. She does not belong to civilized society and lacks the restraints proper to one who does. As always, she functions as a force of nature. Unlike Agnès, she has no sensibility; her love for Dunois seems a wholly physical attraction. She is not depicted as abhorrent, nor is she demeaned; rather, she is a character apart, not quite human, and incarnating attitudes which the worldly poet regarded as unenlightened. We keep our distance from her, by the arrangement of her author.

The ideas of *La Pucelle*

One can then easily see how the preservation of such an earthy individual's virginity becomes an even bigger joke. When it is first raised by Saint Denis, the notion that a maidenhead can save the kingdom of France evokes nothing but rude laughter amongst the military leaders:

> Quand il s'agit de sauver une ville,
> Un pucelage est une arme inutile.

(When it comes to saving a town, a maidenhead is a useless weapon.)[29]

Besides, why didn't Saint Denis bring one of the virgins from Heaven with him? The gratuitous nature of this foolish enterprise is clearly brought home to us. But Saint Denis perseveres, choosing, as we have seen, the most unlikely person for such a fragile honour; and his mystic conception of maidenhead is throughout balanced against the brutally physical world in which Jeanne has to safeguard it. The ceremony in which it is established that she is a virgin and is awarded her 'brevet de pucelle' is a licentious farce;[30] and so the poem will continue. For it is the very notion of chastity as a sacred virtue which Voltaire rejects. The opening of Canto ii makes the narrator's feelings clear. After a mock-heroic first line:

> Heureux cent fois qui trouve un pucelage!

(Happy a hundred times the man who finds a maidenhead!)

he goes on to place the matter in its right perspective. There are greater qualities:

> C'est un grand bien, mais de toucher un cœur
> Est à mon sens un plus cher avantage.
> Se voir aimé, c'est là le vrai bonheur.
> Qu'importe hélas, d'arracher une fleur?
> C'est à l'amour à nous cueillir la rose.

(It is a valuable possession, but touching someone's heart is to my mind a greater gain. Seeing oneself loved, there lies true happiness. What matters it—alas!—if a flower is uprooted? It needs love to gather the rose.)

Here as elsewhere the loss of virginity is reduced to the purely physical notion of uprooting a flower ('vous aurez ma fleur,' Jeanne promises Dunois later),[31] whereas love is equated with the more poetic symbol of plucking the rose, in a manner reminiscent of the medieval *Roman de la Rose* or Renaissance poetry. The distinction is very similar to that which Fielding establishes in *Joseph Andrews* (1742) between chastity and charity; the former is merely a negative attitude, it is the latter which presumes an active quality of good nature. Fielding's attitude springs from the benevolent view that man is not essentially depraved, and so too is it with Voltaire. The narrator intrudes often enough in *La Pucelle*, especially but not exclusively in the exordium of each canto, to impress upon us a true sense of values. His attitude is essentially Epicurean; wisdom lies in the recognition that pleasure, judiciously sought after, is complementary to duty, not its antithesis as the cult of chastity implies.[32] Human nature is well-disposed but frail, not made for the heroic or saintly virtues:

> L'homme et la femme est chose bien fragile,
> Sur la vertu gardez-vous bien de compter.
> Ce vase est beau mais il est fait d'argile:
> Un rien le casse, on peut le rajuster
> Mais ce n'est pas entreprise facile.
> Garder ce vase avec précaution,
> Sans le ternir, croyez-moi, c'est un rêve;
> Nul n'y parvient.

(Man and woman are frail of substance; take good care not to rely on virtue. The vessel is fine but made of clay: a trifle will break it, and though it can be mended the task is not easy. Protecting this vessel with care and keeping it from blemish is, believe me, an idle dream. Nobody manages it.)[33]

The charming Agnès Sorel, Charles VII's mistress,[34] is brutally raped and humiliated by the almoner, and in despair longs for death. But life must go on, and as in *Candide* the instinct for self-preservation gradually reawakens in the form of a desire for food.[35] If then Agnès finds herself falling in love with the young English page Monrose who has saved her life, that is in no way reprehensible and is presented by Voltaire without any cynicism. For love is the natural expression of someone endowed with sensibility.

The poem indeed is a sort of hedonist epic. The erotic principle is expressly apostrophized at the opening of Canto xiv in lines that are an avowed imitation of Lucretius: pleasure brings life and fertility, repelling the darkness of primeval chaos. This philosophy stands in direct contrast to the cult of heroes and chivalry, which leads only to death and destruction. The dramatic confrontation of these two principles reaches its climax in the nineteenth canto with the death of Dorothée, who like Agnès has lived for love. Having been killed by the English captain Tirconel along with her lover La Trimouille, she is, he discovers, his long-lost daughter. Hackneyed as the coincidence is, Voltaire handles it with the utmost seriousness. Surprising though it may seem, *La Pucelle* contains an extended section of deep pathos, as 'ce dur Anglais' who before had been immune to sentiment curses his fate and the fortunes of war. Death, which elsewhere in this poem (as in *Candide*) happens only to others as a kind of backdrop, here becomes instead a personal, felt experience. Charles and Agnès, looking upon the sad sight, are suddenly made aware of their own mortality:

> La belle Agnès, Agnès toute tremblante,
> Pressait le roi qui pleurait dans ses bras
> Et lui disait: mon cher amant hélas!
> Peut-être un jour nous serons l'un et l'autre
> Portés ainsi dans l'empire des morts.

(The beautiful Agnes, Agnes all trembling, clasped the king as he wept in her arms and said to him: 'My dear lover alas! perhaps one day we shall you and I both be borne away thus into the realm of the dead.')[36]

These words seem even to evoke a kind of cathartic reaction among the onlookers:

> A ces propos qui portaient dans les cœurs
> La triste crainte et les molles douleurs

(At these words which carried into every heart sad fear and languid grief).[37]

Jeanne's response is characteristically insensitive: revenge by the sword is for her the only suitable answer. But the last words of the canto are with Agnès:

> Agnès reprit: ah! laissez-moi pleurer!

(Agnes replied: 'Oh! let me weep!')[38]

In short, we are at this moment in the universe of *L'Ingénu* rather than that of *Candide*.

It is significant that this canto was not completed until the end of the thirty years during which *La Pucelle* was being composed.[39] What had begun as an amusement for the intervals between more serious occupations at Cirey[40] had taken on a graver tone. But, though the Dorothea canto is exceptional in its sensibility, a serious polemical aim underlines even the most frivolous sections. Voltaire wishes to assault the whole mystique of heroes, prophets and other such supermen:

> Je ne connais dans l'histoire du monde
> Aucun héros, aucun homme de bien,
> Aucun prophète, aucun parfait chrétien
> Qui n'ait été la dupe d'un vaurien,
> Ou des jaloux, ou de l'esprit immonde.

(In all the world's history I know no hero, no good man, no prophet, no perfect Christian who has not been duped by a rascal, or by jealous men, or the unclean spirit.)[41]

Hence the constant irony at the expense of anything suggesting a providentialist view of the world. Prophets and heroes are automatically suspect, for the former will cheat and the latter will kill in pursuit of their ambitions if they get the chance. Monks and priests are continually lashed for their vile deceits, like the Archbishop of Milan who, though Dorothée's uncle, rapes and then denounces her to the Inquisition.[42] A king like Charles VII is an unheroic monarch, preferring dalliance with Agnès to fighting for France; but what credit he may gain for his pacifism is surely lost when he behaves on the battlefield like an indiscriminate assassin:

> Dunois assomme et le bon Charles tire
> A son plaisir tout ce qui fuit de peur.

(Dunois cudgels and the good Charles at his pleasure shoots at all that flee in fear.)[43]

He is also absurdly credulous, taking the sudden appearance of the *fleurs de lys* for a revelation when they are merely a painting on someone's backside;[44] and in the council of war it is Agnès who, though quietly sewing, appears to be the real power behind the throne.[45] Charles is merely an incompetent idler, far removed from the narrator's ideal king who would exercise justice and keep his subjects in peace;[46] and it is hard to follow M. Vercruysse's view that Charles has politically a 'caractère idéal'.[47] Like all who command power in this work, he is presented in an anti-heroic manner.

The full force of irony, however, as befits this onslaught on the supernatural thesis of history, is reserved for the cult of sainthood.

Saint Georges, the patron saint of England, turns out to be a philis-
tine blockhead incarnating the worst qualities of the nation he
protects; but it is the patron saint of France, Saint Denis, who
receives the more extended treatment and becomes the most
successful comic creation of the poem. Early on we are told that
his trade is a saint ('saint de mon métier'),[48] and that detail cleverly
sets the stage for the appearance of a foolish man whose only
saintly characteristics are that he lives in Heaven and has an ability
to make magic. His language descends below the expected level of
holiness when he castigates the love-making of the French king

> Dont le pays en cendre est consumé,
> Et qui s'amuse au lieu de le défendre,
> A deux tétons qu'il ne cesse de prendre.

(Whose country in ashes is consumed, and who instead of defending it
amuses himself with two tits that he unceasingly clasps.)[49]

The effect is immediately to tarnish the exemplary image of a
figure carrying out his proper patron-like duties. We have already
seen how capriciously he decides on Jeanne as his elect servant and
how he is less than Christian in his desire to kill sleeping men. But
most of the time he is simply a pious fool, leaving Jeanne with the
parting exhortation 'pense à ton pucelage',[50] or praying to his
winged ass to save him from death in the battle against Saint
Georges, having completely forgotten that he is immortal.[51] It is
this battle, indeed, which reduces both combatants to the most
total mockery. After a ritual exchange of heroic insults and homilies,
they begin seeking out the weak points in the other's defence, such
as the halo.[52] The battle gets going, Denis loses an ear and Georges
a nose. It requires the archangel Gabriel to come and chide them
like children, see their wounds restored (the missing flesh is magically
replaced without mark of injury on the respective faces), and take
them off to Heaven where they are given large helpings of nectar![53]
The narrator in his own person has the last word: why should
readers be incredulous, he asks, when Milton has written plausibly
of the battle of the angels in Heaven? For this is no more absurd
than the doings of *Paradise Lost*.[54]

But Saint Denis, total buffoon though he is, controls great power,
watching over Jeanne like a fairy godmother and eventually settling
the war to the advantage of the French. This latter triumph is
achieved not through a feat of arms on earth, but up in Heaven,

where the ode his own team of saints composes wins greater favour with the heavenly host than the one written by the English side;[55] the subsequent liberation of Orléans by Jeanne and the French army will be merely the pre-ordained result of the poetry award. Through such crude interventions Voltaire conveys in *La Pucelle* the same scorn for the concept of a transcendental historicism that he showed more directly in the *Essai sur les mœurs*. Natural change and evolution are replaced by arbitrary metamorphoses. In *Le Taureau blanc* a similar world of fabulous transformations exists; here too miracles can take place at any time, like the return of the muleteer from donkey to human form, evoking in the narrator of *La Pucelle* a comparison with the story of Nebuchadnezzar which is the basis of that *conte*.[56] Indeed, the fantasy-world of *La Pucelle* ridicules the supernatural climate of the Middle Ages in much the same way as *Le Taureau blanc* deflates the myth of the Old Testament. All such gratuitous distortions of natural patterns must of course destroy any human history properly speaking, as Voltaire is at pains to demonstrate.

The form and style of *La Pucelle*

As has become clear, *La Pucelle* allows for the vast sweep of the epic without attempting (except on rare occasions) the serious and elevated tone of that genre. One small detail is important here, given the strongly classical bent of the author: the number of cantos at no stage approximates to the hallowed figure for the epic of twelve or twenty-four.[57] The official edition of 1762 contained twenty cantos, which Voltaire did not scruple to raise to the very odd and unclassical number of twenty-one by the addition of a further section in the editions from 1773.[58] Once again, as in the *contes*, the author has liberated himself from the formal constraints of tradition in order to produce a wholly personal work.

The structure is loose and episodic, as one might expect in so large a composition which took so long to produce, and the resulting flexibility allows for interpolations and additions that at times significantly changes the nature of the original composition. The plot revolves around a series of lightly interwoven motifs, in which the story of Jeanne plays only a limited part. For whole cantos she is completely missing from the stage; equally significant, Agnès is more dramatically highlighted and allowed to lay claim to our sympathies. Jeanne may be the *raison d'être* of *La Pucelle*, but she is not in any sense its heroine. Such a portmanteau structure could hardly fail to be uneven, and there are almost inevitably some mechanical sections, especially when Voltaire is depicting a rather static tableau, as of the Palais de la Sottise in Canto iii. But by and large the interweaving of plots is carried out with much deftness. In the opening canto, for instance, after the exordium which sets the tone, we pass not to Jeanne and the political situation but to the deliciously erotic scene of Charles and Agnès:

> Du lit d'amour ils vont droit à la table

(From the bed of love they go straight to table)[59]

and the fine food, wine and conversation are worthy of the best in eighteenth-century Parisian society, a scenario that might have figured in *Le Mondain*. Only when this picture has been firmly impressed upon us does Charles casually invoke the political situation, nonchalantly letting drop that France is in a state of crisis:

> Mon parlement me bannit aujourd'hui,
> Au fier Anglais la France est asservie;
> Ah! qu'il soit roi, mais qu'il me porte envie

(My parliament banishes me today, France is enslaved to the proud Englishman. Oh! let him be king, but envious of me).[60]

This is the articulation by which Voltaire opens out the canvas on to the real state of affairs and the brutal oppression by the English; from that we pass to Saint Denis in Heaven and the grand design upon which he presently embarks. This inversion of the orthodox approach whereby the private takes precedence over the public has many advantages. The attractive nature of the opening scene is an admirable prologue to a poem that will become a hymn to hedonism. Its deliberately anachronistic quality, furthermore, warns us not to take it too seriously; this is a never-never land.[61] No king, however irresponsible, could so languidly refer to the perils of his situation unless he were totally schizophrenic—and Charles, whatever his defects, seems entirely normal throughout. And it would be embroidering the obvious to ask where all the delicate amenities of life come from in the middle of such an unlovely war.

The scene now passes to the realities of conflict, conveyed with
a proper sense of horror; La Pucelle, though an ironic work, contains many passages where all irony is excluded and the true nature
of things is reported and apprehended directly. But as the poem is
principally aiming to attack its targets by laughter, not compassion,
we return to the ironic mode as Saint Denis comes on to the stage.
This time the technique is more direct, since the worthy figure is to
be the absurd hero of a farce whenever he appears; but the proportions of the canto that are in the comic vein, and the way in
which the serious element is encapsulated within two sections in
which the author's detached amusement is uppermost, establish the
keynotes of the work.

In controlling the mood, the author's presence becomes an
essential element; throughout La Pucelle he is never far away and
does not let us forget that he is manipulating events. We find here
the lineaments of the self-conscious narrator, himself a central
figure in the comedy; he even obligingly lets us know details of
his own life, such as that he too has been an erring mortal, has
enjoyed mistresses in his time and is open to sensibility.[62] He can
be overtly inconsistent, claiming at the opening of Canto x that he
is tired of writing moralistic prefaces to each canto, and then, two
cantos later, admitting that he has changed his mind.[63] All this
encourages the reader to trust him as a man with peccadilloes like
the rest of us but with his heart in the right place. Thus as he gains
our confidence he can express himself with or without irony,
knowing that we now understand where his sympathies lie and
shall not be misled if he occasionally professes the opposite of what
we know he really believes. The confidential tone is increased by
the overtures made to the reader. Not only is the latter privileged
to learn something of the writer's weaknesses, he is appealed to as
a man of equal good sense and feeling. This flattery increases as the
poem goes on. In Canto xx, it is a particularly judicious precaution
to compliment the reader on his taste and moral sanity before
embarking upon the episode of Jeanne and the ass.[64] At the beginning of the final canto also, with the need to justify this scabrous
incident still paramount, the narrator presumes upon the reader's
experience of love and assumes that the latter will know that love
can be either tender or violent. But earlier Voltaire gives the reader
a more positive role to play. In Canto vii, having filled us with
suspense as to whether Dorothée's lover La Trimouille has returned

to rescue her, the narrator interposes his presence to upbraid the reader for his fickleness in being distracted from Jeanne and the situation before the walls of Orléans. But no sooner has he reminded us of our duty to follow the adventures of our nominal heroine than he digresses to chide us much more firmly for forgetting the lovely Agnès.[65] In the next canto, however, we are forgiven. Having complacently announced that Jeanne's tale will triumph over envy and time, the narrator dismisses her airily and charitably allows that it was quite understandable for us to want to follow the love story of Dorothée.[66]

This technique carries several advantages. It permits the use of suspense, swift breaks from one plot to another, the avoidance of monotony. It also offers another opportunity to downgrade Jeanne and her values while ostensibly praising them. But above all, it introduces the reader to a new function; he is placed in a situation not of his choosing and forced to respond to the action. Furthermore, the transparent nature of the device impresses upon us that this is a fiction, a gratuitous product of the author's imagination which follows no fixed or necessary laws. Diderot has been justifiably praised for use of a similar stratagem in *Jacques le fataliste* (1773), and certainly it is there used to a much greater and more varied extent. But Voltaire deserves notice for anticipating this use a good deal earlier in an equally fertile way on a more reduced scale.

The most common form of irony lies in the use of epic statements within a non-epic context; we have seen instances of this in Jeanne's discourse with the ass or the pseudo-heroic nature of the battle between the saints. Louvet, one of the counsellors to the French king, looks the part of a heroic figure:

> grand personnage
> Au maintien grave, et qu'on eût pris pour sage

(an eminent person of solemn bearing, whom one might have taken for a wise man).[67]

But all his dignity is removed when the poet goes on to stress his unawareness of events in his own backyard; his wife is cuckolding him with the English leader Talbot.[68] This comic situation is enhanced at the end of the work, since the denouement depends on it: Charles and Jeanne enter Orléans in triumph because Talbot is in bed with *la présidente* Louvet at the critical hour. Louvet will never know that his wife played, albeit unknowingly, a vital part in the victory:

> Ils [Jeanne et Dunois] vont tous deux de manière engageante
> Au président rendre la présidente.
> Sans nul soupçon il la reçoit très bien,
> Les bons maris ne savent jamais rien.
> Louvet toujours ignora que la France
> A sa Louvet devait sa délivrance.

(They [Joan and Dunois] both go with engaging manner and return his wife to the President. Innocent of all suspicion, he welcomes her back; good husbands are always completely in the dark. Louvet remained for ever unaware that France owed her rescue to his wife.)[69]

It is upon such farces as cuckoldry, or the poetry contest in Heaven, that great events absurdly hang in this mock-epic. Such heroes as these are fools, paraded for our derision.

Other epic devices are also used to exploit the mockery. Bonifoux, Charles's confessor, has a prophetic vision of the heroes of the future—but they are fornicating with their mistresses.[70] The ass in making overtures to Jeanne invokes a noble lineage from Biblical and classical legend.[71] The extended heroic simile appears countless times in support of unsupportable causes; for instance, the confusion in Jeanne's mind and heart as she listens to the ass is given spurious dignity by being compared with the great winds beating in distant and exotic climes.[72] A roll-call of great names overwhelmed by Jeanne in battle degenerates into bathos at the end:

> Et Bartonay qui fit cocu son frère.

(And Bartonay who cuckolded his brother.)[73]

With Voltaire the sting is so often in the tail, as full realization of the truth dawns. It may be a gentle descent from romance to realism, as in Charles's courtship of Agnès:

> Le prince en feu des yeux la dévorait,
> Contes d'amour d'un air tendre il faisait.
> Et du genou, le genou lui serrait.

(The prince passionately devoured her with his eyes, tenderly told her stories of love, and with his knee her knee he pressed.)[74]

It may be sardonic, like the gradual, even seemingly reluctant, admission that Bonneau, who contrived the meeting between

Agnès and Charles and is at first euphemistically described as
'l'ami du prince', is in fact a 'maquereau' (pimp).[75] It may be brutal.
When Charles loses Agnès to the English he summons the necro-
mancers and soothsayers to tell him if she is being faithful to him;
not too surprisingly, their bizarre divinations all lead to the comfort-
ing answer:

> Qu'Agnès est sage et fuit tous les amants.

(That Agnes is virtuous and flees all lovers.)

Voltaire follows up with one ferocious line of comment:

> Puis fiez-vous à messieurs les savants

(Now trust yourselves to learned gentlemen)[76]

and plunges straight into the disclosure that the almoner had already
raped her and that, worse, she would shortly be the willing mistress
of Monrose. Time and time again reality overtakes illusion and
powerfully deflates it.

Voltaire often interweaves this device with the straightforward
presentation of gross absurdities, like the painted *fleurs de lys* which,
as we saw, exercised such an overwhelming effect upon Charles.
Jeanne's warlike accoutrements take this a stage further, since they
are not merely absurd but horrible as well, being notorious weapons
from the Old Testament like the blade with which Judith cut off
Holofernes' head.[77] These are followed by one of the happiest fan-
tasies in the whole poem, because it can be exploited throughout
the story for ironic purposes: instead of a noble steed, Jeanne has to
make do with an ass. Nonetheless it is a noble ass, and winged too;
and we are already warned that it is more than it appears to be. All
these details merely reinforce the absurd disparity. This ass will
however appear most ridiculous when at his most dangerous, in his
attempt to seduce Jeanne, for here Voltaire gives him human
attitudes. He adopts a squatting position at the outset ('doucement
s'accroupissant près d'elle'[78]—the juxtaposition of adverb 'doucement' (gently) and verb is itself somewhat incongruous); but as his
ardour mounts he takes to his knees, suitably arranging his bearing
as he does.[79] Such improbabilities make the seduction scene even
more ludicrous. Fittingly, the ass again kneels, and weeps when
seeking her forgiveness later.[80]

If, as has been recently suggested, the Rococo characteristics in
European literature are 'eroticism, wit, and elegance',[81] then *La*

Pucelle is a very characteristic Rococo work. Wit and elegance, as we have seen, are abundantly in evidence, but perhaps a word more needs to be said about the erotic aspect. Voyeuristic situations are frequent in which the naked limbs of beautiful ladies are displayed before us. A typical instance is that where Monrose looks down on Agnès; she is beautiful, defenceless, half-naked (an open, fluttering dress increases the titillation) and apparently unconscious. But this tableau, worthy of Boucher or Fragonard and enhanced by an orthodox comparison with Venus displaying before Adonis, is undercut like most of the apparently perfect moments in the poem: Venus was not wearing a nightcap as is Agnès and besides

> Son cu d'ivoire était sans meurtrissure

(Her ivory arse was unbruised).[82]

The erotic too is deflated by irony in this poem.

Poetry for Voltaire, it is clear, was not a matter of fresh lyrical imagination as for Hugo, or of densely packed imagery in the manner of Mallarmé. For better or worse, it is a style that rejects mystery, seeing only dangers along that path. The most remarkable quality of Voltairean verse is its harmonious clarity, flowing effortlessly on for thousands of lines. As in his prose works, Voltaire is scarcely ever obscure; when he falls below his own high standards, it is rather into a mechanical flatness. This is, as Vercruysse remarks, a poetry made to be heard rather than read;[83] such was its original function in the evenings at Cirey. One hardly needs to say that the fluency of Voltaire's verse does not happen accidentally; but it is interesting to add that he expressed detailed views on the matter, claiming that poetic musicality comes from

cet heureux mélange de syllabes longues et brèves, et de consonnes suivies de voyelles qui font couler un vers avec tant de mollesse, et qui le font entrer dans une oreille sensible et juste avec tant de plaisir.

(that happy blend of long and short syllables, and of consonants followed by vowels, which make a verse flow so softly and penetrate a sensitive ear with so much pleasure.)[84]

A detailed analysis of *La Pucelle* from this viewpoint would surely demonstrate how positively he put this into effect; it is to be hoped that further research will soon add to our knowledge.

The verse is decasyllabic, a matter of considerable significance,

for in using the alexandrine (as in *La Henriade*) the poet felt himself
constrained by all the formal traditions pertaining to the verse of
Corneille and Racine. Since the caesura divides the line at 6+4 or
more commonly 4+6, Voltaire's verse links flexibility to asym-
metry in a manner which Verlaine was to advocate strongly well
over a century later. In his approach to rhyme, too, Voltaire
curiously anticipates the later poet, who when he proclaimed in
Art poétique (1874) 'O qui dira les torts de la Rime!' (Oh who will
tell of the wrongs of Rhyme!) would have found an enthusiastic
precursor in the *philosophe* who saw 'la gêne de la rime' (the con-
straint of rhyme) as one of the main problems facing French poets.[85]
Voltaire found little value in perfect rhyme, being content with just
enough identity of sounds to please the ear without drawing undue
attention to itself;[86] Vercruysse points out that the rhymes of *La
Pucelle* accord with this dictum.[87] The fact that this is a consciously
taken decision rather than casual negligence is borne out by the
interesting observation of Besterman that the rhyming scheme is
quite complex and varied, which, as he adds, makes the poem
'particularly suitable for reading aloud'.[88] Rhyme too is pressed into
service to reinforce the mock-heroic effect in 'Hudibrastic' fashion:

> Le Richemont se voit incontinent
> Percé d'un trait de la hanche à la fesse,
> Le vieux Saintraille au-dessus du genou,
> Le beau La Hire, ah, *je n'ose dire où*:
> Mais que je plains sa gentille maîtresse!

(Richemont straightway sees himself pierced with an arrow from hip to
buttock, old Saintraille pierced above his knee, the handsome La Hire ah!
I dare not say where: but how I pity his sweet mistress!)[89]

The diction itself likewise can become a comic vehicle in rhyme.
Just as the barbarous tones of the 'château de monsieur le baron de
Thunder-ten-tronckh' in the very opening lines of *Candide* intimate
before anything else that this is not an orthodox fairy tale, so too in
La Pucelle Voltaire enhances the lubricious vision of fornication
down the ages by a superbly bathetic couplet of rhymes dissonant
to the classical ear:

> Charles second sur la belle Portsmouth,
> Georges second sur la grasse Yarmouth.

(Charles II upon the beautiful Portsmouth, George II on the fat Yar-
mouth.)[90]

Long though the poem is, one of its great merits remains concision of detail.[91] So many instances have already been cited that it
would be supererogatory to add many more; but two may be
worth isolated mention because they are not so characteristic of the
comic ironic mode. One sums up by a neatly chosen detail the
demoralization in the English ranks:

> Le preux Chandos toujours plein d'assurance
> Criait aux siens: conquérants de la France,
> Marchez à droite; il dit, et dans l'instant
> On tourne à gauche et l'on fuit en jurant.

(The gallant Chandos ever confident cried to his men: 'Conquerors of
France, march to the right.' He spoke, and on the instant they turn to the
left and flee mouthing curses.)[92]

The other succinctly sums up the brutality of Bedford as he kills
and pillages his way across France, and among his other atrocities

> Livre aux soldats et la mère, et la fille.

(Delivers to the soldiers both mother and daughter.)[93]

The deceptive simplicity of such an evocative symbolic picture is
itself the mark of great artistry.

The final irony of *La Pucelle* is that just when Jeanne has given
her 'fleur' to Dunois, the monk Lourdis (who had earlier in the
poem caused the rout of the English troops by revealing to them
that she is a miracle-working virgin, a piece of information instantly
accepted by his gullible listeners)[94] is still going about crying:
'Anglais! elle est pucelle!'[95] The myth and the imposture go on
just as systems of theology and blind admiration for military
exploits will but, happily, sane and healthy human beings will find
their fulfilment in love, pleasure, kindness. Even the bloodthirsty
Jeanne, now that Saint Denis has gone back to his heavenly base,
may be expected to grow more human again and return to the
fresh spontaneity of her early girlhood in Lorraine. Perhaps too
Charles, now that he has won back both France and Agnès, may
rule as the poet's ideal king would, in justice and peace. In this
fictional world, which has very little to do with France in 1429, it
may yet happen. For it is true, as Vercruysse remarks, that Voltaire
is not being merely denigratory; he is also proposing a moral,
political and philosophical programme.[96] Man must look to himself for his own improvement. Nor does Voltaire's ironic approach

become totally destructive, reducing the whole reality to mere artistic illusion. He stops well short of that. There is a genuine code of conduct to follow in *La Pucelle* and it can be reconciled with the surrounding world if man lives wisely. God is implicitly in His heaven (He never appears in *La Pucelle*); we are here concerned only with those messengers who claim falsely to speak for Him. While one must revolt against notions of transcendental interference in our world, there is no call to revolt against the world as such. The final message, though presented in lighter tones, is the same as in *Candide*; here too the comedy is devastating but never nihilist. This is a view of life as spectacle, with scarcely any claims on our emotional commitment. It does not seek (except in the death of Dorothée) to be lyrical, and the psychological observation is limited to a view of externals, with no pretensions to an intimate sense of subjective consciousness. Ambiguity is eschewed; all is clearly conceived and then lucidly expressed. These are grave limitations; but they still leave a wider and richer area than is commonly supposed. As a comic ironist the poet Voltaire can lay claim to an important place in the development of French verse.

5 | Polemicist and reformer

Although we have looked at Voltaire's contributions to four literary genres and seen abundant evidence of his polemical talents, we have not yet directly concerned ourselves with him as *philosophe*. Yet this is where the majority of his writings are to be found and where we may seek for the essential mainspring of his fight against *l'infâme*. This side of Voltaire's output is however as diverse as it is vast, embracing everything from the briefest of *facéties* (jests) to long and sober dictionary-articles. Pamphlets abound, especially during the Ferney years, 'fusées volantes' or 'petits pâtés' as he called them. Even to enumerate this cornucopia would exceed the compass here, not to mention run the risk of incurring tedium in a domain where, for so much of the time, wit and brilliance prevail. Let us then, as before, dwell upon a few select examples to convey some notion of the wealth. How does Voltaire aim to persuade in this more openly didactic literature? There can be no better place to begin than with one of his acknowledged masterpieces and probably his greatest achievement before *Candide*, the *Lettres philosophiques*.

Lettres philosophiques (1734)

Long before 1734, letters had been popular as a polemical form, and justifiably so. The letter-writer reigns supreme in his world, distributing judgements as he sees fit, mixing description, narrative and dialogue in nicely calculated proportions, proposing himself as a man of sanity and appealing to the equally sensible reader. He is a first-person narrator who has no need to invent a historical background for himself; he is a novelist, but endowed as well with all the intimacy of a personal correspondent. The letter itself may be of any length, style or mood, its connection with its neighbours only tenuous if need be. Pascal had shown what the form could yield in satiric force by his *Lettres provinciales* (1657), where a well-meaning Jesuit father, questioned by an ordinary man genuinely seeking guidance, continually gives the game away for his side with devastating effect.

More directly still, the letter-form was related to the traveller's tale; and the line is subtle indeed between the writer who records his impressions of another land and the one who adapts those impressions to the ends of propaganda. Montesquieu's *Lettres persanes* (1721), a picture of contemporary France as seen through Persian eyes, became a best-seller and the Enlightenment's first major onslaught on the *ancien régime*. The model was not lost on Voltaire when the time came for him to set down his own variant on the theme: the Parisian visitor in London.

But the form and perspective Voltaire adopted were consciously different from Montesquieu's, responding to a markedly new approach. In some 160 letters, Montesquieu had worked out a sinuous narrative running over several years. Voltaire, by contrast, takes an analytical stance and does not exploit the developmental theme. Each letter, unlike Montesquieu's, has an identity and a subject of its own. The total is limited to twenty-four, a sound classical number suggestive of Homer and symmetry.[1] Where Montesquieu had traced the rise and fall of expectations, Voltaire reviews in systematic form the elements of a civilization whose values he had come to know and admire during his period of exile after 1726.[2]

Any suggestion however that Voltaire is merely static should be at once discounted. By general agreement of the commentators, he deals with four major aspects of English life: religion, politics, philosophy (including science) and literature. Far from making a mechanical apportionment of six letters to each, Voltaire intertwines his themes so that outlines are blurred and run together; some letters are brief sketches, others twice or more their length develop a treatise in rigorous form. The first seven letters are on religion, but Letter 7 on the Socinians is virtually an appendix to the others, anticipating the philosophical section (Letters 12–17) with which it has links quite as strong as with the preceding material. The end of this letter moves on to the political plane, preparing the way for the socio-political group that immediately follows—if, that is, they can really be called a group; for Letter 8, a hasty affair about parliament, precedes a much more serious study on government, while Letter 10, on commerce, and 11 on inoculation are as different from their predecessors as from one another. Letters 12–17 are more studiously arranged, moving from Bacon and Locke to Descartes and above all Newton; but the final section on literature shows a return to discontinuity as Voltaire interrupts his march through genres and writers to compose a letter on the social importance of culture in England as compared with France, a theme that will return in the final couple of letters. Nor is the survey to be recommended as a manual of strict objectivity. The Quakers, a tiny sect (and by Voltaire's own admission getting smaller) are given four letters while the Anglicans and Presbyterians have to make do with a fairly brief one apiece. Inoculation is accorded as much space as government. Newton receives his due meed of praise in four letters; but he constitutes the whole of English science, as Locke is the sole standard-bearer of English philosophy. There is time to devote a letter to the relatively obscure writers Rochester and Waller, but no discussion of Milton or Defoe. The *Lettres philosophiques* present a singularly personal view of England in the early eighteenth century.

To some extent this looseness of texture may be related to the way the work was compiled. Many years elapsed after Voltaire left England before the letters appeared, and even then they were first published in an English version in London in 1733, the original French edition not emerging until the following year. The author's project of setting down his views on England goes back to at least 1727, and the letters were almost certainly begun during his English stay. It has indeed been persuasively argued from a close analysis of the English edition that most of the letters were originally composed in English and for an English audience, and that to regard them as a strictly French production is no longer acceptable.[3] Certainly, the *Lettres* were amassed over a number of years in varying circumstances, and their heterogeneity reflects this. Furthermore, they already display what is to become an essential feature of Voltaire's polemical style, the penchant for a form built upon the accumulation of brief episodes, whether they be called letters or dictionary-articles or chapters. Though linked together by subject and repeating the same motifs, these episodes reveal Voltaire's usual casualness about close formal integration. To some extent, the *Lettres philosophiques* may be seen as twenty-four sighting shots on the same target.

What is this target? It is surely the demonstration of English civilization as superior to that in France. Voltaire has been to England and discovered how much better things are ordered there: tolerance of another's point of view, patient and modest empiricism in science and philosophy, concern and encouragement for the value of literature and the importance of writers, justice in government, above all freedom in every sphere—these are the essential ingredients. To this end all the information on England is subordinated; it little matters from Voltaire's point of view if the modest Quakers hold pride of place, provided that in the end the distortion is justified on grounds of propaganda.

Religious tolerance in England

These letters on the Quakers are among the liveliest in the book. Voltaire clearly recognized the need to win his audience's attention from the first, the more so as the Quaker sect was widely derided in both England and France. He saw larger possibilities than merely mocking their eccentric ways. Unique amongst Protestants in having no priest or ritual, they further commended themselves by being simple, modest, brave in the face of authority, egalitarian, tolerant of other creeds. Their religion confronted God directly, unhampered by intermediate obstacles. More important still, they had shown in Pennsylvania that a Quaker state had been established on the principles of tolerance and equality that they professed. Catholicism is subjected to the challenge of a group that does not claim a monopoly of truth, lives in peace with its neighbours, and offers a worthy model for anyone who cares for the social good. Only in Letter 3 does Voltaire satirize Quakerism harshly, and then it is the early history of the sect, its fanatical beginnings, the fraudulent martyrs and miracles on which it flourished. But it is quite consistent with his generally respectful attitude, for this is the portrait of an enthusiasm now largely outmoded; Quakers have lived through their obnoxious infancy to an age of mature responsibility. Besides, in tracing the birth of any religious group, Voltaire has a free hand to make oblique reference to all such beginnings, most notably of the Christian faith itself. George Fox, the founder of Quakerism, a charismatic figure who is constantly in trouble with authority, travels the land with exactly a dozen disciples and offers the other cheek when punished; Voltaire neatly combines the imitation of Christ in Fox's conduct with the suggestion that Christ too must have been just like this, 'de mœurs irréprochables et saintement fou' (of irreproachable morality and a saintly madman).[4]

We are led to the Quakers at the outset by the most beguiling of opening statements: 'J'ai cru que la doctrine et l'histoire d'un Peuple si extraordinaire méritaient la curiosité d'un homme raisonnable.' (I thought that the doctrine and history of such an extraordinary community merited the curiosity of a reasonable man.)[5] It is the man of good sense who will conduct his reader along these curious paths, assuring him from the first that he has already reflected upon his choice ('j'ai cru') before proposing it; besides, the sect is 'si extraordinaire' that one can hardly forbear to inquire about it. Thus Voltaire gently initiates the reader, who is immediately introduced to a solid exemplar of the Quaker faith, a vigorous old man typical of so many of Voltaire's idealized elders. Like the 'bon vieillard' at the end of *Candide* who crucially influences the hero's final decisions, this Quaker lives in the country at peace with himself and his fellows, in a well-ordered and decent household; both are self-sufficient but sociable. Like Jacques, that other heroic character of *Candide*, this Quaker possesses the reassuring quality of having succeeded in business. Voltaire has carefully set the stage for approval. The generalized portrait is developed further and the good Quaker now more specifically emerges—a man of total integrity for whom, in Rousseauist terms, 'être' and 'paraître' are identical. By contrast, our correspondent is, though sensible, a typical Frenchman, bringing his foppish airs and bows with him, as the Quaker quickly points out; not so the English protagonist, direct to the point of shocking his listener because he discourteously addresses him as 'tu' while making no move to doff his hat. He immediately accepts the narrator without any affectation or suspicion, ready to trust him at once and to treat him hospitably because the latter has the saving grace of curiosity.

Voltaire has situated us with care. We are in good hands but it is no superman who guides us; we yet have much to learn. So the discourse may begin, and the rest of Letter 1 is given up to it; from friend the Quaker graduates to teacher. The Quakers, we learn, are opposed to baptism, a Judaic custom the Christians have borrowed without any authority bestowed by Christ's practice. The French listener becomes angry (much as Voltaire himself had once lost his temper with a London Quaker over the same question),[6] splutters threats of the Inquisition, claims that the old man is abusing scripture. But the latter always has an unruffled and effective answer based on Biblical text and after a while the protests die away ('mon Quaker me crut déjà converti'); the dialogue becomes eloquent monologue.

It is at this point, with the battle won, that Voltaire returns to the apparently ridiculous ways the Quaker had shown at their meeting. This strange sectarian has now acquired respectability; it will no longer seem merely a defensive tactic to explain why he acts as he does. Predictably, his reasons are eminently worthy, derived from the purity of primitive Christianity that rejects the false pretensions of the world. The Quaker uses with fine precision the characteristic Voltairean trick of reductionism, whereby an institution or ritual is voided of all meaning and made a parody of itself. His fellow-worshippers, as pacifists and true Christians, refuse to take the king's shilling, seeing the recruiters for what they are: 'des meurtriers vêtus de rouge, avec un bonnet haut de deux pieds, enrôlent des Citoyens en faisant du bruit avec deux petits bâtons sur une peau d'âne bien tendue . . .' (murderers clad in red, with hats two feet high, enrol citizens by making a noise with two small sticks on a taut ass's skin).

If a disproportionate time has been spent on this first letter, it is because here one sees Voltaire's rhetoric of persuasion at its best. The Quakers, tiresome eccentrics though they appear to the indifferent stranger, have been installed as models of conduct, both ethical and social. Voltaire paints the vivid portrait of a Quaker exemplary in appearance and behaviour before he tries to interest us in the tenets of Quakerism. At this stage, the reader's indifference must be suspended and his interest won, so the whole letter aims to please before it instructs; hence the coruscating display. Thereafter Voltaire can afford to fill out the picture in more ambivalent fashion. Letter 2 takes us to a Quaker meeting, from which it emerges that the gentleman we have met is better than the rituals of his religion. The service, compounded of silences, grimaces, sighs, and an incomprehensible 'galimatias tiré de l'Evangile' (farrago taken from the Gospel) offered in a nasal voice as a monologue, is a cameo of Voltairean satire; but even here there is something to be said on the other side. The speakers who make their ridiculous interventions are patiently heard out, for no one can be sure whether divine truth has been revealed to them or not. In metaphysical matters give others the benefit of the doubt: such is the message, to be repeated in many diverse circumstances during the *Lettres*. The Quaker service is vindicated as a fine example of tolerance in action and a price well worth paying for the lack of a priesthood. Once again our Quaker instructor demonstrates that this is true Christianity, based on a direct revelation from God to man.

The Quakers in brief serve many purposes. Being the most pure of Protestants, they are an excellent instrument with which to attack Catholic ceremonies and pretensions; they offer an ideal example of English freedom in action, themselves so tolerant but also themselves as tolerated by other sects; finally and not least, they offer a rich subject of artistic portraiture, arousing in Voltaire a fertile compound of genuine respect and some detached amusement. The other three religious letters offer less promising subjects. The Anglicans (Letter 5) evoke no warm sympathy in the author, and no living human being is presented. Their main interest is sociological. Given the chance they would probably display the same fanatical vices as French Catholics; as it is, bereft of power by the State, they are innocuous and rather dull. Less attractive still are the Presbyterians (Letter 6), an envious, boring and pusillanimous body of men who deny others pleasure by their desolating sabbatarian ways and dislike of culture and entertainment. Like the Anglicans but to an even greater extent, their main virtue in Voltaire's eyes is their existence, which allows him to demonstrate that Britain is truly a pluralist nation in theological matters. In this land there are not just one or two religions but thirty, and because of their very multiplicity 'elles vivent en paix heureuses'. Equally important, such brotherliness permits a flourishing economy, for on the London Stock Exchange men are concerned only with secular criteria: 'là le Juif, le Mahométan et le Chrétien traitent l'un avec l'autre comme s'ils étaient de la même Religion, et ne donnent le nom d'infidèles qu'à ceux qui font banqueroute' (there the Jew, the Moslem and the Christian do business with each other as though they were of the same religion, and give the name 'infidels' only to those who go bankrupt). Paradoxically these, rather than the churches, are the truly 'pacifiques et libres assemblées'. The fact that in 1734 toleration was far from complete, that Catholics, Unitarians, Jews and atheists were excluded from public office, mattered less than the real hopes Voltaire saw for the future in a country where, as he read the signs, sectarian strife was over. Letter 7 on the Socinians adds little except to confirm the point. A new religion would have little chance of success; the world in England, and indeed in France too, is more amenable now to peace and prosperity. Such calamities of the previous century as the Fronde and the Civil War could not be repeated; today Cromwell would be 'un simple Marchand de Londres'.

A land of freedom

From religious Voltaire moves to political matters; but the selection he offers is curious. Letter 8 is formally on parliament, its successor on government; in practice they inevitably mingle together with no clear-cut distinction. If Letter 8 reminds us of the constitutional liberty Englishmen have won through the Civil War, Letter 9 shows the gradual establishment of those rights from the Middle Ages on. It seems that the two letters date from different periods, the first being written in England and the second after Voltaire's return to France.[7] Letter 8 is perhaps superficially tendentious in holding up English political liberty as unique. If there have had to be wars in order to secure this freedom, at least it may be said that Charles I was judicially executed, while in France the assassinations of Henri III and Henri IV are the odious products of fanaticism. Viewed with twentieth-century eyes, this argument might be set down clearly to the advantage of France. We know all too well of the horrible facility with which assassinations can be legalized; whereas the French murders, though influenced by sinister forces, had never been condoned by the law. But Letter 8 gains in limpidity what it lacks in depth. The portrait of 'ce Gouvernement sage, où le Prince, tout-puissant pour faire du bien, a les mains liées pour faire le mal' (that wise government, where the prince, all-powerful for doing good, has his hands tied for doing evil) has contributed one of the most often-quoted phrases from the whole work. Besides, Voltaire's main point is historically correct; the English were unique at that time in having established a constitutional monarchy.

By contrast, Letter 9 represents more serious research and reflection. A historical survey argues that English liberties have gradually evolved and that they had to be fought for; England is not a land of freedom merely through some capricious act of

Providence. Thereafter Voltaire goes on to study the contemporary situation: the ascendancy of the House of Commons over the Lords, the equality of all men before the law and in matters of taxation, the thriving peasantry. Again, the details are highly selective. The historical section ends with Henry VII's alienation of baronial lands, Voltaire concluding complacently: 'Peu à peu toutes les terres changèrent de Maîtres.' (Gradually every estate changed its owner.) A nice Hollywood fade-out, with the power of the nobility definitively broken! Henry VIII's depredations upon Church lands go unmentioned, as do the evils of eighteenth-century politics under Walpole. But again it must be said: Voltaire is not writing a history. He must select and then heighten in simplified form what he selects so as to make his letters truly *philosophiques*, arousing speculation and the desire for reform in his audience. For Voltaire certain lessons can clearly be learned from English political history. The people, like so many others, had been oppressed by the constant warring of feudal lords: 'chaque Peuple avait cent tyrans au lieu d'un maître' (every people had a hundred tyrants instead of one master); they had been dehumanized for the most part: 'espèce de bétail qu'on vend et qu'on achète avec la terre' (a kind of cattle bought and sold with the land). But after Magna Carta the land had begun to free itself of this oppression, with the happy results we have seen. Voltaire's own predilections are becoming clear. For him 'le peuple' are

la plus nombreuse, la plus vertueuse même, et par conséquent la plus respectable partie des hommes, composée de ceux qui étudient les lois et les sciences, des Négociants, des Artisans, en un mot de tout ce qui n'était point tyran.

(the most numerous, the most virtuous even, and consequently the most respectable section of men, made up of those who study the laws and sciences, the merchants, the artisans, in a word, of all who were not tyrants.)

The nobility and clergy had been repressive, unlike the most worthwhile part of the nation, the bourgeoisie who engage in commerce and also in cultural pursuits. This class cannot count on aid from the aristocracy; its hope lies rather in a strong king.

This hostility to a closed aristocratic caste is confirmed in Letter 10 on commerce, where the relationship of trade to prosperity and freedom is made explicit. The English nobles do not disdain trade; hence, unlike their French and German counterparts, they are useful to society. Voltaire's attitude to the nobility, as this detail helps to make clear, is far from being purely antipathetic; his opposition is directed against those who live off the land without making any useful return to society, as do the Court parasites whom he condemns here. On the matter of commerce itself Voltaire is quite unambiguous, and the letter reflects his enthusiasm. Unlike the problems of government, the realities of trade are simple, well known to Voltaire from personal acquaintances,[8] and close to his heart. Typically, he adds an anecdote about how Prince Eugene beat Louis XIV's French armies with the aid of fifty million pounds, raised in half an hour by English merchants. This delightful tale, narrated with pungent economy, is incorrect in several details; but as so often with Voltaire the basic point, which he ascribes to England's great credit, is a true one, and clearly shows that trade can be not merely self-interested but also an effective bastion against military oppression.

The following letter (11, on inoculation) is equally lucid in its perception of a basic English characteristic, but it is more brilliant still, for it focuses attention on a much more hazardous matter. Voltaire exhibits all his flair for isolating a minor phenomenon and giving it major significance. The progress of smallpox inoculation in 1734 was problematical. Was the cure worth the risk? There was opposition on theological grounds too, though this came mainly from England.[9] Inoculation had been fashionable in England about the time of Voltaire's arrival but then fell into disuse around 1730 and did not become established until a decade later. Voltaire, while not ignoring all the unhelpful details, saw the value of the subject as presenting a model example of English empiricism motivated by social utility; the French by contrast are represented as hostile out of pure traditionalism. Voltaire's flair served him well, for the history of attitudes towards inoculation later in the century was to prove him right. While the English phlegmatically re-established the practice without major opposition from clergymen or doctors, it was fiercely opposed by the medical establishment in France until after Louis XV's death from smallpox in 1774.[10] But this concerns us less here than Voltaire's ability to write what might be called a documentary fiction.

He begins with a paradox: 'On dit doucement dans l'Europe chrétienne que les Anglais sont des fous et des enragés' (They say quietly in Christian Europe that the English are madmen and lunatics), and goes on to name the obvious medical objections. The English then have the right to reply, the reply being balanced symmetrically against the other assertion in its opening statement that 'Les autres Européens sont des lâches et des dénaturés' (The other Europeans are cowardly and unnatural), and in the reasons which follow. At this moment we are in a neutral position: 'Pour juger qui a raison' (To judge who is right) the author is ready at hand. First of all comes the strange story, told without adornment, of the Circassian mothers who deliberately give smallpox to their children. Indeed, a year without smallpox is a bad year in that country. Why this dangerous custom? The motives are, surprisingly, universal ones: 'la tendresse maternelle et l'intérêt' (maternal tenderness and self-interest). A partial explanation is supplied, just enough to hold our attention; Voltaire quickly satisfies our curiosity by recounting how the one asset of Circassian families is their daughters' beauty. Destined for the harem, 'these poor creatures' must be brought up to please their 'disdainful masters'. Hence the ravages of smallpox cannot be tolerated. It is a straightforward matter of protecting one's economic interests. Necessity forced the Circassians into empirical verification; when their 'observations naturelles' taught them that a mild attack provided immunity, the conclusions to be drawn were evident.

The scene moves to England. Lady Mary Wortley Montagu, one of the most intelligent of English women, had discovered the practice while in Constantinople and inoculated her son. Religious theory avails nothing against experimental success: 'son Chapelain eut beau lui dire que cette expérience n'était pas chrétienne . . . le fils . . . s'en trouva à merveille' (despite her chaplain telling her that this experiment was unChristian . . . the son . . . felt splendid because of it). On her return to London, Lady Mary tells Princess (now Queen) Caroline. Here is a living instance of the philosophical monarch, 'née pour encourager tous les arts et pour faire du bien aux hommes' (born to encourage all the arts and to do good to men), who had helped Milton's daughter, fallen on hard times, and who had sought to reconcile Clarke and Leibniz. She introduces the practice and it flourishes.

The time has come to leave the parable and draw conclusions. A fifth of the French population is killed or maimed by smallpox;[11] virtually no one in England or Turkey is touched by it; why then are Frenchmen so blind to the obvious?: 'Quoi donc? Est-ce que les

Français n'aiment point la vie? Est-ce que leurs femmes ne se soucient point de leur beauté? En vérité, nous sommes d'étranges gens!' (Good heavens! Don't the French love life? Don't their wives care about their beauty? Really, we are strange people!) The rhetorical questions deliberately simplify the issue to clinch the matter, for the narrator has long since judged for himself 'qui a raison'; and indeed in the final paragraph he reveals that the Chinese nation, 'qui passe pour être la plus sage et la mieux policée de l'univers' (which is thought to be the wisest and the most civilized in the world), have practised inoculation for a whole century. It is an argument of universal wisdom; the Turks have discovered the usage through need, the English through right-minded thinking, and both are confirmed in their good sense by the ancient sagacity of the Chinese.

The letter on inoculation is not the most important or serious in the collection, but there is no better example for showing the Voltairean art of persuasion. The identification of the phenomenon as significant is itself part of the author's genius—the gift, which remained with him throughout his life, of divining what was genuinely important in the world around him. The confidence with which he pursues the subject, refusing to be discouraged by the knowledge that it is momentarily unfashionable, is the mark of a mature writer; and the casual regard for factual details is an integral part of this artistic arrangement of the facts. There still remain to be included all the elements peculiar to Voltaire's polemical style at its best. Invective is absent, as it is generally from the *Lettres philosophiques*; at most the rhetorical questions near the end suggest bewilderment at French foolishness. The tone is genial, courteous, suitable for a reader who has but to be shown the truth to believe it. Lucidity characterizes the expression throughout, as though the logic of the matter were self-evident; rather than attack his opponents' arguments, Voltaire bypasses them as being quite irrelevant. Suspense and paradox enliven the early passages as far as the demonstration, which then unrolls with a direct appeal to 'natural observation' by people intelligent enough to recognize a socially useful custom when they see one. Finally, the concision is remarkable; the whole letter is well under two thousand words. If Voltaire had been completely wrong about inoculation, this would still be one of his finest literary pieces. Paradoxically, it would also remain one of the most 'philosophical', unsurpassed as an illustration of the principles of enlightened freedom which underlie the *Lettres* as a whole.

Locke, Newton and Voltaire

The succeeding letters on science and philosophy, to which Letter 11 constitutes an introduction, are much more serious in tone. No Voltairean survey of a civilization could omit this aspect—indeed, one might argue that Locke's psychology and Newton's science are the key to the whole book, as they are to a large part of the Enlightenment in general. Voltaire is now no longer the umpire or the simple man of good sense, but the pedagogue who expounds the doctrines of his heroes. Bacon, 'le père de la Philosophie expérimentale' (Letter 12), acts as curtain-raiser to Locke (Letter 13), who shines forth by his intellectual modesty. Voltaire reviews a fools' gallery of philosophers who uttered wondrous absurdities about the soul before he comes to Locke, whose wisdom lay in his recording only what he could verify. It is the difference between *roman* and *histoire*,[12] and for the latter, as Voltaire knew, some initial scepticism is required. Locke's achievement was not only in his assertions but in that 'he dares also to doubt'. In so doing he demolished the Cartesian theory of innate ideas and conceded that perhaps matter had the capacity for thought. On this latter point, Voltaire gives Locke's tentative remark a strong materialist emphasis which the English philosopher had never intended. Ending in an agnostic position upon the nature and existence of the soul, he disingenuously claims at the same time that one must believe in its immortality because faith requires us to. This is probably the most radical of the letters[13] and certainly one of the most influential, helping to open the way to Lockean psychology in France as an epistemological science.

Letters 14–17 all deal with Newton. The first of them evaluates him alongside Descartes and begins with a sharp perception of the change in scientific climate when a Frenchman crosses the Channel: 'Il a laissé le monde plein, il le trouve vide' (He has left a full universe, he finds an empty one): in one country the Cartesian cosmos reigns, in the other the Newtonian. Before dealing fully with the English scientist, Voltaire wants due honour paid to Descartes, a great if now outmoded pioneer. To some extent, his fault was to have been born too early, but he accomplished his own downfall by eventually returning to 'system-building' in the worst metaphysical traditions. One should not however forget his earlier merits in decrying false logic and teaching men to reason. While not disguising Descartes's errors, Voltaire wants as ever in these *Lettres* to stress unity rather than division. The reader, persuaded by such reasonableness, can come to the three letters on Newton in a properly receptive frame of mind.

These letters are the most austere in the book, a far remove from the easy accessibility of the early ones on the Quakers; the subject precludes any other approach if the author is to be seriously informative. Even so, he makes sure he does not alienate the reader. If he is here an instructor, he is only a layman himself, no more intelligent than we are: 'Je vais vous dire (si je puis, sans verbiage) le peu que j'ai pu attraper de toutes ces sublimes idées' (I am going to tell you (if I can, without verbosity) the little that I have been able to catch of all these sublime ideas) (Letter 15). The more strictly scientific material will be interspersed with homely anecdotes, most notably the famous story of Newton and the apple, which Voltaire claimed to have heard from the lips of Newton's niece and which is surely the prime contribution of the *Lettres* to scientific folklore.[14] From the account of Newtonian theory emerges Voltaire's unstinted admiration for a man who has attained the sublime, who can say with truth: 'J'ai découvert un des secrets du Créateur.' (I have discovered one of the secrets of the Creator.) Like Locke, Newton is great enough to admit that he might be wrong, and wise enough to restrict his thinking to the knowable. By so doing, he elucidates the laws of the universe, frees man from superstitious terror, uplifts and exalts. Once again Voltaire's influence is far-reaching; as the first popular defence of Newton in France,[15] these letters are a landmark in the growing ascendancy of Newton's physics over the Cartesian universe.

Letters on literature

Finally, Voltaire comes to literature; these letters constitute the most disappointing section of the work. Clearly, no account of a national culture could be complete without some attention to its literature, but here Voltaire is less convinced that the English have much to teach the French. Their tragedy is inferior and Shakespeare an enigma (Letter 18);[16] their comedy, though better, evokes only a

perfunctory response, Voltaire mainly confining himself to recounting the plot and to personal anecdotes (Letter 19); their poets
are treated in a scarcely less mechanical manner (Letter 20). The
opportunity, for instance, to give us a first-hand account of the
London theatre, which he came to know so well, is unfortunately
neglected, as one critic has pointed out.[17] The most striking element
in this final section is the preoccupation Voltaire shows with the
contrast between England, where writers are esteemed, and France,
where they are treated with indifference or worse. In England,
where 'communément on pense' (Letter 20), the aristocracy sets the
tone by cultivating letters; hence the only reason, it would seem,
for giving Rochester and Waller pride of place in a letter devoted
entirely to them (Letter 21). In France culture flourishes only
amongst the professional bourgeoisie or *noblesse de robe* (magistracy)
and in the Church, where an educated mind is needed for one's
daily work. Letter 23, devoted to the 'consideration one owes to
men of letters', as the uncharacteristic title puts it, reminds us that
English writers are encouraged by being given public office; where
this is not possible for a Catholic like Pope, such is the popularity
of literature that he can grow rich on his translations of Homer.
Actresses are honoured, for example Mrs Oldfield, entombed in
Westminster Abbey, not despised like Adrienne Lecouvreur, buried
the same year in unconsecrated ground. Only in one area is France
superior: its Academies, the legacy of that enlightened monarch
Louis XIV, provide institutional encouragement of the arts and
sciences (Letter 24); but even here Voltaire has reservations about
their tedious ceremonial and would like to see the Académie
Française devoting itself to more useful publications.

The *Lettres philosophiques* offer the programme of a whole civilization. It is a remarkable achievement for so brief a work. Certain
specific reforms can be adopted from the English; the French can
abolish, for instance, feudal privileges still remaining in the judicial
and fiscal realms. But the more important lessons are general;
Voltaire's compatriots need to exploit the full consequences of
philosophic freedom to cultivate the scientific method of objective
verification, encourage trade and the arts, exclude matters of faith
from all domains of rational activity. Cosmopolitanism rather than
Anglomania is the keynote throughout. French culture is not
mocked, but its deficiencies are pointed out; with the benefit of

English attitudes it can still flourish. In an age when sectarianism was apparently decaying, there was yet no need for a fiercely polemical approach. One could still expect to work with the liberal elements of Catholicism, notably the Jesuits whom Voltaire hoped to convert to Newtonianism.

It was not to be. While the Jesuit attitude to the *Lettres philosophiques* proved negative, the reaction of official authority was more virulent. The work was burned and Voltaire had to flee to escape arrest. Although he was allowed back to Paris a year later and in the 1740s even occupied for a time an official position at Court, his spiritual exile from the French establishment had already begun.[18]

Discours aux Welches (1764)

Thirty years after the *Lettres philosophiques*, Voltaire is again looking at France with an outsider's perspective. Once again he is in exile from Paris, but this time the sentence seems to be for life. The *Lettres philosophiques* had been prepared for publication by an author restored to France and hopeful still of participating in the mainstream of its destinies. By 1764 he is banished to the frontier and, installed at Ferney, looks in on the French with the eye of one used to observing them from outside, while yet sharing their role and fortunes. This double optic (announced in the opening words: 'O Welches, mes compatriotes!') helps to explain the particular qualities of the *Discours aux Welches*.

The *Discours* is a typical pamphlet of the Ferney period. It is fairly short (about 6000 words), somewhat episodic and rambling. The precise point of departure is not easy to establish. But the sweep is large and effortless, the language clear, the style corrosive. It echoes the *Lettres philosophiques* to the extent that it passes judgement upon a whole civilization, this time the French; but no attempt is made here to apportion equal weighting to the different aspects of that society. The *Discours* bears all the marks of an improvisation, probably struck off in short order by Voltaire, like many another piece in the last two decades of his life.

The brief exordium announces the theme and approach:

O Welches, mes compatriotes! si vous êtes supérieurs aux anciens Grecs et aux anciens Romains, ne mordez jamais le sein de vos nourrices, n'insultez jamais à vos maîtres, soyez modestes dans vos triomphes; voyez qui vous êtes et d'où vous venez.

(O Welches, my compatriots! if you are superior to the ancient Greeks and Romans, never bite the breast of those who suckle you, never jeer at your masters, be modest in your triumphs; see who you are and whence you come.)[19]

The French have nothing to be proud of. Voltaire embarks upon a brief historical sketch of the nation's beginnings, from which it emerges that early French history was a series of inglorious and generally meaningless events. No sense of manifest destiny can be discovered; indeed, the French were lucky in finding the British and the Spaniards occupied with wars at home when they might otherwise have overwhelmed their neighbour. True, Louis XIV's reign was a relief from brutish ignorance, but let us not exaggerate; it was merely 'un moment bien brillant'.[20] Generally, the French nation presents a picture of illiterate fools, subservient to Rome because the Church alone possessed learning and therefore power. Even the cultural improvements which the Renaissance brought about under François I have had little general effect.

Yet though they belong to a provincial backwater the French are insufferably presumptuous. Their historians call them 'le premier peuple de l'univers'; as Voltaire adds with icy sarcasm, 'Cela n'est pas civil pour les autres nations' (That is not courteous to other nations).[21] The historical account now gives way to a survey of the present as the author builds up his theme. What does France amount to, in brief? First of all, it is smaller than many other European lands; it is also infertile over large areas and millions of its peasants are wretchedly poor. It is unique in selling judicial offices and military commissions; and the public exchequer system encourages fraud.

These are merely the opening salvoes. Voltaire on this occasion is less concerned about politics than about culture, as the first paragraph of the work makes clear. He begins with science. All the important discoveries have been made abroad: compass, telescope, printing, logarithms, and a score of others besides. Not only have the French lacked inventiveness; they have opposed countries which possess it. They supported Descartes against Newton until they were the laughing-stock of Europe; they still reject inoculation in the name of theological wisdom.

From science Voltaire passes to literature, which is where he has been tending from the first; the last two-thirds are given over to it. He begins by minimizing one of the great sources of French pride in the eighteenth century, the universality of the language in

European polite society. Even this, he claims, is due to the Huguenot *émigrés* hounded out of France under Louis XIV; this French glory is the result of French oppression. Even so, the language is a strange mixture of Greek derivations and homespun vulgarity. Unlike the elegance of Greek literature, French is full of barbarisms like *cul-de-sac*, with its unfortunate extension of the impolite *cul*.

Nor are French writers so great as is often imagined. Pascal, Bossuet and Fénelon have gone some way, it is true, to raise the French from brutishness, but Pascal's *Lettres provinciales*, for instance, cannot be compared with Cicero; the one is merely concerned with a tedious Jansenist quarrel over religious grace, the other deals with the civil wars of Rome and still instructs Europe today. Bossuet, Fénelon and La Fontaine fall far short of their predecessors. The French language is itself impervious to beauty:

cette langue embarrassée d'articles, dépourvue d'inversions, pauvre en termes poétiques, stérile en tours hardis, asservie à l'éternelle monotonie de la rime, et manquant pourtant de rimes dans les sujets nobles.

(this language obstructed by articles, lacking inversions, poor in poetic terms, sterile in bold expressions, enslaved to the eternal monotony of rhyme, and yet without rhymes in noble subjects.)[22]

Only the theatre has superior merit, but Voltaire refuses to give back his readers their shattered pride. He treats it in a paragraph, then adds a word of praise for Boileau's *Art poétique*, and dismisses the subject curtly: 'Voilà votre gloire, ne la perdez pas.' (Your glory is there, do not lose it.)[23]

Yet there are critics in France who proscribe the literature of antiquity. Voltaire sternly warns his audience against them, painting an evocative picture of the beauties of Greek poetry. French literature by contrast is full of dross. The final lesson is clear: 'respectez vos maîtres, vous dis-je' (respect your masters, I tell you); the author proceeds by way of conclusion to a quiet understatement: 'Croyez, mes frères, que vous ne ferez pas mal de vous en tenir aux belles inventions profanes de vos prédécesseurs.' (Believe me, my brothers, you will not do badly if you abide by the splendid, profane inventions of your predecessors.)[24]

The themes are not new, but they have not been assembled before with such concision or sharpness. As so often elsewhere, Voltaire wants to cut down to size his arrogant countrymen and destroy their sense of being divinely appointed to be the leading nation. It is but another aspect of his war upon the ancient Hebrews, or upon Christians in general, for enjoying this complacent self-centredness, this belief that they are necessarily in the right. But here Voltaire's vendetta takes on a particularly strong tone of invective because his main concern is with something that touches him deeply as a writer. Rarely is he so disparaging of French literary glories. The object of attack, one feels, is not so much the great figures of Louis XIV's age as the intolerable degree of French pride about them.

In order to express his venom with suitable force, he uses a new literary device. Like Swift with the Yahoos, Voltaire demotes the human to the subhuman: the French lose the status of their name and become 'Welches'. The term (it refers literally to the ancient Gauls) is well chosen. Historically, it reduces his compatriots to the level of their primitive forefathers, linguistically it turns them into barbarians. The word itself is odious to the classically trained French ear, especially one so delicately attuned to the elegance of Greece and Rome as Voltaire's. The initial *W* followed by the equally foreign-sounding *elches* with its unattractive orthography: these qualities evoke a sense of the primeval Teutonic, totally at odds with the learning acquired from the cultural heritage of the Mediterranean.

The word itself is shocking. Its use in direct apostrophe is even more so. The audience here is no more the gentle listener of the *Lettres philosophiques* who can be easily persuaded by reason; it is an ignorant mob that must be shown its true image in the mirror. From the second paragraph Voltaire works at building up a picture of grossness in which the reader is asked to acquiesce: 'Mais convenez que vous fûtes toujours un peu barbars.' (But admit that you were always a bit barbaric.)[25] The pretended concession 'un peu' merely heightens the irony by its alliance with so cruel an epithet. Only by these shock tactics, it would seem, can Voltaire demolish the French belief in their own supremacy. He addresses them with an ironic accolade:

Premier peuple de l'univers, songez que vous avez dans votre royaume de Frankreich environ deux millions de personnes qui marchent en sabots six mois de l'année, et qui sont nu-pieds les autres six mois.

(Foremost nation of the world, reflect that you have in your kingdom of Frankreich about two million people who go about in clogs for six months of the year and are barefoot for the other six months.)[26]

The flaunted title is destroyed by the simple truth of so much poverty, the language again being carefully selected. No reference is made to peasants, which might evoke set reactions; the reader is shown them detached from their class structure, tied only to one significant detail that will symbolize their full wretchedness. To crown all, the comfortable associations of 'France' have been removed; in the unfamiliar world of 'Frankreich', it is yet 'votre royaume'. This audience goes on receiving the direct stings of Voltaire's satire. Rhetorical questions are posed that are not even worthy of a direct answer: 'Etes-vous le premier peuple de l'univers pour le commerce et pour la marine? . . . Hélas!' (Are you the foremost nation of the world for trade and navigation? . . . Alas!)[27] The reader is never allowed to escape responsibility. He is accused directly, for instance, of opposing Newton's theory of gravitation with 'le roman impertinent des tourbillons de Descartes' (the irrelevant fiction of Descartes's vortices);[28] of speaking in a vulgar language, even of writing the mediocrities of French literature: 'Avez-vous mieux écrit que Tite-Live . . .?' (Have you written better work than Livy . . .?)[29]

The attack is fierce; it is not however as completely negative as has been sometimes suggested. The final message, after all, is a positive one, as has been seen. In order to reinforce this, Voltaire seems later on to withdraw the derogatory title from his countrymen, or at least to hold it in abeyance. At times they may deservedly enjoy the glory of being Frenchmen: 'O Français! je me fais un plaisir d'admirer avec vous vos grands poètes.' (O Frenchmen! I derive pleasure from admiring with you your great poets.)[30] But their status is at best uncertain, and they can be relegated again if they follow the advice of barbarian critics: 'Gardez-vous bien de les croire, ô Français! vous redeviendriez Welches.' (Take good care not to believe them, o Frenchmen! you would become Welches again.)[31] In the penultimate paragraph they seem to have been returned to their coarse underworld; Voltaire opens once more with 'O Welches!' and goes on to enumerate some of their vulgar names and beliefs. But the final paragraph leaves the way open to salvation: 'Croyez, mes frères . . .'

So the onslaught is tempered. As in *Micromégas*, Voltaire offers a ray of brightness after destroying all the false paths to glory. The French are not written off; they are after all 'mes frères'. Their potential is greater than their achievement, and they are not wholly to be identified with their past follies. If they can banish self-righteousness, they can still hope to become civilized. There is much more disillusionment in the *Discours* than in the *Lettres philosophiques*, as the reader is harangued and called to an awareness of his perilous state. But despite the flashes of irony, Voltaire is no longer in the disruptive mood of *Candide*. The ultimate lesson, as in the *Lettres*, is philosophical. Above all, underlying a true civilization there must be the proper frame of mind. But the prescription is general; no detailed suggestions are offered. The *Discours*, while far from nihilistic in tone, can hardly be called a reformist work.[32]

Avis au public sur les parricides imputés aux Calas et aux Sirven (1766)

The *Discours aux Welches* not surprisingly excited strong reactions in France, and Voltaire quickly wrote a *Supplément* in a much more accommodating tone. There he makes conciliatory distinctions between the Welches as 'ennemis de la raison' and the French as 'les philosophes'.[33] Such a tactical retreat was entirely in keeping with Voltaire's general policy when he felt that he had gone too far; nonetheless, it is not as complete a volte-face as is sometimes claimed, for the distinction is already embryonic in the *Discours*. In any case, the 1760s were not devoted to negative diatribes. Voltaire was discovering where he could intervene decisively in current quarrels. The execution in 1762 of the Protestant merchant Jean Calas for the alleged murder of his son, the hanging of the Protestant pastor François Rochette in the same year for carrying on his ministerial profession, the condemnation of the Sirven parents, likewise Protestant, in 1764 for the alleged murder of their daughter —these and other cases convinced Voltaire that the oppression of Huguenots was one specific area where he could act to overturn abuses of justice. By 1765 Calas was posthumously rehabilitated and Voltaire, through his efforts in the case, had definitely established himself as an avenger of the innocent. The Sirven case, though it dates from 1762 when the arrest of the family was ordered, took more time to evolve, was less dramatic in its development (largely because no one was actually executed, the family wisely fleeing at once to escape arrest), and acquittal was not secured until 1771.

The *Avis*, then, is more immediately concerned with the Sirven affair, but it uses, as the title indicates, the Calas trial as well to make its point—indeed, Voltaire astutely notes the significance of the Calas verdict as a reassuring precedent for the judge in the Sirven case.[34] The tactic is however not solely to intervene on behalf of two unfortunate families, but to indicate the general truths which these matters reveal about the deleterious effects of fanaticism. It is all of a piece with the witchcraft persecutions that have contaminated Christendom for 1500 years. Witchcraft and ignorance have gone hand in hand: 'Plus une province était ignorante et grossière, plus l'empire du diable y était reconnu.' (The more a province was ignorant and uncouth, the more the devil's sway there was acknowledged.)[35] It is already 'une passion bien terrible' to force men to think like us; but it is 'une extrême folie' to think we can win them over 'en les révoltant continuellement par les calomnies les plus atroces, en les persécutant, en les traînant aux galères, à la potence, sur la roue et dans les flammes' (by continually stirring them up with the most heinous slanders, by persecuting them, dragging them to the galleys or the gibbet, on to the wheel or into the flames).[36] And yet the Church goes on whipping up hatred by perpetuating memories of old conflicts, as in Toulouse (the area where Calas, Rochette and Sirven had all been condemned), which in the fateful year of 1762 had celebrated the two hundredth anniversary of a bloody victory over the Protestants in that city during the religious wars. The rituals and attire that went with the procession only exacerbated the passions: 'l'imagination s'enflamme à ces objets, l'âme devient atroce et implacable' (the imagination takes fire at these objects, the soul becomes black and implacable).[37] Voltaire urges men to celebrate instead great deeds of generosity. He later goes on to urge his readers to follow the laws of ancient Rome, neutral in religious matters, and to heed the sermons of Archbishop Tillotson in England or the words of a certain unnamed 'ouvrage ... très philosophique'[38] which turns out to be his own *Poème sur la loi naturelle*. The *Avis* ends with a plea to 'les âmes nobles et compatissantes'[39] to join in and help the Sirven family in their quest for justice. The story of the Calas affair had made abundantly clear who were the friends of the oppressed: 'Pas un de ceux qu'on appelle *dévots*, je le dis avec douleur, n'a essuyé leurs larmes ni rempli leur bourse. Il n'y a que les esprits raisonnables qui pensent noblement. . . .' (Not one of those who are called devout, I say it with sorrow, has wiped away their tears or filled their purse. Only reasonable minds think nobly. . . .)[40]

The *Avis* is not a great literary achievement. Little in it will surprise the reader of Voltaire; there is none of the brilliance of the *Lettres philosophiques* and no device to match the subtle use of the 'Welches' in the *Discours*. It is however not without merit, and that merit grows when one recognizes the *Avis* as entirely characteristic of so much of Voltaire's writing in these years. The tone is less detached than in the *Discours*. A particular crusade is at hand, for which the support of the enlightened is necessary. Voltaire is no longer mordant but angry, and he waxes eloquent in his indignation. The irony that those who know only *Candide* think must be for ever associated with this *philosophe* is almost entirely absent. All is based upon a call to the reader's pity and justice (the two main-springs of all true humanity, in Voltaire's view),[41] generally through the direct techniques of enumeration, repetition, rolling periods mounting to a climax. This is the rhetoric of persuasion in uncompli-cated form, aiming to convince by clarity of thought and simple affirmation above all. Such ornament as is used is low-keyed. If the judge in the Sirven case is made to condemn himself out of his own mouth, the irony is nonetheless unsubtle. Near the end of the work, Voltaire sketches a fable about the sinking ship where, instead of unified action against the imminent peril, all are divided into sects and the ship goes down; the language and rhythms have the simple appeal of a parable from the New Testament.

The author here is manifestly one who cares; his passionate plea for tolerance is divested of all the ingenuity that might make him seem too cold and deliberate. More sophisticated styles of persuasion are left to *L'Ingénu*, written at about the same time. As in the *Lettres philosophiques*, the reader is a potential friend who needs only to see the face of reason in order to appreciate it immediately. Yet the tone carries much of the sombreness of the *Discours aux Welches*, for the world is a dark place and sectarian disputes are not merely ridiculous, they are a contagion, to use the metaphor Voltaire employs and repeats here. The arsenal of Ferney contained more resounding ammunition in its locker; but it was the repeated assaults of pamphlets like the *Avis*, transparent in their logic to the point of banality, simplified in their statement for the meanest of 'esprits raisonnables', and pervaded by the author's concern and alarm at the horrors of persecution, which give the corpus of Ferney works their characteristic flavour. Some, like the *Com-mentaire sur le livre des délits et des peines* (1766) which advocated improvements in the penal laws, are more specifically reformist in nature; others, as we shall see later, pursued a more critical line in attacking the beliefs and rituals of the Catholic Church. The *Avis*, however, typifies in content and form a battle in which Voltaire, his early hopes past but also with the despair of the *Candide* years behind him, set out to 'écraser l'infâme'.

6 | Philosopher and *philosophe*

In preceding chapters, the emphasis has been on the way form and content were intermarried in Voltaire. What precisely Voltaire believed has received little attention; it is time to rectify this. But here one is faced again by the problem of an author elusive in his very voluminousness. Besides, nowhere in Voltaire's work is there a comprehensive or systematic exposition of his philosophy, nothing to match Descartes's *Discours de la méthode*. The thinker is every-where, which is to risk saying nowhere.

Even so, some works come nearer the essential Voltaire than others. In his earlier years the *Traité de métaphysique* stands out. As the title implies, the author is making a rare attempt to set down his world-view in consecutive fashion. It was, furthermore, written for himself and a few friends, not for publication. Since it is a private work, as few public attitudes are struck as is possible in any composition by Voltaire. We may reasonably take the self-examination, devoid of polemics and trying to be fair to different points of view, as authentic. In addition, it is wider in scope and more directly personal in its attitudes than the contemporaneous *Eléments de la philosophie de Newton*, as the editor of the *Traité*, Mrs Patterson, has indicated.[1]

Later in life, Voltaire will write 'un second *Traité de métaphysique*, plus libre et plus personnel que le premier',[2] and entitled, most aptly, *Le Philosophe ignorant*. Already over seventy years of age, Voltaire felt the need of reworking his basic outlook on metaphysics so as to link it meaningfully with the polemical battles of an old man still hoping to 'écraser l'infâme'. Before going on to see Voltaire engaged in his assault on the bastions of Christianity, it is necessary to try to identify and evaluate the universal outlook that motivated this warrior.

Traité de métaphysique (*c.* 1734–7)

One difficulty confronts us immediately: unlike every other major work Voltaire wrote, the *Traité de métaphysique* was never published during his lifetime. The composition may well have been begun as early as 1733.[3] But the essay, though completed by early 1736 when the author offered a presentation copy to his mistress and fellow-philosopher Mme Du Châtelet, was revised again during that and the following year, and it is likely that the manuscript extract which Voltaire sent to Frederick of Prussia in 1737 represented a more advanced stage than the posthumous Kehl edition, which is the only one we possess. But it looks as if the treatise, although evolving a great deal during the 1730s under the influence of Voltaire's new readings and discussions, never reached a final form. This would account for the lack of clear direction in the work as we have it. Its highly abstract quality, so uncharacteristic of Voltaire, gives the impression that he had made a serious effort to elucidate his fundamental premises in general isolation from the amenities of witty example and analogy. It is as if Voltaire needs to be sure for himself of his own ground; in Wade's phrase, 'it is an inventory which he was taking of his basic ideas'.[4] The scaffolding could later be discarded; it remains nonetheless as truly Voltairean as the public edifices he built with its aid.

The *Traité* in its extant form contains an introduction and nine chapters. In the manner made fashionable by Descartes, the author begins with doubt—but about man, not, as Descartes, about his subjective knowledge. Voltaire promises to imagine that he is a visitor from Mars, noting with perfect objectivity the human condition. The immediate impression is twofold: man is only a superior animal; and there are many different species of men. Humankind is not wholly derived from Adam, nor is it uniquely favoured in God's sight. The Christian view of Creation, the Fall and original sin are all implicitly toppled. From man Voltaire moves to God—the order of priorities is as significant as Descartes's (whose solipsism proves his own existence before that of God); for Voltaire it is man who must come first in his considerations, and God is just as effectively relegated to a secondary position. He finds that a belief in the deity is neither universal nor necessary; whether deplorable or not, human beings can get along without knowledge of their Maker.[5] There then follows a lengthy rehearsal of arguments for and against the existence of God. It constitutes the longest chapter of the book, and nowhere in Voltaire's work does he ever again devote so much time and detailed effort to clarifying the subject.[6] The most remarkable side of this chapter is the desire to be fair to atheist opinions. Voltaire states the main reasons for believing in God, allows the opposite view to be put at equal length, then replies to these objections before concluding with the moderate position that the existence of God is not certain but 'la chose la plus vraisemblable que les hommes puissent penser' (the most likely probability that men can conceive).[7]

The arguments for God are two. The first, that from final causes (the order of the universe implies a creator), will be tirelessly repeated throughout Voltaire's life. Here, exceptionally, Voltaire sees a limitation to this reasoning: it proves a superior being, but not necessarily an infinite or omnipotent one. One must however assume that the objections are being scrupulously stated rather than deeply felt, since the philosopher will not use them again in his writings. More space is given to an argument, derived from John Locke and Samuel Clarke (which he will later discount when he comes to see it as aprioristic): 'J'existe, donc quelque chose existe.' (I exist, therefore something exists.)[8] The presence of contingent beings like oneself must be accounted for ultimately by a necessary existence. Voltaire dwells longer on this proof as being the really conclusive one; but already the argument from final causes, which will soon become his favourite because it seems so obviously derived from common sense experience, is, significantly enough, given pride of place.

The difficulties Voltaire raises with regard to a belief in God are equally interesting. God may exist, but the nature of Creation is incomprehensible; final causes work through eternal and immutable laws, not as direct interventions to help out individuals; and the internecine strife among men and animals is a great obstacle to belief in a good God. Already, then, the problem of evil is identified as a direct challenge to any religious faith; this identification will grow through the years, as the evidence of *Candide* alone is sufficient to make clear.[9] But, as in later years, Voltaire distinguishes between what is comprehensible and what is possible. The attributes and essence of divinity are beyond our grasp, as is the question of Creation; but God's existence is demonstrably clear.[10] As for eternal laws, they do not negate God. On the contrary, it was always His prerogative to choose what those laws should be, and even the immutable principles of mathematics were, at first, arbitrary. Lastly, certain criteria can be established for determining final causes: 'quand on voit une chose qui a toujours le même effet, qui n'a uniquement que cet effet' (when one sees a phenomenon which always has the same effect and none other than that effect),[11] then one may scarcely deny that these criteria are being satisfied; and the world is full of such examples. Hence Voltaire has already established the vital distinction between the foolish belief of Pangloss that noses are made to hang spectacles on and the correct view that a nose is the indispensable organ of one of our senses. Evil for its part however remains as great a mystery as Creation; but it is not for us to decide whether God is just, since He surpasses our comprehension.

So then it becomes apparent that while belief in God encounters difficulties, the opposite view leads only to absurdities.[12] The atheist 'attack' has never been in danger of defeating deism; the doubts were tactical, not real.[13] But the God whose existence has been invoked here is not in any way personal or anthropomorphic. In dismissing all human pretensions to decide whether God is just or unjust, Voltaire breaks all links of understanding between mankind and Him. God is a prime mover who has ensured general conditions for human survival; beyond that we cannot go. Lanson cogently defines His nature as an intellectual concept comparable to 'la notion de l'atome'.[14] This is not a deity who by any remote possibility would send His son down to earth to save mankind; still less should any rational human being wish to die for Him.

Once the place and function of Voltaire's God has been established, the philosopher can proceed with his definition of the human role. All men's ideas come through our senses, as Locke had demonstrated. Innate ideas are categorically rejected; the only true philosophy is that which depends on the use of the senses to analyse and verify experience and does not seek to go further. Voltaire thereafter dismisses the sceptical argument that the outer world is an illusion—hardly an attitude ever to appeal to his pragmatic outlook, and one that must be disposed of before man's social relations can be seriously considered. Following Locke once more, he defeats the doubters by invoking the sense of touch, which alone cannot be deceived about external objects.

Rather inconsistently, the *Traité* then goes on to consider whether man has a soul. Here again doubt may be allowed to reign. The existence of a soul is not one of those primary questions about which human beings have to be certain in order to live full lives. As in the thirteenth *Lettre philosophique*, Voltaire follows Locke's opinion that thought is not necessarily a spiritual attribute (as Descartes had maintained). Without being material in nature, thought may nevertheless have been attributed to matter by God. Does this mean that the soul is spiritual and immortal? While not denying the proposition, Voltaire allows his whole argument to be pervaded by hesitations, and he concludes that all the probabilities are against it.[15]

Man, then, moves in a world where comprehensive arrangements have been made for him by a remote but efficacious Providence. Beyond this minimal comfort he can look for few others. He is not a privileged being, only a well-organized animal who, although better equipped than other creatures for thought and self-expression, is subject to the same physical necessities as they. However, Voltaire draws one vital distinction: unlike the rest of creation man is free, that is, he has the power to act, and the proof of this is that he has a subjective intuition of his freedom. Whether the author is referring to physical or moral liberty is never wholly clear; this chapter, an amalgam of incompatible ideas drawn from Locke and Clarke,[16] is the most obscure in the whole essay. But the reader should not be deceived into thinking that Voltaire sees man as unequivocally endowed with freewill. Human liberty is feeble and circumscribed, man can use his rational faculties to improve it but can never hope to make his reason sovereign over all his desires.[17] The debate is so confused that it is hard to see exactly what powers human beings possess, and Lanson plausibly argues that Voltaire has scarcely retained anything of liberty except its name and is already close to denying the whole concept.[18] The argument of the *Traité* here is more affective than rational. Voltaire feels that he is free, and he still deems it essential to retain what he significantly calls 'la santé de l'âme'[19] if his moral code is to have any chance of success.

For it is morality to which the author is tending. He says as much when he sends a summary of the *Traité* to Frederick: 'Je ramène toujours, autant que je peux, ma métaphysique à la morale.' (As far as I can, I always bring back my metaphysics to morality.)[20] The last two chapters are addressed to this essential aspect. Is man a social animal? Voltaire's answer is unhesitatingly affirmative. Here again man is different from other creatures, who possess only the instincts of sexuality and self-preservation; in addition to those faculties, man has a natural benevolence towards his fellows. This predisposes men to form social groups, and the predisposition is reinforced by the human passions of pride, avarice and envy, which though unattractive in themselves play an important social role, since they motivate men into actions where by helping themselves they promote the good of all. The passions, then, also have a teleological purpose, fitting into the divine framework of general Providence. This much established, Voltaire moves to the last chapter, on virtue and vice. They are defined in terms relative to their particular social context, according to the criterion of public utility; hence an act such as murder or incest, reprehensible in itself, may be a good deed if it proves the saving of the nation.[21] At the same time, the author avoids the trap of falling into a total relativism by his insistence on a universal natural law. God has revealed no specific instructions to men, nor told them what is good or evil in an absolute sense; but He has given men presents— reason, self-esteem, benevolence, needs and passions—which are enough if rightly used for them to construct a just society. The *Traité* concludes on a note of optimism which can properly be called activist.

Not the least of Voltaire's problems in this concluding section is the necessity to reconcile the universal with the relative. If, as he has argued, there are in man no innate ideas of moral right, what is to prevent 'situation ethics' related only to local place and time? Voltaire replies that man has the latent possibility within him of understanding that one must be just, and that this possibility becomes more effective as the rational faculty matures. The distinction between this view and the theory of innate ideas is not clear, the more so as Descartes, strongly attacked by Voltaire on this very point, had intended much the same thing by his own concept of innate ideas. But logic enters little into the matter; on this question Voltaire's passions run deep. He apparently wants to keep human beings free of direct divine intervention. God, having laid down the basic rules in both the physical and the moral domain, retires to outer space and leaves man the entire job of interpreting them. The consequence is that, as Pomeau puts it, human beings are able to do good just as they can breathe and digest, without reference to God.[22] It is a naturalist moral code, separate from theology and faith (except for the simple need to adore God). It is positive, related only to the sublunar world and based on the belief that man is made for action. It will clear the decks for empirical inquiry and social reform. Metaphysics consists of a great many subjects about which one must remain for ever ignorant and of a few where one has a moral certainty; only the latter, providentially, are necessary for man's welfare.

The problem of freewill is already causing Voltaire great difficulties, even though he still resolves it optimistically. For the moment equanimity also prevails over the existence of atheists. They may be misguided but they present no dangers. As yet Voltaire, separating faith from morality, does not worry about the social consequences of unbelief. The ordinary man has no need to be threatened by eternal sanctions, since he will be sufficiently restrained by the fear of society's punishment and by the desire to win the esteem of his fellow-men.[23] This attitude will change. So too will Voltaire's views on evil grow more sombre. But all these issues have already occurred to him as obstacles, and his later pessimism represents not so much a volte-face as a gradual recognition that his earlier complacency had underestimated the implications.

But Voltaire will never again undertake a discussion of such abstract rigour. He is a *philosophe* rather than a philosopher, for whom ideas have import only if they open out on to committed action. The *Traité* assimilates French and English influences, the one through Montaigne, the seventeenth-century *libertins* and Bayle, the other through the rationalism of Locke, Clarke, Shaftesbury, Mandeville; it also draws on the sceptical and Epicurean strains of antiquity.[24] What emerges is a kind of constructive deism not unlike Matthew Tindal's *Christianity as Old as the Creation* (1730) in outlook. For all its weaknesses, the treatise reveals the hand of the master who embraces so much in so little space; and in doing so Voltaire delineates for himself the basic orientation of thought upon which his life will, with few exceptions, be hereafter based.

Le Philosophe ignorant (1766)

Thirty years later, Voltaire will attempt another profession of faith. *Le Philosophe ignorant* is less dense in texture than the *Traité de métaphysique* and even more wayward in construction. Apart from brief flashes of pyrotechnics, it lays little claim to literary distinction;

but as with the earlier essay it is a wide-ranging philosophical survey and serves to illuminate Voltaire's views on metaphysics and morality at the time. The structure of *Le Philosophe ignorant* is casual; fifty-six sections of varying length (most of them containing no more than a few paragraphs) weave a loosely embroidered theme with many recapitulations, almost as if, once completed, the author had never given it a second glance. One may discern, however, four segments into which the whole work broadly divides. The essay begins with an extended development (i–xii) of the idea that man is ignorant on almost all metaphysical questions: the nature of thought, its relationship to the body, the nature of substance, our own psychological make-up, souls human and animal, and so forth. In all this, however, one doubt seems to be missing: Voltaire's scepticism never extends so far as to query his own existence.[25] But the element of doubt has acquired a new flavour since the *Traité*. Voltaire still maintains that it is not essential for human beings to know the answers to such problems, but now he is not quite so happily resigned to the situation. For he himself is insatiably curious, these problems cause him anxiety and despair at his ignorance: 'nous sommes effrayes de nous chercher toujours, et de ne nous trouver jamais.' (We are frightened at seeking ourselves always and finding ourselves never.)[26] Other works of the 1760s, like the *Histoire d'un bon Bramin* (1761) and *L'Homme aux quarante écus* (1768), reveal the same attitude, while in 1770 Voltaire will write to Frederick that 'le doute est un état désagréable'.[27] Passionate inquiry has replaced the detachment of yore.

This broad range of doubts gives way to a more precise subject. Voltaire starts with the question of freewill and uses it as a preamble to the existence and nature of God (xiii–xx). His views on human liberty have now decisively changed, thanks to his reading of Anthony Collins' *Philosophical Inquiry concerning Human Liberty* (1717), as he readily admits. The change to determinism had begun as early as 1738, the morrow of the *Traité de métaphysique*, so by now it was merely the ratification of an old decision. Collins' argument seems irrefutable: every effect has a cause; hence our will and therefore our actions are always determined by our judgement, which itself is subject to the sensory experience received from outside. Voltaire's concept of freedom is equated, as in the *Traité*, with the capacity to act: 'Quand je peux faire ce que je veux, voilà ma liberté.' (When I am able to do what I want, that is my freedom.)

But now he sees more clearly than before that 'je veux nécessaire-ment ce que je veux' (I want necessarily what I want). Liberty is a matter of walking when one wants to and is not prevented by the gout.[28] There is no room in the universe for gratuitous happenings —chance does not exist, and man must fit into the overall pattern. Nonetheless, we must be content with 'cette mesure de liberté', even though it is limited; such as it is, the stars do not possess it; Voltaire makes no greater claim than this very modest one, refusing to become involved in deciding whether animals have as much freewill as man.

Enslaved as man is to eternal laws, he should logically consider what those laws are and how they operate. More firmly than in the *Traité*, the author decides that since matter cannot be made out of nothing, it must be co-eternal with God, and furthermore must always have been organized. The Biblical notion that the earth was without form and there was void until the spirit of God moved upon the face of the waters is not consonant with human reasoning— though Voltaire makes a formal bow to Holy Scripture by acknow-ledging that we must believe what faith tells us. Here again man's intellect can go no further. More fruitfully, however, one can discern that the cosmic order irresistibly points to a God; and though His properties remain unknown to men, that ignorance does no harm to ethics but serves only to make men more subject to Him. Though Voltaire is somewhat less agnostic on the points he considers demonstrable, nothing here runs essentially counter to the *Traité*. One new analogy, however, is striking: the philosopher argues that the world has always emanated from the prime mover, 'comme la lumière émane du soleil'.[29] Once again it is the abstract, impersonal link between man and God which stands out; but the association of the deity with light is not accidental. There are few moments in Voltaire which approach the mystical, but most of those that do are associated with the experience of luminosity: a rising or a setting sun,[30] or the stars at night as in *Zadig*[31] (which are matched by a similar incident that, significantly, happened *later* in Voltaire's life).[32] It seems at times as if Voltaire is actually worship-ping the sun,[33] a detail which is all the more piquant when one recalls Zadig counselling Sétoc to avoid sun-worship as being idolatrous.[34] God, like light (or gravity, as Lanson puts it)[35] is every-where. Small wonder that in comparison with this flawless, ineffable vision the world is so often, as here[36] (or the *Traité de métaphysique*),[37] likened to a heap of mud; it is not, he will say a little later on, for earthworms to limit the power of the Supreme Being.[38] The Voltairean God is perfect because inhuman; He will not be tarnished with what Voltaire regards as the mediocrity, and absurdity, of the Christian Incarnation.

But Voltaire has not lost sight of the theme that God is also incomprehensible, and a smooth transition is made to the next set of preoccupations, where he returns to the subject of ignorance (xxi–xxx). Some enigmas, like man's capacity to think, have been heard before; but most are new. This time, too, the author is more polemical in approach, working through a list of fallacious philosophies (Manicheism, Spinoza, Christian doctrines of the Trinity and transubstantiation, Platonist and Leibnizian Optimism, Cudworth's theory of plastic forms) before arriving at the truth of Locke. Not all of these of course are handled in the same manner. Christianity, Optimism, Cudworth are targets for outright mockery, but the others receive better treatment. Manicheism had long been a source of fascination to Voltaire, since it seemed at first sight to represent a common sense solution to the problem of evil. Was not the easiest answer to postulate two divinities, one good, the other bad, and ceaselessly at war with each other? In that way alone, one might seem to find a rational way of eluding the dilemma; for otherwise it seemed hard to avoid making God the author of sin and pain and death, with the consequent risk of serious damage to His benevolence or His omnipotence or both. Influenced by Bayle's cogent arguments on behalf of Manicheism, Voltaire had long found himself attracted to the thesis and had made countless references to it, particularly after 1750 as his views on evil became more gloomy. Martin in *Candide* is a Manichean who is allowed many a strong argument against Optimism, and the hypothesis appears in other *contes* as well.[39] But Voltaire always stops well short of conversion to the doctrine, and the main argument is the one adduced here: the harmony of the universe is inconsistent with the notion of two warring gods.[40] As he says in the *Homélie sur l'athéisme* (1767), Manicheism can be applied only to this planet, for all the millions of worlds that move in ordered regularity through space are clearly not subject to the influence of any evil principle.[41] Harmony and good are thereby equated, and as ever the manifest design of the cosmos is Voltaire's bulwark against all doubts about God.

Spinoza's philosophy never elicited Voltaire's sympathy, but by the 1760s he has moved from a position of general indifference and is trying hard to come to terms with it, despite his fragmentary knowledge of Spinoza's metaphysics and the limitations imposed by undue respect for Bayle's cramping view of the Dutch philosopher.[42] But what concerns us here is less the technical dispute about modalities and parts[43] than Voltaire's essential reason for rejecting Spinozism: it is in his view an atheistic philosophy 'dans toute la force de ce terme',[44] because it recognizes no Providence, ignoring all the final causes around us, whereas Spinoza should have noticed the divine plan every time he breathed and felt his heart beat.[45] This tireless insistence upon cosmic order as the essential crux in metaphysics needs to be noted by those who would see a *conte* like *Candide* as absurdist philosophy in eighteenth-century clothing.[46]

It is, naturally, Locke who wins the most applause, and Voltaire admiringly sets forth his main propositions. Here again is the truly modest philosopher who does not try to affirm what he cannot know. Locke's help, added to Voltaire's own reasoning, has given the latter four or five truths, banished a hundred errors, and conferred a vast quantity of doubts.[47] What matters is to use this self-education in order to find a moral principle. Thus the author manages the transition to the final and all-important subject of his inquiry.

After all the dubious statements that have prevailed so far, the tone now becomes positive. Without question, all men share the same basic moral code, founded on 'une notion grossière du juste et de l'injuste' (a rough notion of what is just and unjust).[48] It seems therefore that this idea of justice was necessary for mankind and that the Creator took care to provide it in order that the human race might survive. Without justice society could not exist. All peoples show respect for parents and detest perjury, calumny and murder: such are the elements of this universal ethic, so much so that even malefactors pay homage to it by pretending that they are acting in accord with the principle of justice even as they kill and steal. Wickedness must arise from delusion, in Voltaire's opinion; his mind seems closed to the possibility which the marquis de Sade was shortly to explore, that men could and indeed should engage in systematic evil-doing. Even in *Candide*, as we have seen, the kindly Jacques refuses to accept that men are inherently vicious.[49] There is always a moral norm underlying human activities, no matter how many deviations may be found. But the problems of establishing that norm are great. Voltaire, pursuing his point that there is universal agreement on morality, asks himself why then belief in magic and the occult, which also has occurred among every nation, is not equally valid. The only answer he can offer is that such beliefs are not necessary to the human race. 'Necessity' is clearly defined according to a strictly rationalist criterion; it never occurs to him that these 'perversions of reason', as he calls them, could also play a vital part in the psychic and therefore the social well-being of a community.[50]

But now he has to oppose his admired Locke, who has taken rejection of innate ideas to the point of arguing that there can be societies without a sense of justice, for example those of cannibals. Voltaire makes a brave effort to rationalize cannibalism (lack of good food, belief that victors have right of life and death over vanquished); but essentially his defence of natural law is the same as in the *Traité de métaphysique*: reason develops with age, teaching men a belief in God and the necessity for justice.[51] Indeed, it turns out a little later that men have acquired their concept of justice not only through reason but through sentiment as well.[52] The difference from Rousseau's moral outlook, in purely theoretical terms, seems very small.[53] Building up towards his climax, Voltaire explicitly recognizes what is already evident, that his zeal for social justice is felt with deep passion. As Peter Gay points out, in rejecting Locke's arguments Voltaire rejects the very theory of knowledge that would make it possible to support natural law. Gay goes on to suggest, with some plausibility, that Voltaire did not fully examine the implications of natural law, being more concerned as a practical reformer with getting to work on social evils than with wasting much time on 'fine-spun theoretical arguments that divert men from action'.[54]

So to the coda. Zoroaster, the Brahmins, the ancient Greeks, all developed foolish metaphysical theories; their morality was no less pure for that. To them may be joined the more noble examples of such as Confucius, Epicurus, the Stoics.[55] No link at all binds dogma to virtue. The prescription then is obvious: with men's freedom of action, limited but real, let them get back to tolerating people for their opinions as in the days of ancient Rome. Let them not become embroiled in futile persecution of one another over matters beyond their knowledge like the ancient history of the French nation and the Catholic Church. The final paragraph is a stirring call to action. Reason is beginning to make genuine progress at last; let men help it on its way by affirming the truth.[56]

This is the philosophy underlying the attack on *l'infâme*. As the *Traité de métaphysique* was an inventory of the Cirey period, so does this represent the theoretical stocktaking at Ferney. The mood will still have time to change somewhat in the last decade of Voltaire's life. A few months after publishing *Le Philosophe ignorant*, the execution of the young chevalier de la Barre would remind him that the monsters of fanaticism were more virulent than he had thought. A new threat, too, is developing, particularly after the publication of d'Holbach's *Système de la nature* (1770) makes materialist atheism fashionable in intellectual circles. Voltaire's final years witness a battle on two fronts, against the dogmatic and socially subversive atheists as much as against the abominations of Christian intolerance. *Le Philosophe ignorant* does not echo every one of Voltaire's philosophical concerns. What is mainly absent is any concentration on the 'Dieu rémunérateur et vengeur', who plays such a large part in Voltaire's thinking from the 1750s. Without a God to threaten eternal punishments, it seemed to the *philosophe* and Ferney landowner that one could not keep the anarchic mob or unbridled prince under control. He himself did not of course believe in such a God, taking the pragmatic, even cynical, view that such a belief was necessary for the majority in order to hold civilized society together. On this particular issue, however, Voltaire is linking faith and morality, contrary to the professions of *Le Philosophe ignorant*. But then, as its title indicates, this work is not written for the people at large but for the *philosophes*, who will not require the threat of divine sanctions to make them accept the laws in force while they are also working to amend those laws in the direction of the greater good. It is this outlook, modified and in some respects clarified since the *Traité de métaphysique* but essentially little changed, that will support the *philosophe* in the role where he is more at home, actively combating *l'infâme*. The originality of Voltaire's philosophical ideas is not great; what is original, as Pomeau makes clear,[57] is the passion of his faith and the fervour with which he proselytizes. No one ever attacked the whole of revealed religion with more religious passion than Voltaire.

THE *philosophe*

The article 'Philosophe', published in 1765 in Voltaire's *Dictionnaire philosophique*, begins thus: 'Philosophe, *amateur de la sagesse*, c'est-à-dire *de la vérité*' (Philosopher, *lover of wisdom*, that is to say *of truth*).[58] Hardly anything here to affright the most traditionalist of philosophers; it is the way in which Voltaire interprets this dictum that matters. In the article itself Voltaire is at his most tolerant. Even so, certain unconventional criteria emerge: Confucius outranks all ancient philosophers in the importance he is accorded and Bayle all modern ones, while Catholic apologists like Aquinas of course figure nowhere. Why this order of priorities? Above all because of the moral teachings of these thinkers, the criterion one might expect from the future author of *Le Philosophe ignorant*. But Voltaire develops another theme as well: all modern French philosophers except Montaigne have been persecuted, Bayle notably so. Philosophy, in brief, has become a dangerous occupation, because the pursuit of truth commits one to a critical outlook. In Gusdorf's elegant phrase, 'Penser librement, c'est penser *contre*.' (Free-thinking is thinking *against* something.)[59] Voltaire the *philosophe* will follow no other course.

Examen important de milord Bolingbroke (1767)

It is possible that a draft of the *Examen important* dates from Voltaire's stay at Cirey, though there is no proof of its existence. What is certain is that Voltaire, while using materials from his studies of Biblical criticism at Cirey, did not publish the work till 1767, and it is one of the most extended documents in Voltaire's battle against *l'infâme* during the Ferney period.[60] The false attribution by Voltaire of his study to the English thinker and political figure was a typical subterfuge used by him in bringing his militant works before the public eye. Few people were deceived for very long, but the pseudonymous device, usually followed by loud protests from Voltaire that he had had nothing to do with it,[61] spared him embarrassing attention from the authorities. He had learned once and for all with the treatment his *Lettres philosophiques* had received after publication[62] never openly to sign his name to a work of social criticism again. Rousseau had made the same painful discovery as recently as 1762 when by openly publishing *Emile* he had exposed himself to

the threat of imprisonment and the reality of exile. The precise
attribution of this self-styled 'important examination' by Voltaire
to Bolingbroke may however be seen also as an act of homage to
the man who in the 1720s 'was the first of Voltaire's friends to
exhort him to take a more serious approach to philosophy'.[63]

There is little doubt that Voltaire regarded the *Examen important*
as a key work in the philosophic struggle. The *Avis* indicates this
clearly, in stating that it is the 'livre le plus éloquent, le plus profond,
et le plus fort qu'on ait encore écrit contre le fanatisme' (the most
eloquent, most profound and most powerful book that has yet been
written against fanaticism).[64] The *Avant-propos* which follows is a
justification of the enterprise: the choice of a religion is the most
important decision, yet it is irrationally made; the author will
therefore examine the religion nearest home, the Christian faith.
The work itself, made up of thirty-eight chapters,[65] divides into
two roughly equal sections, the first dealing with the Old and
New Testaments, the second with the history of the Catholic
Church.

It would be tedious to relate at length the criticisms Voltaire
levels at the Bible; let us look simply at the leading strands of the
argument. The early chapters (i–ix) deal with the Old Testament in
Voltaire's most denunciatory manner. Jewish history, far from
being the sacred word of a sacred people, is filled with the petty
doings of a rascally, absurd nation who moreover borrowed most
of their essential lore and custom from other races like the Egyptians
and Phoenicians. Once again, this is not the Voltaire of shrewd
irony whom the readers of *Candide* know; he is more like the Old
Testament God whom he so detests, breathing fire and brimstone.
Every trait of Jewish history is 'une hyperbole ridicule, un mensonge
grossier, une fable absurde'.[66] The *philosophe* is appalled that the
ridiculous barbarities of Moses and his people, written by madmen,
commented upon by imbeciles and taught by rascals, should have
to be learned by heart by little children.[67] The Judaic doctrine,
supposedly communicated direct by God to His chosen people, did
not even contain belief in the immortality of the soul;[68] Voltaire
was to consider this the most powerful of all objections to giving
the Jewish law a special status.[69] The Jews, in short, were originally
no more than a band of wandering Arabs who set themselves up in
Palestine through brigandage.[70] Voltaire's indignation is particularly
reserved for the link which Christianity has made with this odious

race, and he vents his wrath upon the thesis that the Jews are the precursors of Jesus[71] (who was, be it noted in passing, descended from a Jewish prostitute!).[72]

The attack is blatant and overwhelming, intended to abolish any claims to a privileged position by the Old Testament and Judaism. Drawing upon Biblical scholarship (which really began in 1678 with the erudite Richard Simon's *Histoire critique du Vieux Testament*), he attempts to introduce scientific standards of exegesis into an area which had suffered from the vaguenesses of allegorical and mystical interpretation. In Voltaire's opinion it was positive fact that counted: what real evidence, for example, is there that Moses ever existed?[73] Or how in the desert could Saul have amassed an army of 300 000 men?[74] But inevitably, short of scholarship and driven by strong passions,[75] the author castigates the early Jews with an antagonism that does little justice to the specific qualities they possessed as a tribe rich in culture if also primitive in manners. Critics have never been wanting to point out these defects, and only in recent years has a scholar undertaken to investigate in detail the nature of Voltaire's attacks with respect to the apologetic traditions and to see precisely what his strategy is. The conclusion of Bertram Schwarzbach's useful study[76] is that the *philosophe* performed valuable services in this domain by clearing away 'the exegetical debris of centuries to expose the Bible in a relatively pristine form' and by bringing to bear perceptions that would later be incorporated into the higher criticism. Schwarzbach further claims that Voltaire did all this with intellectual honesty and that he needs to be absolved of the unfair reputation he has acquired in this respect.

The onslaught is transferred to the New Testament and the founding of the Christian Church (x–xx). First of all, Christ is subjected to a bitter attack as Voltaire tries to construct an entirely secular explanation for the extraordinary events surrounding his life and influence. No Jew was expecting or desiring a messiah. The new sect established itself by fanatical preaching to the lowest classes, ever full of malcontents and eager to accept some miraculous new thing. One of the most constant complaints made against Christianity by Voltaire throughout his works is that it was plebeian in origin and therefore based on superstitious quackery suited to the illiterate. With Christ's death the cause gained a martyr as well. Yet according to the *Toldos Jeschut*, an early biography, Jesus had been a bastard who became embittered against the priests because of his illegitimacy and eventually after a quarrel with Judas was arrested and executed (by hanging, not crucifixion). No glory attaches to his life or person. His quarrel was partly over a matter of self-interest and after his arrest he began weeping and attempted in vain to obtain a pardon.[77] To this unremarkable rebel was post-humously added a new reputation by various gospels which appeared; they introduced the extravagant idea of the Holy Ghost, of Christ the Son of God, worker of miracles (many of them patently foolish or absurd) and author of ridiculous parables, the man who was executed publicly but rose from the dead in secret and ascended to Heaven in the presence only of his disciples and no one else. But the real Christ, though obviously more intelligent than most of his peers, was clearly an ignorant man from 'la lie du peuple' (the dregs of the populace) and probably illiterate as well.[78] It was his preaching of equality that flattered the riff-raff who listened to him. The same unenlightened segment of society spread the word after his death; and for the first century Christianity was a low-class phenomenon, a marginal Jewish sect on uneasy terms with other Jews. The Christians' gospels were full of contradictions, their ceremonies indecent, while Saint Paul was a power-crazy fanatic. The Second Coming was at first expected imminently and only after many centuries did it become the mystic vision of the New Jerusalem which would descend from on high.

Voltaire's indignation, scarcely concealed at any time, breaks out here again at the thought of how many have suffered for this and similar opinions, how half the world has been ravaged, principalities delivered into the hands of fraudulent priests, Europe bathed in blood and Charles I executed on the scaffold.[79] The rhetoric mounts finally to a paroxysm, the cry of a man who is acutely sensitive to what Camus would in our century call legitimized murder.[80] It contrasts with the foregoing tone of sober examination which at least appears to invite the reader to use his intellect, even though the cards are stacked; at the end the author indulges in unashamed emotion to remind the reader, as he notes these petty details of far-off stupidities, how tragically they have affected the world ever since.

One of the difficulties of Christianity arises from the fact that its founder never wrote a single line. Hence occurred a void that the early Church filled with such nonsense as allegorical interpretations of the Old Testament, which then became directly linked to the

New as a prophetic and figurative precursor. With the proliferation of fraudulent documents establishing Christian authority this sorry tale of the primitive Church is complete. It all comes down to ignorance generating superstition, the gullibility of the uneducated calling forth a spate of impostures from the clergy who are only too ready to gratify such a foolish hunger.

But fraud of itself will not entirely explain why Christianity eventually became a social and political force amongst the upper classes, and Voltaire will devote the latter half (xxi–xxxviii) to elucidating this problem. The change begins in the second century A.D. with Saint Justin, who gives the unsophisticated absurdities a philosophical cast based on Platonism. This is where the doctrine of the Trinity is first heard, for Christ himself had never preached any such message.[81] Gradually the concept, though valueless for morality, will gain currency with Clement and become fully elaborated by Origen.[82] Concomitantly, Voltaire notes the sociological evolution of the new sect. Like other nonconformists excluded from public office for their beliefs, the Christians resorted to trade and grew rich on the proceeds.[83] Their religion was broadening its base. Already it was troubling authority by its zealous intolerance of other sects; but so far the Roman Empire was indulgent and few Christians had been executed. Meantime the Fathers of the Church multiplied their extravagances: Tertullian, Clement, Irenaeus, Origen—at the end of which Voltaire perfunctorily adds: 'En voilà, je pense, assez pour faire connaître les Pères. . . .' (That is enough, I think, to make the Fathers known. . . .),[84] as though an odious duty had been accomplished. The very telling of this tale seems painful. Occasionally the author savours a particularly absurd miracle such as the lubricious account of Bacchus in Hell,[85] where the ironist's detachment is given play. But such amusement is rare, and significantly this particular miracle is a pagan one. The nonsense of the Christian tradition has caused too much trouble for frivolity to be permitted in discussing it.

The pattern is now sufficiently clear and will merely be confirmed in the remaining chapters. Christians, though themselves insatiable troublemakers, are surprisingly little harassed by the Roman emperors. Eventually under Constantine, that notorious tyrant and murderer, they achieve status as the official religion of the Empire, and once in a position of power begin pursuing and massacring their enemies. Much of the time they are killing one another, since the Church is quickly rent by heresies and schisms. For a brief moment Julian the Apostate, a philosopher-king who renounces his Christian baptism and whom Voltaire describes as perhaps the greatest man who has ever lived,[86] seems likely to establish a cult of pure deism, but his premature death renders this impossible. Meanwhile Mohammedanism is born, a more sensible religion which does not worship a Jew while holding all Jews in abhorrence, does not call a Jewess mother of God or say that three gods are one god or devour God.[87] Voltaire is particularly appalled by the notion of a god become man who dies and is resurrected, and by the subsequent dogmas of the Trinity and transubstantiation.[88] The last two are merely absurd metaphysics, while the first involves the supreme majesty of God in the most humiliating physiological functions such as all human beings must perform on our 'tas de boue'.[89] The personal warmth and immediacy of the Incarnation are lost on a thinker who needs to see his God as a remote being in order to adore Him.

The Christian faith, corrupt from the start, has been constantly accompanied by war and intolerance. To say that it is a good tree which has sometimes borne bad fruit is to underestimate the issue; no tree which has carried such terrible poison could possibly have been planted by God.[90] Nor has any other religion ever demonstrated such a continuous series of barbarities. The Catholic Church is pre-eminent in crime because of its wealth and power and pre-eminent in debauchery because of priestly celibacy which, by preventing marriage, goes against nature and encourages obscenity.[91]

The indictment is complete. Voltaire has cried scandal on every aspect of the Christian religion—its forbears, its founder, its scriptures, its doctrines, its morality. The conclusion is straightforward: 'tout homme sensé, tout homme de bien, doit avoir la secte chrétienne en horreur' (every sensible man, every good man, must abhor the Christian sect).[92] Instead men should become theists. But the message is not subversive. The hold of Christianity is now so great that it would be politically dangerous to overthrow it; the people are not yet ready. For the present, the Church should be kept within limits by being made subject to civil legislation and its independent position within the State removed. Gradually men may then move towards a better religion and society.[93]

The *Examen important* is a direct assault on Christianity and also upon the reader's sensibilities. Voltaire's voice thunders forth, brooking no interference, unambiguously urging his audience to see things in the only true way. Every detail is planned to help demolish any sympathetic link one may feel with the practices of one's own religion. It is probably, as Schwarzbach says, Voltaire's most virulent attack on Christianity.[94] After a while such unmitigated vehemence wearies, and it must be said that the *Examen important* holds the reader's attention with difficulty today. But the work represents an essential side of Voltaire, the side which tends to be known only at second-hand. It is easy to forget that the last twenty years of his life were in no small measure devoted to this sort of propaganda, totally committed and often ferocious.

Le Dîner du comte de Boulainvilliers (1767)

The polemic against Christian corruption was not however always conducted in tones of such straightforward denunciation. Another common strategy was the philosophical dialogue, of which over thirty were published in the years after 1750.[95] Unlike in Diderot's more open-ended use of the same form, there is scarcely ever any doubt as to who is speaking for Voltaire; but the need for some dramatic presentation, however limited, involves the author in a certain amount of stylization with pleasing results, as in *Le Dîner du comte de Boulainvilliers*.

Le Dîner appeared in December 1767, some months after the *Examen important*, but these were by no means Voltaire's only productions during that prolific year. Appalled by the La Barre affair and momentarily silenced by this and other troubles,[96] he returns in 1767 to a spate of composition that will go on unabated until 1772. The wonder is not that there is so much mechanical writing in works tossed off with scarcely a second glance, but that their author continues to turn out propaganda at such a high level of synthesis and clarity. *Le Dîner* is a philosophical play in three acts, the dinner sequence in the middle being flanked by a brief *apéritif* and *digestif*. Boulainvilliers and Fréret, the main protagonists, were long since dead, the former in 1722, the latter in 1749; they were both remembered as freethinkers who had been active during the Regency period in a coterie that was probably run by the Count himself.[97] Against them is ranged, as defender of the faith, the obscure figure of the abbé Couet, who had been *grand vicaire* to the cardinal de Noailles and had been assassinated in 1736. No very good reason can now be seen for this choice, though he may have been, as Grimm claims in the *Correspondance litrétaire*, a Jansenist[98] and as such particularly antipathetic to Voltaire; but as we shall see he is not portrayed in a totally unattractive light. The only other character is the Countess,[99] who serves mainly to keep the *mise en scène* alive. But she does make some pertinent observations, and to that extent gives extra variety to the propaganda because she expresses these ideas not as a *philosophe* but as an ordinary intelligent woman. She may well have been included to impress the feminine audience in the *salons* whom Voltaire probably also had in mind.

The first dialogue, before the dinner,[100] sees the abbé take up the attack on very broad lines: can philosophy be as useful as the Catholic religion? To which the Count replies that it is much older, being more eclectic in its code, which consists only in loving wisdom and a God who rewards virtue and punishes crime. When the abbé readily agrees to this, the Count willingly accepts him into the ranks of the *philosophes*. Why then are there expressions of intolerance in the gospels? Why so many other foolish and contradictory statements in these books? When the Count quotes a submissive-sounding prayer such as a Christian might have uttered, the abbé falls for the trap, only to learn that it comes from the Stoic Epictetus. The abbé, drawn into discussing virtuous pagans, admits that they were often fine people but were unfortunately ignorant of theology; they did not know, for instance, how to discriminate between efficacious grace and sufficient grace. What a pity the Ciceros and Catos never learned of the Trinity and such fine truths! But when the Count presses the abbé to say whether these pagans are in Hell, the latter is torn between his dogma, which tells him they are, and his personal desires, which are to wish they are not. It is time to go to table. In direct exchange with the abbé, the Count has forced him on to the defensive and revealed him as a better man than his theology.

During the dinner Fréret and to some extent the Countess join in the attack. After some preliminary skirmishing on dietary and marital restrictions established by Catholicism, the Countess invites Fréret's opinion. His opening remark is portentous: 'Je me tais, madame, parce que j'aurais trop à dire.' (I am silent, Madame, because I would have too much to say.)[101] But when the abbé incautiously challenges him to attack the glory and truth of the Church, Fréret is drawn into the argument. The Christians, he asserts, are essentially Jews and idolaters in their ritual: baptism, Easter, the psalms demonstrate the first, the cult of saints and relics and the Mass the second. The Mass is a particularly odious farce, celebrated by debauched monks dressed up like actors, muttering a foreign language, making farcical gestures, and eating and drinking God, whom they will evacuate later. The abbé of course has no useful reply to make. As the dinner continues, the familiar attack develops upon the usual orthodox positions: prophecies, miracles, martyrs, comparison with Islam, the suspect origins of Christianity and its subsequent history of bloodshed. Fréret, the more radical opponent, claims, as Voltaire had done in the *Examen important*, that the tree has always borne poisonous fruit and must be cut out root and branch.[102] The Count's view is more moderate: to do this would inaugurate a new era of massacre. There is only one remedy in his view, to make religion totally dependent upon the sovereign and the magistrates; and Fréret agrees, while adding that the magistrates themselves must be enlightened. The latter is all for sending in the army to break up religious disturbances if they occur, but the Count would prefer to try educating the zealots before punishing them.[103] On the other hand the Count, hearing the tale of the Moslem ruler who rewarded his slave when the latter had accidentally scalded him because the prince wished to win glory in Paradise, complacently accepts it as an edifying tale about the good Moslems of early times; but Fréret reminds him that the prince's motives were unworthy, since he should have been disinterested when he was doing good.[104]

So to the coffee. The onslaught on Christianity has spent itself. A wider issue emerges. The abbé asserts that one must have a religion and this wins general assent. The problem is *which* religion, and their viewpoints are not yet reconciled, for the abbé remains sceptical of man's capacity to live with a pure doctrine. You would be stoned in Paris, he says, if in rainy periods you refused to carry Saint Geneviève's bones through the streets as a supplication for better weather. 'Une religion de philosophes n'est pas faite pour les hommes.' (A religion for *philosophes* is not made for men.)[105] The others however argue that progress has already been made in uprooting superstition and that while retaining the name of Christianity one can move towards purifying its form. As for the dangers of crime emanating from unbelief, an effective curb already exists in the cult of God who will punish and reward in the afterlife. The Count sounds the final note: 'prêchez Dieu et la morale, et je vous réponds qu'il y aura plus de vertu et plus de félicité sur la terre' (preach God and morality, and I assure you that there will be more virtue and happiness on earth).[106] And all agree.

Le Dîner, being more subtle than the *Examen important*, is also more persuasive. If the Voltairean version of the truth emerges just as clearly by the end, it does so in a way calculated to seduce the reader rather than bludgeon him into submission. Somewhat differing emphases within the deist creed by Fréret and Boulainvilliers make it seem more flexible, more human and therefore more appealing. The abbé is mocked throughout, as one might expect in a propaganda piece by Voltaire. Foolish enough to initiate the argument, he is never a match for his opponents, sometimes does not even recognize when he has been trounced, and spends much of the crucial argument in the middle section making himself ridiculous by calling for more to drink. When the Countess tells him that he is like a certain duchess who was called a prostitute, he accepts the rather crude insult with complacency.[107] As the representative portrait of a Christian, it is of course wildly unfair. But the characterization is a little less crude than these instances would make it appear. The abbé is no villain, his heart is in the right place; he is in short a deist under the skin and is suitably converted at the end. More significantly, he raises one of the main obstacles to a belief in deism: can human nature be trusted to follow the good? Voltaire was far less confident in his answer to this question than are Fréret and Boulainvilliers. Indeed, when the latter rebukes the abbé for wishing to deceive men[108] and then later supports the idea that religion can be a salutary curb on immorality through the threat of divine sanctions[109] (which Voltaire himself is known to have thought a necessary deception to practise on the masses), it is clear that an inconsistency is being perpetrated. Not that the abbé can ever hope to realize how fragile are the defences in this area; but the fact of such critical questioning points to a debate rather than a pure exposition. When one adds that this debate is carried on in lively language, especially during the sections where there are quick exchanges of speech, it becomes clear that the *Dîner* is more carefully crafted than the *Examen important*.

But the work still remains above all a polemical vehicle, and the more positive side supporting deism which develops apace as it progresses is less effective than the ironic deflation of Christian ways in the earlier parts. In particular, the long sermons which Fréret and then Boulainvilliers are allowed at the end represent a descent to the mechanical again; one is perversely tempted in the face of such pomposity to feel much more sympathy for the abbé and his insouciance! The author's seriousness of purpose is conveyed all too unsubtly. By its tripartite structure, *Le Dîner* is reminiscent of a more famous philosophical dialogue, Diderot's *Le Rêve de d'Alembert*. The latter, composed two years later, may even owe something to *Le Dîner* in general inspiration, the use of real figures in an imaginary philosophical discussion and a sketchy interior setting; the very titles are similar. But the comparison can only do Voltaire's work an injustice. Diderot's *Rêve* is one of his outstanding productions, Voltaire's *Dîner* no more than a run of the mill composition. Even so, it is one of the shrewdest of the *philosophe*'s many direct attacks during the Ferney period upon *l'infâme*.[110]

7 | Correspondent

The eighteenth century was the golden age of letter-writing. Some intimate correspondence from classical times remains, for instance the letters of Cicero to his daughter, and the Middle Ages have yielded us a few outstanding examples such as the love letters of Abelard and Héloïse. But the form begins to attain importance only at the Renaissance, and in France the epochal name is that of Mme de Sévigné (1626–96). By the eighteenth century, the private letter has become the form in which above all men and women in society can communicate freely and informally with one other.[1] In England Horace Walpole, Chesterfield, Boswell all adorned the genre, as did Diderot and Rousseau in France; but among all the letter-writers in this glorious period Voltaire can fairly lay claim to be pre-eminent.

As is so often true of Voltaire, the statistics are themselves impressive, and Theodore Besterman has gathered them with loving care.[2] The correspondence stretches from 1711 to Voltaire's death in 1778. He had 1200 correspondents, of whom thirty-five maintained an uninterrupted link for twenty years and a score (all outside his family) for more than thirty. There are letters in French, English, Italian, Latin, German and Spanish, and in all about 17 000 are extant,[3] yet Dr Besterman estimates that probably as many again have been irremediably lost. But these are merely the bare bones. What astonishes the modern reader is the vast range of these letters and the abundant vitality which almost everywhere suffuses them. For his correspondence alone Voltaire would remain a major figure of his times. Lanson admirably sums up this side of Voltaire's output: 'tout est vif, rapide, léger, mesuré' (it is all lively, swift, light, measured), going on to call them, with perhaps a slight though pardonable exaggeration, Voltaire's least contested masterpiece.[4]

One of the most impressive features of this correspondence is that from first to last it sparkles. There are no juvenilia and there is no falling off at the end; Voltaire the letter-writer seems to have entered fully-grown upon the scene at sixteen and remained so till a few days before his death. In August 1711 he wrote to his school companion Fyot de La Marche (who was to remain a friend till his death in 1768) with news of the ceremonies to celebrate the ending of the school year, and incidentally Voltaire's own schooldays, at the Jesuit Collège Louis-le-Grand in Paris. It seems to have been a curious mixture, as speech days continue still to be, and the weather did not help. Voltaire captures the atmosphere with mature skill:

Une grosse pluie a fait partager le spectacle [the performance of a tragedy by one of the Jesuit teachers, Père Lejay, which was the high-point of the day] en deux après-dîners, ce qui a fait autant de plaisir aux écoliers que de chagrin au père Lejay; deux moines se sont cassé le cou l'un après l'autre si adroitement qu'ils n'ont semblé tomber que pour servir à notre divertissement; le nonce de sa sainteté nous a donné huit jours de congé; M. Thevenard a chanté; le père Lejay s'est enroué; le père Porée a prié Dieu pour obtenir un bon temps; le ciel n'a pas été d'airain pour lui, au plus fort de sa prière, le ciel a donné une pluie abondante; voilà à peu près ce qui s'est passé ici.

(A downpour divided the entertainment into two afternoon sessions, which gave as much pleasure to the pupils as vexation to Father Lejay; two monks fell flat on their faces with such dexterity that they appeared to tumble only for our entertainment; the nuncio of His Holiness granted a week's holiday; M. Thevenard sang; Father Lejay got hoarse; Father Porée prayed to God for fine weather; the heavens were not brazen for him, at the height of his prayer they granted him a good soaking; that is more or less what took place here.)[5]

He ends with one of those graceful flourishes of compliments at which he will continue for nearly seventy years to be so adept. Here already is the concision, the care not to write a single dull word; here too the balance and antithesis that are inseparable from his style. The wit and irony are recognizably Voltairean, the future crusader against Christian superstition already noting with glee the way Heaven rewards Père Porée's request for fine weather with an immediate deluge of rain. More striking perhaps is the clever word-play that follows: 'le ciel n'a pas été d'airain pour lui'. 'D'airain', literally 'of bronze', usually has the metaphorical sense of 'implacable', but here Voltaire has turned the image upside down.

The sky, far from being brazen, was full of clouds and moisture, and gives forth generously despite the good Father's prayer. The vignette ends with perhaps a clue that the scene has to some extent been improved for Fyot's benefit: 'voilà *à peu près* ce qui s'est passé ici'. Long before he has assumed the pseudonym Voltaire,[6] the artist has already taken his own licence with events. The joke itself betrays no more than a clever sixth-former enjoying the pompous absurdities of the grown-ups' world; but the style of the joke reveals the master in embryo.

Take, by contrast, two of Voltaire's very last letters, mere snippets from a dying man and yet imbued with elegance, both in word and manner. To Mme de Saint-Julien he is gallant even in the knowledge that his end is near:

Je sais bien ce que je désire mais je ne sais pas ce que je ferai. Je suis malade, je souffre de la tête aux pieds, il n'y a que mon cœur de sain, et cela n'est bon à rien.

(I know clearly what I desire but I don't know what I shall accomplish. I am sick, in pain from head to foot, only my heart is sound, and that is useless.)[7]

That very eighteenth-century combination of friendship with overtones of sexual desire, which the sophisticated man of society in France regarded as a civilized ideal in his relations with women, comes out clearly here.[8] But the gracefulness gains poignancy from the simple realities which underlie the courtliness: his whole body is racked, and worse yet, his heart which alone remains sound 'n'est bon à rien'. Even the most banal statement of human mortality by one who knows his time has run out is turned into a crafted object.

Similar cadences are achieved in the much better-known letter to the chevalier de Lally-Tollendal, more famous because it is probably Voltaire's very last, coming only four days before he died, and because it records a final victory for the *philosophe* during his lifetime in securing a posthumous repeal for Lally's father:

Le mourant ressuscite en apprenant cette grande nouvelle; il embrasse bien tendrement M. de Lally; il voit que le roi est le défenseur de la justice; il mourra content.

(The dying man recovers life in learning this great news; he embraces M. de Lally most tenderly; he sees that the king is the defender of justice; he will die content.)[9]

The 'calm of mind, all passion spent' is moving as it takes on the Voltaire rhythms for a final time with the same assured art and economy as ever. From paradox ('le mourant ressuscite') to describe his joy, he moves to simple statement, then on to the political perspective, and lastly to the philosophical leave-taking of his correspondent in particular and the world at large. When one reflects on the probable circumstances in which this letter was tossed off in a moment's thought by a debilitated figure, and sees how yet the result could serve as well for a stylistic analysis as a passage from *Candide*, then one grasps something of the extra-ordinary capacities in a mind that so spontaneously conceived its thoughts with ordered and limpid elegance.

How then to give any focus in brief space to such a huge collection of letters, when even two or three brief ones can take the reader so far? Auerbach and Spitzer both concentrated on just one a mere ten lines in length,[10] and the temptation is strong to do likewise. But Voltaire's letters are important for their themes as well as their form, and single examples cannot sufficiently convey the full flav-our for the purpose here. It seems wise to take a cross-section, such as the run of letters for a whole year, preferably one of the great years at Ferney when the author was at the height of his powers. Even so, at best only the quintessence of such wealth can be captured.

VOLTAIRE'S LETTERS: 1766

The year 1766 saw some of Voltaire's best-known works completed, notably the *Avis au public sur les Calas et les Sirven*, *Le Philosophe ignorant* and the *Commentaire sur le livre des délits et des peines*; in addition, much of the author's energy was invested in a play, *Les Scythes*, which the contemporary world and posterity have alike refused to value at his own high estimation of it. When not writing, Voltaire was intervening in the internal difficulties of Geneva, in attempts to rehabilitate Sirven and Lally-Tollendal, in denunciations of Rousseau; and above all 1766 was ever to be remembered by him as the year in which French authority had barbarously executed the nineteen-year-old chevalier de La Barre. All these activities are reflected in his letters, over five hundred in all, which have come down to us. These letters are distributed among well over a hundred people, with only eight of them receiving ten or more. So one further remarkable facet of this correspondence becomes clear; the large number is not based simply upon repeated letters to a limited circle. Voltaire's Parisian agent Damilaville, who received ninety-five letters, and his publisher Cramer, who got thirty-eight, owe their high figures to Voltaire's necessary business relationships with them. Of his friends, the only ones who stand out in this respect are the comte and comtesse d'Argental, his 'guardian angels' as he calls them, to whom he sends sixty-three in that year alone. It is this friendship which overshadows all others in Voltaire's life, lasting from schooldays until his death; and the letters here show that to them he could confide personal hopes and prides with a degree of intimacy rarely shown to others. But it would be wrong to deduce that all his other relationships were cool and casual. Though he might write a mere handful to most of his correspondents, over and over again they reveal his warm spontaneity and his ability to pick up a friendship where it had been left off some months before; and on occasion one finds him chiding some tardy correspondent from whom he has heard nothing in months.

Voltaire's efforts to make peace between the different factions in Geneva did not meet with conspicuous success. Not only was he unwelcome as an outsider; it seems that he underestimated the seriousness of the conflict. He is found writing to the Duchess of Saxe-Gotha on 4 March that

Ces troubles sont fort pacifiques, les Genevois sont malades d'une indigestion de bonheur. Leurs petites querelles n'aboutissent qu'à de mauvaises brochures qu'eux seuls peuvent lire.

(These disturbances are very peaceful, the Genevans suffer from a surfeit of happiness. Their petty squabbles lead only to bad pamphlets that they alone are capable of reading.)[11]

Clearly there is a measure of stylization here, and Voltaire is creating for his German correspondent an antithesis with the way they order things in Germany, for as he goes on to say, a dispute there is 'plus sérieuse' and generally costs the lives of two or three hundred thousand men. But an element of condescension still creeps in, here and elsewhere. The Genevans are seeking a French mediator to come and arbitrate, and Voltaire repeatedly implores d'Argental to accept. When the latter eventually declines, his friend at Ferney is deeply hurt, as a note to Hennin, the French Resident in Geneva, shows;[12] but he quickly recovers his spirits, briefly tells d'Argental how sorry he feels, and immediately moves on to other things.[13]

It is a good instance of Voltaire's talent at keeping friends. He had set his heart on attracting d'Argental and the disappointment went deep; but he does not wear his heart on his sleeve or utter vain reproaches. The tact which he shows in managing the incident helps to explain why this friendship lasted as long as his life.

But so far as the Genevans were concerned Voltaire, despite protestations to the contrary, could not keep from offering his good offices. Auzière, leader of the *natifs* rebelling against the patricians in the city, sought and obtained the *philosophe*'s advice, the latter giving useful suggestions about how to present a petition that was wholly candid while yet refraining from being offensive or, worse still, tedious.[14] But a few days later Auzière was in prison with his friends, and Voltaire intervenes to ask authority not to be too harsh on them.[15] Yes, he had written a *petit compliment* for them to address to the ruling *Petit Conseil*, just as he had once done for the fishwives of Paris to send to the king. But the king was much more receptive: 'c'est apparemment que messieurs des vingt-cinq sont plus grands seigneurs que le roi' (it seems that the twenty-five gentlemen [of the *Petit Conseil*] are greater lords than the king). The moral of the tale is clear:

je vous demande votre protection pour de pauvres diables qui ne savent ce qu'ils font. . . . Tout en riant, honorez ces bonnes gens de vos bontés compatissantes. . . .

(I ask your protection for poor devils who know not what they do. . . . Despite your laughter, honour these good people with your kind sympathies. . . .)

Voltaire aims to play down the situation, to urge that compassion, a sense of balance and humour be brought to bear. Here he is, trying to help all ranks in Geneva who seek him out ('j'ai prêché la paix à tous'), while keeping a proper sense of detachment ('tout ceci est une comédie'). It is yet another revealing incident for those who imagine Voltaire always crusading with fire and thunder and brilliant irony. He understood too the gentler path and could tread it with delicacy. But unfortunately on this occasion no letter however carefully worked could undo the harm Voltaire had already caused by his interventions. The reply he receives the next day informs Voltaire that the most useful thing he can henceforth do is to wash his hands of the whole business.[16] For a while the *philosophe*, irrepressible, defends himself; but the comedy has gone sour on him. To the d'Argentals he complains that all parties make complaints about him and for his part he is tired of the whole pack of them: 'L'esprit de contumace est dans cette famille.' (The spirit of perversity is in that family.)[17]

The Genevan troubles were a matter of intense frustration; La Barre's death was something else again. When Voltaire first learns of the affair La Barre is still alive, and he is sanguine about a happy solution. After all, enlightenment is spreading into the provinces and younger magistrates bear witness to the progress made.[18] On 6 July he is similarly optimistic,[19] so when the awful news comes the next day his reaction is all the more overwhelming:

Mon cher frère, mon cœur est flétri; je suis atterré. . . . Je suis tenté d'aller mourir dans une terre où les hommes soient moins injustes. Je me tais, j'ai trop à dire.

(My dear brother, my heart is stricken. . . . I am tempted to go and die in a land where men are less unjust. I hold my peace, I have too much to say.)[20]

For months his correspondence will resound with shock and horror; La Barre becomes an obsessive theme. The clock has been put back to barbarism: 'Une telle horreur est digne du douzième siècle. L'inquisition de Portugal ne serait pas si cruelle.' (Such horror is worthy of the twelfth century. The Portuguese Inquisition would not be so cruel.)[21] Voltaire rounds on d'Alembert for reacting ironically: 'Ah! mon cher ami, est-ce là le temps de rire? . . . Je vous embrasse avec rage.' (Ah! my dear friend, is this the time for laughter? . . . I embrace you in rage.)[22] The reaction of *Candide*, it would seem, is deemed unworthy of such a calamity. What particularly offends Voltaire is that a nation apparently so sophisticated at the same time could be so primitive. One image recurs frequently: France is 'un pays de singes qui deviennent si souvent tigres' (a land of monkeys which so often turn into tigers).[23] The French are both frivolous and cowardly; after an initial protest they relapse into the lethargy of everyday banalities: 'On gémit, on se tait, on soupe, on oublie.' (They groan, say nothing, sup, forget.)[24] As in *Candide*, a good meal is enough to reconcile people to horrible injustices.

So, as Voltaire had suggested in his first reactions to the news, flight from French soil seems the only practical answer. He could go to Cleves, where Frederick II would welcome him. But Voltaire does not envisage solitary exile. From this mood of despair about France rises the vision of a *philosophe* society which could publish and export without hindrance its views to the world. As always with Voltaire, resilience comes to his aid, and with it the hopes of acting positively. He appeals to Damilaville, in terms whose optimism seems so extreme that one feels a balanced judgement has momentarily been lost:

Soyez très sûr qu'il se ferait alors une grande révolution dans les esprits, et qu'il suffirait de deux ou trois ans pour faire une époque éternelle. Les grandes choses sont souvent plus faciles qu'on ne pense. Puisse cette idée n'être pas un beau rêve.

(Be quite certain that then there would be a great revolution in men's minds, and that two or three years would be enough to create an eternal age. The great things are often easier than one imagines. May this thought not be just a beautiful dream.)[25]

The last sentence has a prayer-like tone which indicates the urgency of Voltaire's plea. The key figure who needs persuading is not Damilaville, but Diderot. His fellow-*philosophe*, however, saw life differently, and was not to be convinced that exile (which unlike Voltaire he had always avoided) should now be undertaken for the good of the cause. Despite Voltaire's impatience, Diderot did not hasten to reply, and when he did the letter in which he declined to cooperate delayed in arriving until 7 November.[26] For Voltaire it is the last real hope of a concerted attack upon *l'infâme*, though he goes on for a while longer maintaining that he would move to Cleves if others were interested;[27] henceforth he will know that he must depend upon himself alone for the kind of reforms he envisages.

Thus the agitation over La Barre's fate diminishes, and Voltaire gradually returns to the qualified optimism which he had felt before July. Even before he has heard from Diderot, he has become reconciled to the value of what 'le petit nombre de sages répandus dans Paris' can achieve. Books alone are not enough; close social relationships between the enlightened are more productive:

La raison est victorieuse à la longue, elle se communique de proche en proche. Une douzaine d'honnêtes gens qui se font écouter produit plus de bien que cent volumes. Peu de gens lisent, mais tout le monde converse, et le vrai fait impression.

(Reason is triumphant in the end, it spreads by degrees. A dozen gentlemen who are listened to do more good than a hundred volumes. Few read, but everyone talks, and truth makes an impression.)[28]

Even allowing for the fact that Voltaire is writing to a Parisian society hostess, the change of mood fits in with what one might call a recovery of nerve. La Barre may be dead, but the fight to rehabilitate Sirven can go on as before (it would eventually end in victory some years later), while new cases of injustice demanding attention constantly arise. One such comes to Voltaire's notice in September. A Protestant, Jean Pierre Espinas, had been condemned in 1740 for giving hospitality to a Huguenot preacher. Having served a sentence of twenty-five years in the galleys and survived to re-emerge in society, Espinas found himself and his family reduced to penury. Here was a situation worthy of Voltaire's advocacy. As he puts it with compassionate irony in soliciting the powerful aid of the duc de Richelieu: 'Vingt-trois ans de galères pour avoir donné à souper sont une chose un peu dure. Jamais souper ne fut si cher.' (Twenty-three years in the galleys for inviting someone to supper is a bit hard. Never was a supper so expensive.)[29] The *philosophe*'s crusade for mercy and justice has refurbished one of its most effective weapons as indignation once more becomes tempered with Voltairean wit.

By the end of the year, Voltaire has re-entered his former role with self-assurance; the scourger of all false and foolish men, physically frail but spiritually debonair, he returns in double measure the assaults made on him, accepting that the world is both absurd and tragic by turns:

> Pour moi, chétif, je fais la guerre jusqu'au dernier moment. Jansénistes, Molinistes, Frérons, Pompignans, à droite, à gauche, et des prédicants, et J.-J. Rousseau. Je reçois cent estocades: j'en rends deux cents et je ris. Je vois à ma porte Genève en combustion pour des querelles de bibus, et je ris encore; et dieu merci je regarde ce monde comme une farce qui devient quelquefois tragique.
>
> Tout est égal au bout de la journée, et tout est encore plus égal au bout de toutes les journées.
>
> (As for me, puny though I am, I am waging war until the last breath. Jansenists, Molinists [Jesuits], Frérons, Pompignans, to right and left, and Protestant preachers, and J.-J. Rousseau. I receive a hundred thrusts; I return two hundred and I laugh. I see at my gate Geneva on fire over arguments about quiddities, and I laugh again; and thanks be to God I look upon this world as a farce that sometimes becomes tragic.
>
> It is all one at the end of the day, and is even more so at the end of all our days.)[30]

Here in the last phrase is foreshadowed the stoical equanimity of the man who will a decade later write that 'il mourra content'. It is, too, fascinating to see the reversal of attitudes. The man who could, five months earlier, consider it intolerable of d'Alembert to end a letter about persecution with the words 'Je rirai',[31] can now himself write 'je ris' and 'je ris encore' as he contemplates the world.

The year 1766 is not however to be limited to a few basic themes. The very diversity of Voltaire's correspondence is one of its most attractive features. In part this was because he was so ready to listen and help. He saw that d'Alembert lacked this capacity, being one of those 'qui aiment mieux instruire que plaire, qui veulent se faire écouter, et qui dédaignent d'écouter' (who prefer to teach than give pleasure, who want to be listened to and scorn to listen).[32] Being more approachable, Voltaire was approached by those like the young dramatist Chabanon, who was seeking useful criticism of his play. Voltaire's reply blends discretion with honesty: the subject is almost impossibly difficult; it might be best to put it aside for a while and then judge it anew with fresh eyes; perhaps the plot could be improved, since that is what matters most on the stage. All this is intimated most circumspectly, 'avec la juste défiance que je dois en avoir' (with the proper diffidence I must have about it), but perhaps a random word from him may cause new beauties to spring up in the mind of a genius.[33] In reality, Voltaire had little doubt that the play was a failure, as a letter to the d'Argentals on the same day makes clear.[34] But something more complex than the mere need for tact is at work here. No one knew better than Voltaire the anguish of writing a play which others thought bad, and much of the kindness surely comes from a genuine sympathy for the problems of a fellow-dramatist struggling to make good. Before the year is out, Voltaire will himself be similarly involved.

With *Les Scythes* he feels that he has created something worthwhile. On 5 November, he hints to the d'Argentals that another tragedy may be on the way,[35] on the 8th he apparently sends them Act 1,[36] and by the 19th he has completed the play, as he announces with pride to the same friends:

une tragédie faite en dix jours! me direz-vous, aux petites maisons, aux petites maisons, de bons bouillons, des potions rafraîchissantes comme à Jean-Jacques.
. . . Zaïre ne me coûta que trois semaines. Mais cinq actes en vers à 73 ans et malade! J'ai donc le diable au corps? . . .

Des larmes! on en versera, ou on sera de pierre. Des frémissements! On en aura jusqu'à la moelle des os ou on n'aura point de moelle. . . .

(a tragedy written in ten days! You will tell me, off to the lunatic asylum, good broths, restorative potions, just as for Jean-Jacques.

   . . . Zaïre took me only three weeks. But five acts in verse at 73 and ill as well! Am I possessed? . . .

   Tears! People will weep torrents, if they're not made of stone. Tremors! People will feel them to the marrow, if they've any marrow at all.)[37]

It is as much a hymn of triumph over old age as anything else. But of equal interest is a tone which is rarely associated with Voltaire and scarcely ever emerges even in his correspondence—one of simple naïveté. Only among intimate friends did he lower the mask with such complete candour and admit almost fatuously to the simple pride of authorship coursing through him. *Les Scythes*, alas! was to prove a disappointment. Others did not share his admiration and the dramatist suffered a long process of mortification before resigning himself at last to public opinion many months later.[38]

   Voltaire is already, as we have seen, an old man, and his infirmities are particularly evident in the winter months, when he never leaves his fireside or even, he claims, his bed for months on end. It is for this reason that he misses Mozart when that ten-year-old prodigy comes to Geneva.[39] But he dwells little on the meditations of an old man about ageing and death, and when he does it is in reply to the despairing questions of Mme Du Deffand, old and blind, who asserts that she has only one abiding thought and sorrow, the affliction of ever having been born.[40] Can Voltaire, she asks, share with her the truths he has discovered and teach her a way of enduring life? It is the disciple's approach to a guru, the more curious because Mme Du Deffand in her brittle way maligned Voltaire when she wrote to Horace Walpole.[41] Voltaire rarely played the guru's part; it was not in his nature to seek or relish such a solemn pontificatory role. But Mme Du Deffand was one of that special circle whose friendship dated back over several decades, and for her he was willing to expound his world-view in his letters. Ignoring her despair, he claims to be agreeing with her that one should love life and hate death, however unhappy one is. The positive note once struck, he enlarges upon it. Although metaphysical knowledge is both incomprehensible and useless, nevertheless it is pleasant to ask oneself such questions, for they exercise the mind. The loss of one's eyesight helps at least towards spiritual meditation. In order not to make this sound complacently unfeeling, the author adds that he too profits in this way from those occasions when 'mes fluxions sur les yeux m'empêchent de lire' (inflammation of my eyes prevents me reading). He deflates the solemnity with a delicate gallantry: 'Je voudrais surtout passer ces temps avec vous.' (I would like above all to spend those hours with you.)[42] Once again, the recipient must be borne in mind when one evaluates this letter. Voltaire may well have been affecting a greater optimism for Mme Du Deffand's sake than he really felt, and the whole letter is redolent of that discreet kindness which we have seen in other contexts when he was writing to d'Argental or Chabanon. But the picture he paints fits in well enough with the outlook of *Le Philosophe ignorant*. Besides, being more personal it is a more remarkable statement of confidence and inner resources in a man aged and infirm but whose life-force flows with undiminished vigour.

There is energy enough in reserve to denounce Rousseau when the latter accuses Voltaire of plotting against him. In invective worthy of his best polemical pamphlets, Voltaire rages against the unfortunate Jean-Jacques:

Voyez Jean-Jacques Rousseau, il traîne avec lui la belle Mlle Le Vasseur sa blanchisseuse âgée de cinquante ans, à laquelle il a fait trois enfants qu'il a pourtant abandonnés pour s'attacher à l'éducation du seigneur Emile, et pour en faire un bon menuisier.

(Look at Jean-Jacques Rousseau, he trails around with him the beautiful Mlle Le Vasseur, his washerwoman fifty years old, by whom he has got three children that he has nonetheless abandoned so that he can devote himself to educating the lord Emile and making him into a good carpenter.)[43]

Like all good satire, its unfairness contains enough basic truths about the inconsistencies in Rousseau's life to make a sharply valid point. But the real misfortune of Rousseau's impossible character is that he has split the *philosophe* ranks: 'Quel beau rôle auraient joué les philosophes, si Rousseau n'avait pas été un fou et un monstre!' (What a fine part the *philosophes* would have played if Rousseau had not been a madman and a monster!)[44] For then they might have been so much farther forward with causes like Sirven's.

Still, courage was all; the remark about Rousseau is immediately followed by the exhortation: 'Mais ne nous décourageons point.' Despite recurring crises (including a discovery by the authorities at the end of the year that he was attempting to smuggle some of his works into France), the struggle goes on unabated, as Damilaville, d'Alembert and d'Argental are pressed into service on his account in the French capital whenever possible. The tone of this correspondence, filled as it is with words and actions employed to improve the human lot, is caught in a simple phrase which suddenly arises within a letter full of diverse mundane details: 'Oh! que j'aime cette philosophie agissante et bienfaisante!' (Oh, how I love this philosophy of action and goodwill!)[45] It can hardly be called a self-conscious statement, so spontaneously does it seem to spring from Voltaire's thought. Happiness lay at the heart of these multifarious campaigns, and he knew it. That is essentially why, despite the repeated alarms, these letters convey so much life, so much concern for mankind and (the La Barre reactions notwithstanding) so much essential cheerfulness.

VOLTAIRE'S WORLD-VIEW

The world, as we saw above, is for Voltaire both absurd and tragic; this is the viewpoint of *Candide*, and it is the paradoxicality of tragic farce that makes *Candide* so memorable. But the dual thread runs right through Voltaire's work, though the relationship of the one element to the other keeps changing. From the first Voltaire was maligned as a cynical mocker of persons and ideas; as early as 1735 an anonymous pen-portrait had spread the myth.[46] Latterly, we have begun to rediscover the man of feeling, and a very recent book has been devoted to a rehabilitation of this side.[47] But Voltaire can be truly seen only if the elements of sensibility and irony are constantly interrelated. As one of his most perceptive analysts has put it, he was 'un dionysiaque qui voulut être apollonien' (a Dionysiac who wanted to be Apollonian).[48] The extraordinary emotivity by itself would have made him no more than a failure, like the broken genius whom Diderot brilliantly records as the eponymous hero of *Le Neveu de Rameau*. It was the capacity to harness this intense feeling and transform it into superb ridicule which gave him his mordant edge. Without the reserve of sentiment the grin would indeed have been as hideous as Musset (in line with other uncomprehending Romantics) claimed it was. Not a work we have considered lacks this sensibility; even in the abstract *Traité de métaphysique* it is only just beneath the surface. When equilibrium is destroyed, it is in the direction of too much emotion, whether that be pity or rage. If there is excess, it is not one of dryness.

Tragic farce has however become a province of the absurd in contemporary literature; it is for instance the precise sub-title which Ionesco gave to his play *Les Chaises* (1952). This is not Voltaire's view of things. If the world was both sad and mad, that did not place the meaning of life in jeopardy. Voltaire would not have shared Camus's attitude in *Le Mythe de Sisyphe* (1942) that the only important question to ask oneself is whether one should commit suicide. For Voltaire the question is simply not posed. Men do not commit suicide, save for a few misfits or particularly unfortunate persons, and that is a fact of life, though not necessarily a cheerful one. We must just get on with it, for there is plenty to be done; here is established the groundwork for 'cette philosophie agissante et bienfaisante' which made Voltaire a giant in his day.

But a giant only of his day? Let us hope not. The time is out of joint for a Voltaire. We live in an age of deep faiths, like the Middle Ages. Voltaire had a firm religious belief, true, but it was minimal, a basic guarantee of values and no more. One did not live by absolutes, for that was what had caused so much suffering to the world. Voltaire did not always free himself from *a priori* positions, as we have seen, but the whole tenor of his existence was to do so, to find human and secular criteria for the decisions one took. The balance (it would be modish to call it dialectic, but deplorable because we would be moving into an ideology such as he would have deprecated) between anguish at life's horrors and joy in the vital energies of living is not easy to maintain without constant recourse to some transcending principle. It requires deep sophistication, since detachment and commitment have to be reconciled and one knows that there can be no final resolution of any kind. Amongst modern French writers Camus has perhaps exemplified it best, though in Camus's case the social commitments were more prudent and equivocal, in the post-war years at least. It is hard not to end by turning one's back on the human hurly-burly as meaningless and hopeless; Voltaire never did.

This world-view still has to be articulated, however, if Voltaire is to be a great artist as well as a great man. Here one supreme gift supported him throughout life in all his many-sided activities: lucidity. He was often wrong in his views (especially on scientific matters as he grew older), there were realms like Newtonian physics where even his clear thinking could not completely penetrate; but when he saw a matter whole, he conveyed the essence of it with unfailing clarity. Besides, he stylized the situation to engrave it on the mind: Newton's apple to make gravitation more comprehensible, Joan of Arc's virginity to make all saints and miracles ridiculous. It is fitting to finish with a little Voltairean drama, which however comes from Bertrand Russell's autobiography; but Russell, as he generously acknowledged, owed something to Voltaire[49] and had a deep affinity for him. Here brought up to date is the wit and malice of the *philosophe*, conveyed with the same balance and rhythms. It may give us hope that Voltaire's particular contributions to life and literature will endure:

... pandemonium broke loose. Everybody had to escape as best they could while the police looked on calmly. Two of the drunken viragos began to attack me with their boards full of nails. While I was wondering how one defended oneself against this type of attack, one of the ladies among us went up to the police and suggested that they should defend me. The police, however, merely shrugged their shoulders. 'But he is an eminent philosopher,' said the lady, and the police still shrugged. 'But he is famous all over the world as a man of learning,' she continued. The police remained unmoved. 'But he is the brother of an earl,' she finally cried. At this, the police rushed to my assistance.[50]

Notes and references

Chapter 1. DRAMATIC CRITIC AND DRAMATIST

1. Even with Racine, however, Voltaire professed reservations; cf. E. P. Kostoroski, *The Eagle and the Dove*, *Studs. Volt.*, xcv (1972), pp. 95–142.

2. *La Mort de César*, Ed. A.-M. Rousseau, Paris, SEDES, 1964, p. 7.

3. The passage is quoted from the earliest edition of the *Lettres*, which was published in English as *Letters concerning the English Nation*, London, 1733. It is to be found in *Voltaire on Shakespeare*, Ed. T. Besterman, *Studs. Volt.*, liv (1967), p. 44. For ease of reference, all quotations relating to this subject are taken from this source.

4. ibid., p. 50.

5. *Discours sur la tragédie* (1730), ibid., p. 51.

6. ibid., p. 53.

7. *Dissertation sur la tragédie ancienne et moderne* (1748), ibid., p. 57.

8. *Appel à toutes les nations* (1761), ibid., pp. 63–80.

9. 'Translation of *Julius Caesar*' (1764), ibid., p. 156.

10. La Place had been the first to translate, albeit mechanically, some of Shakespeare's work in his *Théâtre anglais* (1745–9). In 1769 Ducis presented his version of *Hamlet*, the first of his adaptations that helped to make Shakespeare better known. In 1776, Le Tourneur's complete translation of Shakespeare's plays began to appear.

11. *Lettre à l'Académie Française* (1776), *Voltaire on Shakespeare*, pp. 186–209. In fairness to Voltaire it needs to be said that he is replying spiritedly to Lord Kames's *Elements of Criticism* (1762), where the Scottish critic had compared these two lines and with an insularity equal to Voltaire's had found Shakespeare's line acceptable but not Racine's. cf. ibid., pp. 87–8.

12. F. C. Green, *Literary Ideas in 18th Century France and England*, New York, Ungar, 1966 (originally published in 1935 under the title *Minuet*), p. 103. The author deals with the Ducis *Hamlet* in some detail and sketches an interesting account of 'Shakespeare and the French Dramatic Tradition' as a framework for 'Shakespeare and Voltaire' (pp. 54–129).

13. *Lettres philosophiques*, Ed. G. Lanson, revised by A.-M. Rousseau, 2 vols., Paris, Didier, 1964, ii, pp. 90–1.

14. 'I have wept for her death, and I would be with her. Life is but a dream full of starts of folly, and of fancied, and true miseries. Death awakes us from this painful dream, and gives us, either a better existence or no existence at all.' Letter to Thieriot, 26 Oct. 1726, *Voltaire on Shakespeare*, p. 43.

15. ibid., p. 227.

16. Many of these are taken from the Besterman introduction to his *Voltaire on Shakespeare*, pp. 29–30.

17. Gildon, *Remarks on the Plays of Shakespeare*, London, 1710; cited in R. S. Ridgway, *La Propagande philosophique dans les tragédies de Voltaire*, *Studs. Volt.*, xv (1961), p. 83.

18. cf. letter to La Marre, 15 Mar. 1736, Best. 997.

19. A detailed examination of Voltaire's views on taste is to be found in R. Naves, *Le Goût de Voltaire*, Paris, Garnier, 1938; D. Williams, *Voltaire: literary critic*, *Studs. Volt.*, xlviii (1966).

20. J. Lough, *Paris Theatre Audiences in the Seventeenth and Eighteenth Centuries*, OUP, 1957, provides comparative figures (p. 178).

21. Indeed, the actual name Voltaire was known even less; the author François-Marie Arouet had begun using it only in that year.

22. By his own profession, the play had been begun when he was only nineteen years of age (Moland ed., ii, p. 11).

23. 'J'ai fait des souverains, et n'ai point voulu l'être' (I have made kings, and not wished to be one) (II. 4).

24. Moland ed., ii, p. 536.

25. ibid., p. 542.

26. cf. R. Fargher's account of Belloy's *Le Siège de Calais* (1765) in the context of French patriotic tragedy (*Life and Letters in France: The Eighteenth Century*, London, Nelson, 1970, pp. 117–27).

27. 'Voilà les premiers pleurs qui coulent de mes yeux' (V. 8).

28. *Lettre à d'Alembert sur les spectacles*, Ed. M. Fuchs, Lille/Geneva, Giard/Droz, 1948, p. 73.

29. Giraudoux sums it up neatly in the words of a character in *Siegfried* (1928): 'mon drame débute par où finissent les mélodrames, par la croix de ma mère . . .' (I. 6). cf. also Anouilh's *Pauvre Bitos*, act 1 (Ed. W. D. Howarth, London, Harrap, 1958, p. 33).

30. Moland ed., ii, p. 534.

31. cf. infra, p. 81.

32. P. M. Conlon, *Voltaire's literary career from 1728 to 1750*, *Studs. Volt.*, xiv (1961), p. 98.

33. R. Ridgway rightly points out that *Mahomet* is the first major attack on *l'infâme* (p. 130).

34. 'The Historical philosophy of the Enlightenment', *Studs. Volt.*, xxvii (1963), p. 1683.

35. cf., e.g., letter to Frederick II of Prussia, 9 Apr. 1741, Best. 2308.

36. Lanson ed., i, p. 33.

37. Ridgway cites several instances of dramatists, all of them second-rate, who laboured on this particular genre from 1758 onwards (p. 196).

38. 19 Nov. 1766, Best. 12789.

39. Letter to d'Argental, 25 May 1767, Best. 13303.

40. *Préface* to *Les Scythes*, Moland ed., vi, p. 267.

41. Letter to Thieriot, 19 Dec. 1766, Best. 12858.

42. cf. infra, p. 75.

43. 8 Dec. 1766, Best. 12829.

44. The phrase is borrowed from Ridgway (p. 210), who argues that the play however avoids this pitfall and that there is a consistently primitivist outlook. He upholds this viewpoint with his usual cogency and effectively

destroys the opposing school of thought which maintains that *Les Scythes* is pro-French; but he passes too readily over the ferocity of the several statements (not just one isolated passage, as he claims) by Obéide expressing her loathing for the Scythian way of life.

45. Moland ed., vi, p. 269.

Chapter 2. HISTORIAN

1. The standard work on this side of Voltaire's writings remains J. H. Brumfitt, *Voltaire Historian*, OUP, 1958. Other useful major studies are F. Diaz, *Voltaire storico*, Turin, Einaudi, 1958, and C. Rihs, *Voltaire: Recherches sur les origines du matérialisme historique*, Geneva/Paris, Droz/Minard, 1962. *Histoire de la guerre de 1741* has recently been published in a good edition by J. Maurens, Paris, Garnier, 1971. The most useful edition for the rest of the historical works collectively remains that of R. Pomeau, *Voltaire: Œuvres historiques*, Paris, NRF, Bibliothèque de la Pléiade, 1957.

2. For a more detailed account of the complex textual history, cf. *Essai sur les mœurs et l'esprit des nations et sur les principaux faits de l'histoire depuis Charlemagne jusqu'à Louis XIII*, Ed. R. Pomeau, 2 vols., Paris, Garnier, 1963, i, pp. ii–xviii. All references will be to this edition unless otherwise stated.

3. *Voltaire*, London, Longmans, 1969, p. 220.

4. Moland ed., xxiv, p. 477.

5. 4 vols., Rotterdam, art. 'Blondel (François)'; cf. I. O. Wade, *The Intellectual Development of Voltaire*, Princeton University Press, 1969, p. 459.

6. Moland ed., xxvii, p. 237.

7. Pomeau ed., i, p. 196. This is however preceded by a brief look at China, India, Persia and Islam, further confirming the contrast in approach with Bossuet's work.

8. ibid., ii, p. 395.

9. ibid., i, p. 195. The 'vous' in the first instance would have been Mme du Châtelet; but the retention of this address in all the printed versions after her death indicates a more general literary stratagem, of which Voltaire shows himself master on numerous occasions elsewhere.

10. ibid.

11. ibid., i, p. 781.

12. ibid., i, p. 708.

13. cf. the chapter 'Civilisation' (pp. 333–48) in G. Gusdorf, *Les Principes de la pensée au siècle des Lumières*, Paris, Payot, 1971, where the author cites the research of Lucien Febvre and Benveniste. This section offers a most stimulating account of what the Enlightenment understood by the concept of civilization.

14. Pomeau ed., ii, p. 812.

15. ibid., ii, p. 804.

16. ibid., ii, p. 662.

17. ibid., ii, p. 804.

18. ibid., ii, pp. 283, 290.

19. ibid., i, p. 509.

20. Bellessort, *Essai sur Voltaire*, Paris, Perrin, 1925; cited in *Voltaire et la critique*, Ed. J. Sareil, Englewood Cliffs, New Jersey, Prentice-Hall, 1966, p. 41.

21. Pomeau ed., ii, p. 806.

22. ibid., i, p. 197.

23. ibid., i, p. 408.

24. ibid., i, p. 600.

25. ibid., i, p. 761.

26. To quote a few examples: in fourteenth-century Paris it was a luxury to be conveyed by cart (ibid., i, p. 760); when Henry VIII met François I on the Field of the Cloth of Gold in 1520, their display of magnificence was quite extraordinary and could not have been put on by anyone but heads of state (ibid., ii, pp. 166–7); in seventeenth-century Spain, great lords had much silver plate and a large retinue of servants, but comfort and convenience were unknown (ibid., ii, pp. 632–3.)

27. Turgot's essays on social and economic progress, hitherto somewhat inaccessible, have recently become available in a good English version, translated and edited by R. L. Meek: *Turgot on Progress, Sociology and Economics*, Cambridge University Press, 1973.

28. Pomeau ed., i, p. 540.

29. ibid., i, p. 393.

30. ibid., i, p. 616.

31. ibid., ii, p. 101.

32. ibid., ii, p. 548.

33. ibid., ii, p. 558.

34. ibid., ii, pp. 545–6.

35. ibid., ii, p. 60.

36. ibid., ii, p. 471.

37. The chapter on Richelieu reveals a fascination with this odious figure who, despite being universally hated, was never dispossessed of power during his lifetime.

38. These opinions are expressed on many occasions, but perhaps most cogently in chapter xcvi, 'Du gouvernement féodal après Louis XI', Pomeau ed., ii, pp. 17–21.

39. ibid., ii, p. 679.

40. ibid., i, p. 505.

41. ibid., ii, p. 808.

42. ibid., ii, p. 779.

43. ibid., ii, p. 243.

44. ibid., ii, pp. 644–5.

45. P. Gay, *Voltaire's Politics: The Poet as Realist*, 2nd ed., New York, Vintage, 1965, p. 181.

46. cf. *Œuvres historiques*, Ed. Pomeau, p. 22.

47. Best. 7090.

48. Letter to Frederick II, 6 Jan. 1778, Best. 19818.

49. cf. Brumfitt, op. cit., pp. 160–1.

50. Pomeau ed., i, pp. 199, 215.

51. L. Gossman, 'Voltaire's *Charles XII*: history into art', *Studs. Volt.*, xxv (1963), pp. 691–720.

52. ibid., p. 720: author's italics.

53. ibid., p. 717. A similar line of attack is developed by G. Murray, *Voltaire's 'Candide': the Protean gardener, 1755-1762*, *Studs. Volt.*, lxix (1970), esp. pp. 245-99.

54. cf. supra, p. 34.

55. Two examples taken at random will serve as typical. In the *Avant-Propos* the reader is told: 'En vous instruisant en philosophe de ce qui concerne ce globe, vous portez d'abord votre vue sur l'Orient . . .' (In instructing yourself as a philosopher about what concerns this planet, you cast your eye first of all upon the East . . .) (Pomeau ed., i, p. 197). The final paragraph of chapter ii begins: 'Je me réserve à jeter les yeux sur Siam . . .' (I reserve for later to cast my eye on Siam . . .) (ibid., i, p. 226).

56. 31 Oct. 1738, Best. 1571.

57. Pomeau ed., i, p. 511.

58. ibid., ii, p. 2.

59. ibid., i, p. 512.

60. ibid., i, p. 688.

61. ibid., i, pp. 404-5.

62. ibid., i, p. 405.

63. ibid., i, p. 338, n.

64. ibid., ii, p. 225.

65. ibid., i, p. 27.

66. *Voltaire: Zadig and Other Stories*, Ed. H. T. Mason, OUP, 1971, p. 175.

67. Pomeau ed., ii, p. 756.

68. ibid., ii, p. 779.

69. Gossman, art. cit., p. 715.

70. Pomeau ed., i, p. 754.

71. ibid., ii, p. 735.

72. cf. *Religion, érudition et critique à la fin du XVIIᵉ siècle et au début du XVIIIᵉ*, Paris, P.U.F., 1968.

73. cf. H. T. Mason, *Pierre Bayle and Voltaire*, OUP, 1963, pp. 128-33; Brumfitt, op. cit., pp. 32-4.

74. Moland ed., xvi, p. 123.

75. Pomeau ed., i, pp. 328-9.

76. ibid., i, pp. 399-400.

77. ibid., i, p. 748.

78. ibid., i, p. 806; ii, p. 724.

79. E.g. the Spanish ambassadors' naïve amazement at the frugality of the Dutch, ibid., ii, p. 727.

80. cf. Pomeau's remarks, ed., i, pp. xxi-xxii.

81. ibid., ii, p. 802.

82. ibid., i, pp. 62-3, nn.

83. *La Philosophie de l'Histoire*, Ed. Brumfitt, in *The Complete Works of Voltaire*, Ed. T. Besterman, vol. 59, Geneva, Institut et Musée Voltaire, 1969, p. 49.

84. Pomeau ed., i, p. xxiii.

85. G. Lanson, 'Notes pour servir à l'étude des chapitres 35-39 du *Siècle*

de Louis XIV de Voltaire', *Mélanges offerts à M. Charles Andler*, Strasbourg/
Paris, Istra, 1924, pp. 171–95.
86. G. Lanson, *Voltaire*, 2nd ed., Paris, Hachette, 1910, p. 168.
87. Pomeau ed., i, p. 120.
88. ibid., ii, p. 810.
89. ibid., i, p. 87.
90. ibid., ii, p. 64.

Chapter 3. *Conteur*

1. I. O. Wade's work on these years has definitively rehabilitated them as
of major importance for Voltaire's work. cf. *Voltaire and Madame Du Châtelet:
An Essay on the Intellectual Activity at Cirey*, Princeton University Press, 1941;
Studies on Voltaire, Princeton University Press, 1947.
2. cf. J. Van den Heuvel, *Voltaire dans ses contes: De 'Micromégas' à 'L'Ingénu'*,
Paris, Colin, 1967, for a lively demonstration of the author's apprenticeship
as a *conteur* (pp. 15–50). A discussion of Voltaire's treatment of the *conte* is
given in Ed. H. T. Mason, *Zadig and Other Stories*, OUP, 1971, pp. 9–21.
3. Best. 1944.
4. I. O. Wade's critical edition (*Voltaire's 'Micromégas': A Study in the
Fusion of Science, Myth, and Art*, Princeton University Press, 1950) first established the case for dating it to 1739. This has been confirmed by Van den
Heuvel's own investigations (op. cit., pp. 76–8, n.).
5. U. Schick, *Zur Erzähltechnik in Voltaires 'Contes'*, Munich, Wilhelm Fink,
1968, includes a useful comparison of vocabulary employed in *Micromégas* and
in *L'Ingénu*.
6. Ed. H. T. Mason, *Zadig and Other Stories*, p. 58.
7. ibid.
8. ibid., p. 63.
9. Wade ed., p. 7.
10. Mason ed., p. 55.
11. ibid., p. 67.
12. ibid., p. 70.
13. Letter to Cardinal de Bernis, 14 Oct. 1748, Best. 3304.
14. Mason ed., p. 74.
15. ibid., p. 84.
16. The political background to the story is well handled by V. L. Saulnier
in his edition (Geneva/Paris, Droz, 1956).
17. Mason ed., pp. 100–1; my italics.
18. ibid., p. 101. Nature imitated art when Voltaire himself underwent a
similar experience some months later, his coach having broken down one
starry night in the open country; cf. Longchamp and Wagnière, *Mémoires*,
2 vols., 1826, ii, p. 168, and the discussion of this episode in R. Pomeau, *La
Religion de Voltaire*, Paris, Nizet, 2nd ed., 1969, pp. 216–17.
19. Van den Heuvel's discussion of this point is particularly helpful (pp.
164–5). Leibniz maintained that this world must be the best of all possible
worlds, for it is the work of God who knew all possibilities and chose the best
of these.

20. Pope had already expressed such a point of view in unforgettable terms in Epistle I of his *Essay on Man* (1733):

All Nature is but Art, unknown to thee;
All Chance, Direction which thou canst not see;
All Discord, Harmony, not understood

21. Mason ed., p. 148.
22. ibid., p. 90.
23. Van den Heuvel, p. 194.
24. Mason ed., p. 94.
25. ibid., p. 73.
26. ibid., p. 130.
27. C. Thacker rightly points out that Zadig's almost miraculous cleverness takes away that total passivity which makes Candide the truly transparent hero, more completely representative of suffering humanity (ed., *Candide*, Geneva/Paris, Droz, 1968, p. 65).
28. The literature on this complex subject is legion. Amongst the more useful studies are the critical editions by A. Morize (Paris, Didier, 2nd ed., 1957) and R. Pomeau (Paris, Nizet, 1959), W. H. Barber's *Voltaire: 'Candide'* (London, Arnold, 1960), I. O. Wade's *Voltaire and 'Candide'* (Princeton University Press, 1959) and W. F. Bottiglia's *Voltaire's 'Candide'*, *Studs. Volt.*, viiA, 1964. A useful introduction is provided by J. H. Brumfitt in his edition (OUP, 1968); all textual references are to this version.
29. cf. Chapter 6 for a closer look at Voltaire's philosophical thought.
30. Brumfitt ed., p. 107.
31. Voltaire to Elie Bertrand, 18 Feb. 1756, Best. 6066.
32. Brumfitt ed., p. 66.
33. Van den Heuvel, p. 261.
34. 'The Quality of "Candide"', *Essays Presented to C. M. Girdlestone*, Newcastle-upon-Tyne, King's College, 1960, pp. 338, 340, 346.
35. Brumfitt ed., p. 84.
36. 'On ne meurt point dans ce monde-là. . . . Le monde de *Candide* est un monde où l'on vit' (One does not die in that world. . . . The world of *Candide* is a world where one lives), Pomeau, *La Religion de Voltaire*, p. 311.
37. Brumfitt ed., p. 71.
38. ibid., pp. 110–11; my italics.
39. ibid., p. 110.
40. ibid., p. 111.
41. ibid., p. 112.
42. ibid.
43. ibid., p. 114. Though Voltaire flirted with the Manichean hypothesis of evil, especially around the period when *Candide* was written, he never accepted it; cf. H. T. Mason, 'Voltaire and Manichean dualism', *Studs. Volt.*, xxvi (1963), pp. 1143–60.
44. ibid., p. 148.
45. ibid., p. 114.
46. G. Murray admirably demonstrates this point: *Voltaire's 'Candide': the Protean gardener, 1755–1762*, *Studs. Volt.*, lxix (1970), pp. 349–84.

47. Interestingly enough, Voltaire seems to consider the great to be if anything worse off. As Martin says: 'Le doge a ses chagrins, les gondoliers ont les leurs. Il est vrai qu'à tout prendre le sort d'un gondolier est préférable à celui d'un doge; mais je crois la différence si médiocre que cela ne vaut pas la peine d'être examiné.' (The doge has his sorrows, the gondoliers have theirs. It is true that taking everything into consideration the fate of a gondolier is preferable to that of a doge; but I think the difference so unimportant that it does not merit the trouble of examination.) Brumfitt ed., pp. 129–30.

48. ibid., p. 147.

49. ibid., p. 104.

50. ibid., p. 150.

51. Letter to Louise de Cormenin, 7 June 1844; cited in Van den Heuvel, p. 277: author's italics.

52. For a comprehensive discussion of the gardens in *Candide*, cf. W. F. Bottiglia, op. cit. He discovers eight in all.

53. Ed. R. Barthes, *Romans et contes de Voltaire*, Paris, Club des Libraires, 1958, p. 28; cited in Van den Heuvel, p. 277.

54. Brumfitt ed., p. 65.

55. ibid.

56. Murray, p. 365.

57. Brumfitt ed., p. 106.

58. ibid., p. 107.

59. Wade, *Voltaire and 'Candide'*, pp. 176–7.

60. Letter to Le Bault, 18 Nov. 1758, Best. 7234; Brumfitt's comments are also interesting (ed., p. 179, n. 1).

61. Pomeau, *La Religion de Voltaire*, p. 310.

62. Brumfitt points the parallel well, ed., p. 174, n. 5.

63. ibid., p. 69.

64. ibid., p. 81.

65. cf. R. Federman and J. Fletcher: *Samuel Beckett: his works and his critics. An essay in bibliography*, Berkeley, University of California Press, 1970, p. 5. The matter is briefly discussed in J. Fletcher, *The Novels of Samuel Beckett*, London, Chatto and Windus, 1964, p. 20.

66. Brumfitt ed., p. 82.

67. cf. supra, p. 53.

68. Brumfitt ed., p. 87.

69. ibid., p. 93.

70. E. P. Grobe, 'Aspectual Parody in Voltaire's *Candide*', *Symposium*, xxi (1967), pp. 38–49.

71. A. Camus, *L'Homme révolté, Essais*, Ed. R. Quilliot and L. Faucon, Paris, Bibliothèque de la Pléiade, 1965, p. 668.

72. Auerbach, *Mimesis*, New York, Doubleday Anchor, 1957, p. 361.

73. R. S. Crane, 'The Concept of Plot and the Plot of *Tom Jones*', *Perspectives on Fiction*, Ed. J. L. Calderwood and H. E. Toliver, London, 1968, p. 306; cited in E. Dipple, *Plot*, London, Methuen, 1970, p. 15.

74. *Messages*, Paris, Gallimard, 1926; cited in E. Muir, *The Structure of the Novel*, London, Hogarth Press, 1954, pp. 119–21.

75. cf. H. T. Mason, 'Voltaire and Manichean dualism', p. 1151.

76. Auerbach, *Mimesis*, p. 355.

77. He himself expressed a distinct preference for *L'Ingénu* over *Candide*: 'L'Ingénu vaut mieux que Candide, en ce qu'il est infiniment plus vraisemblable' (*L'Ingénu* is better than *Candide* because it is infinitely more true to life), letter to Gabriel Cramer, [June/July 1767], Best. 13360.

78. For the historical background to *L'Ingénu*, one should consult the excellent study by F. Pruner, 'Recherches sur la création romanesque dans *L'Ingénu* de Voltaire', *Archives des lettres modernes*, xxx (1960). For Voltaire's personal reaction as seen in his correspondence, cf. infra, pp. 163–4.

79. 15 Sept. 1766, Best. 12673.

80. Letter to Moultou, [Oct./Nov. 1766], Best. 12753: my italics.

81. Moland ed., xxv, p. 527.

82. cf. supra, n. 77.

83. Moland ed., xxxii, p. 349.

84. The matter is gone into in H. T. Mason, 'The Unity of Voltaire's *L'Ingénu*', *The Age of the Enlightenment: Studies Presented to Theodore Besterman*, Ed. W. H. Barber et al., Edinburgh and London, Oliver and Boyd, 1967, pp. 93–106.

85. *L'Ingénu* and *Histoire de Jenni*, Ed. J. H. Brumfitt and M. I. Gerard Davis, Oxford, Blackwell, 1960, p. 1. All references will be to this edition.

86. ibid., p. 57.

87. ibid., p. 30.

88. ibid., p. 48: author's italics.

89. ibid., p. 57.

90. ibid., p. 45.

91. ibid., p. 14.

92. ibid., p. 48.

93. ibid., p. 58.

94. ibid., p. 37.

95. For a fuller discussion of this and other matters related to this *conte*, cf. H. T. Mason, 'A Biblical "Conte Philosophique": Voltaire's *Taureau blanc*', *Eighteenth-Century French Studies*, Ed. E. T. Dubois et al., Newcastle-upon-Tyne, Oriel Press, 1969, pp. 55–69. It has recently been argued that *Le Taureau blanc* was not written over several years, since an acquaintance of Voltaire, the baron de Montelieu, refers to it as 'un conte nouveau' in Sept. 1773 (E. Mass, *Le Marquis d'Adhémar: la correspondance inédite d'un ami des philosophes a la cour de Bayreuth*, *Studs. Volt.*, cix (1973), pp. 49, 189); but this scarcely seems a persuasive piece of evidence.

96. cf. *Le Taureau blanc*, Ed. R. Pomeau, Paris, Nizet, 1956, pp. 74–7.

97. H. T. Mason ed., *Zadig and Other Stories*, pp. 195–6. All references are to this edition.

98. ibid., p. 211.

99. ibid., p. 227.

100. ibid., p. 230.

101. Unfavourable observations on human sacrifice in the Old Testament, as demonstrated by this story, are to be found in the *Dictionnaire philosophique*, Moland ed., xix, pp. 497–500, and in *La Bible enfin expliquée*, Moland ed., xxx, pp. 141–3.

102. Mason ed., p, 223.

103. ibid., p. 230.

104. ibid., p. 217.

105. ibid., p. 198.

106. ibid., p. 205.

107. ibid., p. 224.

108. *Notebooks*, Ed. T. Besterman, *The Complete Works of Voltaire*, vol. 81, 1968, p. 106.

109. V. Mylne, 'Literary techniques and methods in Voltaire's *contes philosophiques*', *Studs. Volt.*, lvii (1967), p. 1075. This article provides a useful discussion in what is still a little-treated area, the formal aspects of Voltaire's tales.

110. I should like to make grateful acknowledgement to the Clarendon Press for permission to reproduce some of the material used in my edition of *Zadig and Other Stories*.

Chapter 4. POET

1. G. Lanson, *Voltaire*, makes this point (p. 84).

2. Ed. T. Besterman, *The Complete Works of Voltaire*, vol. 2, 1970, p. 212.

3. ibid., pp. 226–31.

4. Lanson, op. cit., pp. 89–91.

5. cf. D. Williams, 'Voltaire and the language of the gods', *Studs. Volt.*, lxii (1968), p. 60.

6. Moland ed., ix, p. 470.

7. ibid., pp. 566–8.

8. ibid., p. 361; cf. I. O. Wade, 'The *Epître à Uranie*', *PMLA*, 47 (1932), pp. 1066–1112.

9. cf. the critical edition by André Morize, *L'Apologie du luxe au XVIIIe siècle et 'Le Mondain' de Voltaire*, Paris, Didier, 1909, pp. 135–6.

10. Sénac de Meilhan remarks in his novel *L'Emigré* (1797) that it now seems inconceivable Voltaire could ever have been in danger of exile for such remarks; but his very awareness of the situation indicates that it had lived on in men's consciousness throughout the century.

11. Morize ed., op. cit., pp. 153–4. The inventiveness of this little drama won Frederick of Prussia's applause when he received the poem (letter to Voltaire, 23 Jan. 1737, Best. 1208).

12. Ed. T. Besterman, *The Complete Works of Voltaire*, vol. 7, 1970.

13. Even as recently as 1971, an article in *Le Figaro Littéraire* made the point that in France many things, including some that are even very old and respectable, may be attacked, provided one does not touch Saint Joan (D. Jamet, 26 Feb. 1971; cf. R. J. Buyck, 'Chateaubriand juge de Voltaire', *Studs. Volt.*, cxiv (1973), p. 262).

14. R. Aron, *Histoire de la libération de la France*, 2 vols., Paris, Fayard, 1959, ii, p. 302.

15. For fuller details, cf. J. Vercruysse, 'Jeanne d'Arc au siècle des Lumières', *Studs. Volt.*, xc (1972), pp. 1700–03.

16. Canto ii, 31–5. All textual references are to the Vercruysse edition.

17. Canto ii, 200.

18. Canto ii, 193–4.
19. Book i, Fable 2.
20. Canto iv, 407–17.
21. In a manuscript version which is certainly from Voltaire's hand, she appears actually to succumb, though the poet leaves it somewhat ambiguous as to whether she was saved in the nick of time. The pirated editions are quite explicit, describing the seduction in detail that leaves nothing to the imagination. It was this scene, as one may readily imagine, which has particularly shocked the commentators.
22. Canto xx, 278–81.
23. cf., e.g., Canto ii, 445–50.
24. Canto xxi, 87–91.
25. Canto xxi, 457–60.
26. Canto ii, 269–92.
27. Canto xxi, 384–6; 400–01.
28. Canto xviii, 41–69.
29. Canto i, 344–5.
30. Canto ii, 420–3.
31. Canto xxi, 91.
32. Canto ii, 10–14.
33. Canto xx, 1–8.
34. Another deliberate anachronism: the historical Agnès, only seven years old at this time, was not to become Charles's mistress until many years later.
35. Canto x, 175–210; cf. *Candide*, ch. xvi.
36. Canto xix, 286–90.
37. Canto xix, 293–4.
38. Canto xix, 314.
39. Vercruysse ed., p. 19.
40. cf. letter to Cideville, 26 June 1735, Best. 858; T. Besterman, *Voltaire*, p. 375.
41. Canto xviii, 1–5.
42. Canto vii.
43. Canto xxi, 402–03.
44. Canto xii, 371–7.
45. Canto xxi, 309–12.
46. Canto iv, 1–4.
47. Vercruysse, art. cit., p. 1704.
48. Canto i, 315.
49. Canto i, 319–21.
50. Canto ii, 496.
51. Canto xi, 285–6.
52. Canto xi, 306.
53. Canto xi, 313–79.
54. Canto xi, 380–92.
55. Canto xvi, 1–243.
56. Canto iv, 553–62.
57. It is true, as we have seen, that a few editions appeared in twenty-four cantos, but this was due solely to what M. Vercruysse calls 'un découpage

fantaisiste' (ed., p. 57) of the text by certain misguided editors of pirated editions and in no way corresponds to Voltaire's intentions.

58. cf. Vercruysse ed., p. 243.

59. Canto i, 130.

60. Canto i, 173–5.

61. The use of anachronism of a more or less blatant kind is a common device in *La Pucelle*. Among the most striking, apart from examples already mentioned, is the reference to pistols, underlined by Voltaire himself in a footnote (xii, 124), and the onslaught on contemporary writers in Canto xviii.

62. Canto vii, 359–64.

63. Canto xii, 1–6.

64. Canto xx, 71–4.

65. Canto vii, 327–64.

66. Canto viii, 30–2.

67. Canto i, 261–2.

68. Canto i, 267–74.

69. Canto xxi, 445–50.

70. Canto xiii, 294–404.

71. Canto xx, 179–212.

72. Canto xx, 255–66.

73. Canto iv, 38.

74. Canto i, 74–6.

75. Canto i, 56–60.

76. Canto x, 106–07.

77. Canto ii, 222–5.

78. Canto xx, 166.

79. Canto xx, 177.

80. Canto xxi, 369–74.

81. H. Hatzfeld, *The Rococo: Eroticism, Wit, and Elegance in European Literature*, New York, Pegasus, 1972.

82. Canto vi, 197.

83. Vercruysse ed., p. 138.

84. *Dictionnaire philosophique*, art. 'Art dramatique'; cited in R. Naves, *Le Goût de Voltaire*, pp. 252–3.

85. ibid., art. 'Vers et poésie', cited in D. Williams art., p. 71, n.

86. cf. Naves, *Le Goût de Voltaire*, p. 252, n. 107.

87. Vercruysse ed., p. 138.

88. Besterman, *Voltaire*, p. 375.

89. Canto iv, 146–50: my italics.

90. Canto xiii, 398–9.

91. René Pomeau summed up this paradox most felicitously in describing Voltaire as 'interminablement bref', a general phrase about the author which could apply particularly well to *La Pucelle*; cf. *La Religion de Voltaire*, p. 471.

92. Canto iv, 75–8.

93. Canto i, 191.

94. Canto iv, 45–70: Lourdis is a particularly cunning monk, even in a profession noted for its low trickery: 'Le moine, enfin, le plus moine du monde' (xxi, 239).

95. Canto xxi, 462.
96. Vercruysse, art. cit., p. 1704.

Chapter 5. POLEMICIST AND REFORMER

1. The *Lettres philosophiques* now of course run to twenty-five; but the twenty-fifth, entitled 'Remarques sur Pascal', is in no sense about England. It does not appear in some of the early editions, and not until 1733 did Voltaire think of attaching it to the *Lettres* as originally conceived (cf. letter to Formont [*c.* 1 June 1733], Best. 596). The remarks on Pascal are best seen, in every way, as an appendix to the main work.

2. A fascinating article on the relationship of the work to both the travel and the letter-form has become available since this chapter was written: R. Pomeau, 'Les "Lettres philosophiques", œuvre épistolaire?', in *Beiträge zur Französischen Aufklärung und zur Spanischen Literatur: Festgabe für Werner Krauss zum 70. Geburtstag*, Ed. W. Bahner, Berlin, Akademie-Verlag, 1971, pp. 271–9. With characteristic deftness, M. Pomeau points out Voltaire's originality in adding a new approach to traditional modes; but he tends to overstress the didactic elements at the expense of the author's equal concern with entertaining while instructing.

3. H. Brown, 'The composition of the *Letters concerning the English Nation*', in *The Age of the Enlightenment*, pp. 15–34.

4. For useful discussions on Voltaire and Quakerism, cf. R. Pomeau, *La Religion de Voltaire*, pp. 133–9; W. H. Barber, 'Voltaire and Quakerism: Enlightenment and the inner light', *Studs. Volt.*, xxiv (1963), pp. 81–109.

5. All quotations are taken from the edition by G. Lanson, revised by A.-M. Rousseau, 2 vols., Paris, Didier, 1964; punctuation and spelling have been modernized.

6. Lanson ed., i, pp. 19–22.

7. cf. H. Brown, pp. 24–5, 33.

8. 'Toute cette *Lettre X* s'inspire d'un idéal vivant, dont Voltaire partagea longtemps l'intimité et qui le marqua pour la vie.' (The whole of this *Letter X* is inspired by a living ideal, whose close friendship Voltaire long enjoyed and who marked him for life.) (A.-M. Rousseau note, in Lanson ed., ii, p. 317, n. 31). In particular, Voltaire was closely acquainted with the Fawkener family and especially his host Everard, an important City merchant who was later to be knighted and become the English Ambassador in Constantinople; cf. supra, p. 20.

9. G. Bonno, *La Culture et la civilisation britanniques devant l'opinion française (1713–1734)*, Philadelphia, American Philosophical Society, 1948, p. 148. For illustrations, cf. Lanson ed., i, p. 144, n. 18.

10. For a succinct history of smallpox inoculation in England and France during the eighteenth century, cf. R. Waldinger, 'Voltaire and medicine', *Studs. Volt.*, lviii (1967), pp. 1800–05; cf. also J. Mayer, *Diderot homme de science*, Rennes, Imprimerie Bretonne, 1959, pp. 377–81; A. Magnan, 'Un épisode oublié de la lutte des médecins parisiens contre Théodore Tronchin', *Studs. Volt.*, xciv (1972), pp. 417–29.

11. As Lanson shows (ed., i, p. 147, n. 27), Voltaire, never the most reliable

arithmetician, falls into errors of transcription; but it little matters, for the seriousness of the disease was well documented.

12. Bacon makes much the same distinction in *The Advancement of Learning* (1605), Book ii, Section iv, 1–2.

13. It was the only one which the censor had not approved; cf. *Lettres philosophiques*, Ed. F. A. Taylor, Oxford, Blackwell, 1961, p. xxvi.

14. Lanson ed., ii, p. 32, n. 25. As A.-M. Rousseau remarks, the story 'place V. parmi les journalistes de génie' (ibid., p. 320, n. 50).

15. The first Newtonian apology had appeared in Maupertuis's *Discours sur les différentes figures des astres* in 1732.

16. cf. supra, pp. 11–12.

17. T. J. Barling, 'The Literary art of the *Lettres philosophiques*', *Studs. Volt.*, xli (1966), p. 44. The whole article (pp. 7–69) offers a very useful discussion of this generally neglected aspect of the work.

18. The *Lettres philosophiques* have been viewed here essentially within the line of Voltaire's development as a polemical writer. Among other works which have proved useful on the *Lettres philosophiques*, one must mention the edition by R. Naves, Paris, Garnier, 1956; P. M. Conlon, *Voltaire's literary career from 1728 to 1750*; P. Gay, *Voltaire's Politics: The Poet as Realist*; and I. O. Wade, *The Intellectual Development of Voltaire*.

19. Moland ed., xxv, p. 230; all references will be to this edition.

20. ibid., p. 232.

21. ibid., p. 231.

22. ibid., p. 241.

23. ibid., p. 246.

24. ibid., p. 247.

25. ibid., p. 230.

26. ibid., pp. 233–4.

27. ibid., p. 234.

28. ibid., p. 235.

29. ibid., p. 238.

30. ibid., p. 242.

31. ibid., p. 246.

32. Very little notice has been taken of the *Discours aux Welches*, although it is among the most interesting of Voltaire's brief polemics. Recently however, an excellent article has been devoted to it by P. B. Daprini, 'Le *Discours aux Welches* ou la France vue de Ferney', *Studs. Volt.*, xcviii (1972), pp. 47–60. M. Daprini most usefully sets the *Discours* in the context of Voltaire's life at the time. He tends however in my view to overstress the critical aspect of the work at the expense of the more subtly constructive elements.

33. Moland ed., xxv, p. 250.

34. ibid., p. 518; all references will be to this edition.

35. ibid., p. 522.

36. ibid., p. 523.

37. ibid., p. 527.

38. ibid., p. 535.

39. ibid., p. 536.

40. ibid., pp. 536–7: author's italics.

41. cf. G. R. Havens, 'The Nature Doctrine of Voltaire', *PMLA*, 40 (1925), pp. 852–62.

Chapter 6. PHILOSOPHER AND *philosophe*

1. Ed. H. Temple Patterson, *Traité de métaphysique*, Manchester University Press, 2nd ed., 1957. All references will be to this text.
2. Pomeau, *La Religion de Voltaire*, p. 394.
3. I. O. Wade, *The Intellectual Development of Voltaire*, pp. 342–3; cf. also Wade, *Studies on Voltaire*, pp. 56–114.
4. *Studies on Voltaire*, p. 113.
5. Ch. ii, p. 7.
6. The article 'Dieu' in the *Questions sur l'Encyclopédie* (1770) is longer, but being more committed to a deist position and more polemical, it is rather a review of other erroneous opinions than an attempt at profound self-analysis.
7. Ch. ii, p. 18.
8. ibid., p. 8.
9. cf. W. H. Barber, *Leibniz in France, from Arnauld to Voltaire*, Oxford, Clarendon Press, 1955, pp. 210–43; H. T. Mason, *Pierre Bayle and Voltaire*, pp. 55–77.
10. Ch. ii, p. 14.
11. ibid., p. 15.
12. ibid., p. 17.
13. Pomeau develops this view eloquently (*La Religion de Voltaire*, p. 205).
14. Lanson, *Voltaire*, p. 64.
15. Ch. vi, p. 42.
16. cf. Patterson ed., p. 50, which also draws on the important study of this question by J. Hahn, *Voltaires Stellung zur Frage der menschlichen Freiheit in ihrem Verhältnis zu Locke und Collins*, Borna-Leipzig, Noske, 1905.
17. Ch. vii, p. 46.
18. Lanson, *Voltaire*, p. 66.
19. Ch. vii, p. 46.
20. [*c.* 15 Oct. 1737], Best. 1315.
21. Ch. ix, p. 59.
22. Pomeau, *La Religion de Voltaire*, p. 232.
23. Ch. ix, pp. 62–3.
24. Preface, p. xii.
25. This point is made by J. L. Carr in his useful edition of *Le Philosophe ignorant*, University of London Press, 1965. All references will be to this text.
26. xi, p. 51; cf. also iv, p. 47.
27. 12 Oct. 1770, Best. 15677.
28. xiii, p. 54.
29. xx, pp. 59–60.
30. Pomeau cites some revealing accounts of Voltaire's religious exaltation at moments like these (*La Religion de Voltaire*, pp. 416–18).
31. cf. supra, pp. 53–4.
32. cf. Pomeau, *La Religion de Voltaire*, pp. 216–17.
33. ibid., p. 418.
34. Mason ed., *Zadig and Other Stories*, p. 107.

35. Lanson, *Voltaire*, p. 177.
36. xxix, p. 74.
37. Ch. i, Patterson ed., p. 3.
38. xxix, p. 75.
39. cf. H. T. Mason, *Pierre Bayle and Voltaire*, pp. 67–77; 'Voltaire and Manichean dualism', *Studs. Volt.*, xxvi (1963), pp. 1143–60.
40. xxiii, p. 61.
41. Moland ed., xxvi, p. 319.
42. P. Vernière, *Spinoza et la pensée française avant la Révolution*, 2 vols., Paris, P.U.F., 1954, has a masterly section on Voltaire's relationship to Spinoza (ii, pp. 495–527). The role played by Bayle is studied in some detail in H. T. Mason, *Pierre Bayle and Voltaire*, pp. 104–11.
43. xxiv, pp. 64–5.
44. ibid., p. 65.
45. ibid., p. 66.
46. cf. supra, pp. 63–5.
47. xxx, p. 76.
48. xxxi, p. 76.
49. cf. supra, p. 65.
50. xxxiii, p. 80.
51. xxxv, p. 81.
52. xxxvi, p. 84.
53. Carr has some interesting pages (pp. 31–3) on the influence exerted by Rousseau upon *Le Philosophe ignorant*. He sees the work as in part a riposte to Rousseau's *Profession de foi du vicaire savoyard*, which had appeared in *Emile* (1762).
54. Gay, *Voltaire's Politics*, p. 346.
55. xxxix–xlvii, pp. 85–90.
56. xlix–lvi, pp. 91–4.
57. Pomeau, *La Religion de Voltaire*, p. 220.
58. Moland ed., xx, p. 195: author's italics.
59. G. Gusdorf, *Les Principes de la pensée au siècle des Lumières*, p. 217: author's italics.
60. The genesis of the *Examen important* has been the subject of some debate between Wade and Pomeau. The former having argued that the Biblical section (the first half) was written 1736–46 (*Voltaire and Madame du Châtelet*, p. 150), Pomeau replied that in its present form, the work is certainly posterior to the publication of Bolingbroke's *Philosophical Works* posthumously in 1754–5, and that the idea for the work does not appear until a letter by Voltaire in 1759 (*La Religion de Voltaire*, pp. 180–1). But Pomeau allows that Voltaire would have used the products of his research at Cirey, albeit enriched by later readings; and Wade, while disagreeing with various details of the Pomeau argument, has accepted this general view (*The Intellectual Development of Voltaire*, pp. 554–6).
61. In this instance, cf. letter to d'Alembert, 24 May 1769, Best. 14683.
62. cf. supra, p. 124.
63. Wade, *The Intellectual Development of Voltaire*, p. 130.
64. Moland ed., xxvi, pp. 195–6; all references will be to this text.

65. The final chapter was not added until 1771, cf. Moland ed., xxvi, p. 195, n.

66. Ch. i, p. 201.

67. Ch. ii, p. 204.

68. Ch. iii, p. 205.

69. ibid., p. 205, n. (footnote appended in 1771).

70. Ch. v, p. 209.

71. Ch. viii, p. 216.

72. Ch. vii, p. 211.

73. Ch. ii, pp. 201–02.

74. Ch. viii, p. 214.

75. The question of Voltaire's anti-semitism has often been debated. It is hard to deny that his hatred of the Jews is more than just a part of his attack on Christianity and that it springs from deeply emotional roots. As a recent student of the question has put it, Voltaire regarded the Jews as a race apart from others (A. Hertzberg, *The French Enlightenment and the Jews*, New York, Columbia University Press, 1968, p. 285).

76. B. Schwarzbach, *Voltaire's Old Testament Criticism*, Geneva, Droz, 1971.

77. Ch. x, p. 223.

78. Ch. xi, p. 227.

79. Ch. xvii, p. 244.

80. *L'Homme révolté*, 'Introduction', in Camus, *Essais*, Ed. R. Quilliot and L. Faucon, Paris, N.R.F., Bibliothèque de la Pléiade, 1965, pp. 413–20.

81. Ch. xxi, p. 252.

82. Ch. xxv, pp. 259–63.

83. Ch. xxii, p. 254.

84. Ch. xxv, p. 263.

85. Ch. xxiii, p. 257.

86. Ch. xxxiii, p. 288.

87. Ch. xxxv, p. 292.

88. Ch. xxxviii, p. 298.

89. Ch. xxxv, p. 291; cf. supra, p. 51.

90. Ch. xxxvii, p. 296.

91. Ch. xxxviii, p. 296.

92. Conclusion, p. 298.

93. ibid., pp. 299–300.

94. Schwarzbach, op. cit., p. 18.

95. They are handily compiled in Ed. R. Naves, *Voltaire: Dialogues et anecdotes philosophiques*, Paris, Garnier, 1966.

96. cf. Pomeau, *La Religion de Voltaire*, pp. 351–2.

97. I. O. Wade, *The Clandestine Organization and Diffusion of Philosophic Ideas in France from 1700 to 1750*, Princeton University Press, 1938, p. 98.

98. *Correspondance littéraire*, 16 vols., Paris, Garnier, 1877–82, viii, p. 9.

99. I shall not deal with the postscript in which, after the discussion is concluded, other guests arrive and the abbé de Saint-Pierre reads his 'Pensées détachées' to the gathering. While repeating in more schematic form some of the ideas in the preceding dialogue, it is not a summary and has a gratuitous air; the *Dîner* as a literary and philosophical vehicle would be better without it.

100. Moland ed., xxvi, pp. 531–7. All references will be to this text.
101. ibid., p. 539.
102. ibid., p. 550.
103. ibid., p. 551.
104. ibid., pp. 551–2.
105. ibid., p. 555.
106. ibid., p. 557.
107. ibid., p. 541.
108. ibid., p. 551.
109. ibid., p. 556.
110. No published study of *Le Dîner* exists to my knowledge, but a very useful analysis of the work has been undertaken by C. Milward (M.A. thesis, University of East Anglia, unpublished, 1969); it has been helpful in the preparation of this section.

Chapter 7. CORRESPONDENT

1. A useful article on the subject is G. May, 'La littérature épistolaire date-t-elle du dix-huitième siècle?', *Studs. Volt.*, lvi (1967), pp. 823–44, though it tends to be over-schematic on the preceding period.
2. T. Besterman, 'Le vrai Voltaire par ses lettres', *Voltaire Essays and Another*, OUP, 1962, pp. 74–113.
3. The Besterman edition of the *Correspondence* runs to over 20 000 letters, but of these a sizable minority come from other pens or are exchanged between third parties.
4. Lanson, *Voltaire*, p. 161.
5. [*c.* 7 Aug. 1711], Best. 6: as throughout with quotations from the Correspondence, punctuation and spelling have been modernized.
6. He did not change his name from Arouet until 1718; cf. T. Besterman, *Voltaire*, pp. 70–1.
7. [?May 1778], Best. 20030.
8. L. Spitzer has some interesting comments to make on this phenomenon in 'Pages from Voltaire', *A Method of Interpreting Literature*, Smith College, Northampton, Mass., 1949, pp. 94–7.
9. 26 May 1778, Best. 20046.
10. E. Auerbach, *Mimesis*, pp. 362–4; L. Spitzer, art. cit.
11. Best. 12323.
12. [18 Jan. 1766], Best. 12251.
13. 20 Jan. 1766, Best. 12255.
14. [22 or 23 Apr. 1766], Best. 12390.
15. To chevalier de Taulès, 30 Apr. 1766, Best. 12402.
16. Taulès to Voltaire, 1 May 1766, Best. 12406.
17. 12 May 1766, Best. 12418.
18. To d'Alembert, 26 June 1766, Best. 12494.
19. To Mme d'Epinay, Best. 12513.
20. To Damilaville, 7 July 1766, Best. 12514.
21. To Duchess of Saxe-Gotha, 25 Aug. 1766, Best. 12630.
22. 23 July 1766, Best. 12557.

23. To d'Alembert, 18 July 1766, Best. 12545.
24. To d'Alembert, [*c.* 10 Aug. 1766], Best. 12599.
25. 25 July 1766, Best. 12565.
26. cf. Best. 12773; Diderot's letter is at Best. 12719.
27. To Damilaville, 1 Dec. 1766, Best. 12816.
28. To Mme d'Epinay, 26 Sept. 1766, Best. 12703.
29. 15 Sept. 1766, Best. 12673; as the quotation shows, Voltaire has been misinformed and somewhat underestimates the extent of the punishment.
30. To cardinal de Bernis, 22 Dec. 1766, Best. 12865.
31. To d'Alembert, 23 July 1766, Best. 12557.
32. To Mme Du Deffand, 20 Jan. 1766, Best. 12257.
33. 13 Jan. 1766, Best. 12239.
34. Best. 12238.
35. Best. 12764.
36. cf. Best. 12789.
37. ibid.
38. cf. supra, pp. 27–8.
39. To Damilaville, 7 Nov. 1766, Best. 12773.
40. 28 Feb. 1766, Best. 12315.
41. cf., e.g., Best. 12699, Commentary; Best, 12782, Commentary.
42. 12 Mar. 1766, Best. 12333.
43. To Chabanon, 3 Nov. 1766, Best. 12757.
44. To Damilaville, 29 Dec. 1766, Best. 12888.
45. To Damilaville, 19 Mar. 1766, Best. 12338.
46. cf. R. A. Leigh, 'An anonymous eighteenth-century character-sketch of Voltaire', *Studs. Volt.*, ii (1956), pp. 241–72.
47. R. S. Ridgway, *Voltaire and Sensibility*, Montreal and London, McGill-Queen's University Press, 1973.
48. A. Delattre, *Voltaire l'impétueux*, Paris, Mercure de France, 1957, p. 33.
49. B. Russell, 'Voltaire's influence on me', *Studs. Volt.*, vi (1958), pp. 157–62.
50. B. Russell, *The Autobiography of Bertrand Russell*, 3 vols., London, Allen and Unwin, 1967–9, ii, p. 32.

Selected bibliography

Studs. Volt.= *Studies on Voltaire and the Eighteenth Century,*
Ed. T. Besterman, Geneva and later Banbury, 1955–.

BACKGROUND AND GENERAL STUDIES

Barber, W. H., et al., Ed., *The Age of the Enlightenment: Studies Presented to Theodore Besterman,* Edinburgh and London, 1967.
Besterman, T., *Voltaire,* London, 1969.
Conlon, P. M., *Voltaire's literary career from 1728 to 1750, Studs. Volt.,* xiv (1961).
Delattre, A., *Voltaire l'impétueux,* Paris, 1957.
Gay, P., *Voltaire's Politics: The Poet as Realist,* 2nd ed., New York, 1965.
Green, F. C., *Literary Ideas in 18th Century France and England,* New York, 1966 (originally published in 1935 as *Minuet*).
Lanson, G., *Voltaire,* 2nd ed., Paris, 1910.
Naves, R., *Le Goût de Voltaire,* Paris, 1938.
Pomeau, R., *La Religion de Voltaire,* 2nd ed., Paris, 1969.
Schwarzbach, B., *Voltaire's Old Testament Criticism,* Geneva, 1971.
Wade, I. O., *Voltaire and Madame Du Châtelet: An Essay on the Intellectual Activity at Cirey,* Princeton, 1941.
Wade, I. O., *Studies on Voltaire,* Princeton, 1947.
Wade, I. O., *The Intellectual Development of Voltaire,* Princeton, 1969.

EDITIONS

Œuvres complètes, Ed. L. Moland, 52 vols., Paris, 1877–85 (referred to as Moland ed. throughout notes).
The Complete Works of Voltaire, Ed. T. Besterman, Geneva and later Banbury, 1968–.
Vol. 2. *La Henriade,* Ed. O. R. Taylor, 1970.
Vol. 7. *La Pucelle,* Ed. J. Vercruysse, 1970.
Vol. 53. *Commentaires sur Corneille,* vol. i, Ed. D. Williams, 1974.
Vol. 59. *La Philosophie de l'histoire,* Ed. J. H. Brumfitt, 1969.
Vols. 81–2. *Notebooks,* Ed. T. Besterman, 1968.
Vols. 85–. *Correspondence,* Ed. T. Besterman 1968–.
Œuvres historiques, Ed. R. Pomeau, Paris, 1957.
Correspondence, Ed. T. Besterman, 107 vols., Geneva, 1953–65 (referred to as Best. throughout notes).
Candide, Ed. A. Morize, 2nd ed., Paris, 1957.
Candide, Ed. R. Pomeau, Paris, 1959.

Candide, Ed. I. O. Wade (*Voltaire and 'Candide': A Study in the Fusion of History, Art, and Philosophy*), Princeton, 1959.

Candide, Ed. J. H. Brumfitt, Oxford, 1968.

Essai sur les mœurs, Ed. R. Pomeau, 2 vols., Paris, 1963.

Lettres philosophiques, Ed. G. Lanson, revised by A.-M. Rousseau, 2 vols., Paris, 1964.

Micromégas, Ed. I. O. Wade (*Voltaire's 'Micromégas': A Study in the Fusion of Science, Myth, and Art*), Princeton, 1950.

Le Mondain, Ed. A. Morize (*L'Apologie du luxe au XVIIIe siècle e 'Le Mondain' de Voltaire*), Paris, 1909.

La Mort de César, Ed. A.-M. Rousseau, Paris, 1964.

Le Philosophe ignorant, Ed. J. L. Carr, London, 1965.

Le Taureau blanc, Ed. R. Pomeau, Paris, 1956.

Traité de métaphysique, Ed. H. T. Patterson, 2nd ed., Manchester, 1957.

Voltaire on Shakespeare, Ed. T. Besterman, *Studs. Volt.*, liv (1967).

Zadig, Ed. G. Ascoli, revised by J. Fabre, 2 vols., Paris, 1962.

Zadig and Other Stories, Ed. H. T. Mason, Oxford, 1971.

SPECIFIC CRITICISM

Barber, W. H., *Voltaire: 'Candide'*, London, 1960.

Barling, T. J., 'The Literary art of the *Lettres philosophiques*', *Studs. Volt.*, xli (1966).

Bottiglia, W. F., *Voltaire's 'Candide'*, *Studs. Volt.*, viiA (1964).

Brumfitt, J. H., *Voltaire Historian*, Oxford, 1958.

Daprini, P. B., 'Le Discours aux Welches ou la France vue de Ferney', *Studs. Volt.*, xcviii (1972).

Gossman, L., 'Voltaire's *Charles XII*: history into art', *Studs. Volt.*, xxv (1963).

Murray, G., *Voltaire's 'Candide': the Protean gardener, 1755–1762*, *Studs. Volt.*, lxix (1970).

Mylne, V., 'Literary techniques and methods in Voltaire's *Contes philosophiques*', *Studs. Volt.*, lvii (1967).

Ridgway, R. S., *La Propagande philosophique dans les tragédies de Voltaire*, *Studs. Volt.*, xv (1961).

Sareil, J., *Essai sur 'Candide'*, Geneva, 1967.

Topazio, V. W., *Voltaire: A Critical Study of His Major Works*, New York, 1967.

Van den Heuvel, J., *Voltaire dans ses contes: De 'Micromégas' à 'L'Ingénu'*, Paris, 1967.

Weightman, J. G., 'The Quality of *Candide*', in *Essays Presented to C. M. Girdlestone*, Newcastle-upon-Tyne, 1960.

Williams, D., *Voltaire: literary critic*, *Studs. Volt.*, xlviii (1966).

For a useful anthology of criticism on Voltaire, see *Voltaire et la critique*, Ed. J. Sareil, Englewood Cliffs, 1966.

Chronology

1637   Publication of Descartes's *Discours de la méthode*.

1690   Publication of Locke's *Essay concerning Human Understanding*.

1694   (21 November) Voltaire born in Paris, as François-Marie Arouet.

1704   Entered Jesuit college of Louis-le-Grand; remained there till 1711.

1716   (May to October) Voltaire exiled from Paris to Sully-sur-Loire, accused of a satire against the Regent.

1717   (May) Imprisoned in Bastille for nearly a year on account of another satire.

1718   (12 June) First letter by the author to carry his new name 'Voltaire'. (18 November) First play, *Œdipe*, established him as successful tragic dramatist.

1721   Publication of Montesquieu's *Lettres persanes*.

1726   Voltaire exiled to England (arriving in May) in consequence of quarrel with the chevalier de Rohan.

1728–9   Returned to France.

1731   Composition of *La Mort de César*.

1732   Publication of *Zaïre*.

1733–4   Publication of Pope's *Essay on Man*.

1734   (March) Published *Lettres philosophiques* in France. The *Lettres* were condemned by the Parlement of Paris, and Voltaire fled the capital, eventually settling at Cirey, in the château of Mme Du Châtelet, where much of the following decade was spent.

1741   Publication of *Mahomet*.

1745   (April) Appointed Historiographer to King at Versailles.

1747   (June) Publication of *Zadig* (under title of *Memnon*), the first of Voltaire's *contes* to appear in print. (November) The period of favour at Court ended when indiscretions forced his flight.

1748   Publication of Montesquieu's *De l'esprit des lois*.

1749   (September) Death of Mme Du Châtelet.

1750 (June) Voltaire left Paris for Frederick the Great's Court at Potsdam on the latter's invitation.

1751 Publication of Volume I of *Encyclopédie* edited by Diderot and d'Alembert.

1752 Publication of *Micromégas*.

1753 (March) Voltaire left Frederick's Court after growing hostility between the two men. A desolate period of wandering ensued.

1755 (March) Settled at Les Délices on the outskirts of Geneva.

1756 First complete official text of *Essai sur les mœurs* published.

1759 (January-February) Publication of *Candide*.
(February) Voltaire acquired the château of Ferney near Geneva, henceforth to be his home.

1762 Publication of Rousseau's *Contrat social* and *Emile*.
First text of *La Pucelle d'Orléans* authorized by Voltaire published.
Beginning of long campaign to rehabilitate Jean Calas, who had been broken on the wheel by order of the Parlement of Toulouse. This was but the most renowned of a whole series of defences and polemical writings which was to occupy Voltaire for the rest of his life.

1764 Publication of *Discours aux Welches* and first edition of the *Dictionnaire philosophique*.

1766 Publication of *Les Scythes*, *Avis au public sur les parricides imputés aux Calas et aux Sirven* and *Le Philosophe ignorant*.

1767 Publication of *L'Ingénu*, the *Examen important de milord Bolingbroke* and *Le Dîner du comte de Boulainvilliers*.

1772 Last volumes of *Encyclopédie* appeared.

1774 Publication of *Le Taureau blanc*.

1776 Publication of Adam Smith's *The Wealth of Nations*.

1778 Voltaire made a triumphal return to Paris, virtually an apotheosis, and died there on 30 May.

Index